Nedra Glover Tawaab

communication
+ Boundaries

Dr Pham - neuropsych
~~referral~~

homework
→ PCP talk
→ reschedule Pdoc
→ read her

~~July 28~~, Friday, August 13
Friday 7/23   10 am
10 am

What to
Say *Next*

What to
Say *Next*

SUCCESSFUL COMMUNICATION
IN WORK, LIFE, *and* LOVE
with AUTISM SPECTRUM DISORDER

SARAH *and* LARRY NANNERY

TILLER PRESS

New York   London   Toronto   Sydney   New Delhi

TILLER PRESS

An Imprint of Simon & Schuster, Inc.
1230 Avenue of the Americas
New York, NY 10020

First Tiller Press hardcover edition March 2021

TILLER PRESS and colophon are trademarks of Simon & Schuster, Inc.

For information about special discounts for bulk purchases, please contact Simon & Schuster Special Sales at 1-866-506-1949 or business@simonandschuster.com.

The Simon & Schuster Speakers Bureau can bring authors to your live event. For more information or to book an event, contact the Simon & Schuster Speakers Bureau at 1-866-248-3049 or visit our website at www.simonspeakers.com.

Manufactured in the United States of America

1   3   5   7   9   10   8   6   4   2

Library of Congress Cataloging-in-Publication Data
Names: Nannery, Sarah, author. | Nannery, Larry, author.
Title: What to say next : successful communication in work, life and love —with autism spectrum disorder / by Sarah and Larry Nannery.
Description: New York : Tiller Press, 2020. | Includes bibliographical references.
Identifiers: LCCN 2020016765 (print) | LCCN 2020016766 (ebook) | ISBN 9781982138202 (hardcover) | ISBN 9781982138219 (ebook)
Subjects: LCSH: Autism spectrum disorder—Patients—Life-skills guides. | Autism spectrum disorder—Patients—Language. | Autistic People—Life-skills guides. | Autistic people—Language. | Communication.
Classification: LCC RC553.A88 N364 2020 (print) | LCC RC553.A88 (ebook) | DDC 616.85/882—dc23
LC record available at https://lccn.loc.gov/2020016765
LC ebook record available at https://lccn.loc.gov/2020016766

ISBN 978-1-9821-3820-2
ISBN 978-1-9821-3821-9 (ebook)

For Sirus and Emmeline

In pursuit of being your best self,
never forget you are already perfect.

Table of Contents

"The truth of who we are is innate goodness, and the whole journey is really about removing any obstacle or false belief that keeps us from knowing that."

—ALANIS MORISSETTE

Introduction

> Need your help with a work thing when you have a min . . .

I typed feverishly into the open instant messenger tab on my work desktop as soon as I got back to my desk at the office.

This was the fourth such SOS message I had sent to my husband in the last week, and it was only Wednesday.

> What's up?

Larry typed back, prompt as ever.

Struggling to find the delicate balance between too few and too many details, I tried to give him just the right amount of information to make the exchange quick and useful for both of us, trusting that he would ask for more if he needed.

"I met Deborah in the pantry just now," I explained through IM. "And she asked me for more details on a report I sent yesterday. She needs them by this afternoon for a conversation she's having with a Board member to-morrow morning. This is going to take me away from the financial report that Adam needs by tomorrow for the Board meeting in two weeks."

Three little dots appeared next to Larry's avatar, letting me know that he was already responding. "Deborah's need is higher priority," he answered simply. "Are you saying this means you won't be able to finish what Adam needs by tomorrow?"

"Yes—I will probably need until Friday now for the financial report."

"Anything that you can give to Tanesha?"

I had to think about that one for a minute. Would she be able to help me with anything for either report? She'd only just started two months ago, and I hadn't trained her yet on either of these types of reporting. She wouldn't know where to look to get the data, she wouldn't know how to put it together the right way . . .

"No," I typed back, feeling a little defeated. "It would take too long to train her to give me the kind of help I would need right now."

"OK," Larry pinged back. "So tell Adam that something's come up from Deborah, and you need extra time on his report. Give him your projected timeline. He should understand."

Adam was my boss. Deborah was Adam's boss. It made sense to me—now that Larry had helped me think it through logically—that a last-minute, time-sensitive request from Deborah would trump a previously known time-sensitive need from Adam, especially when Deborah's request was more urgent than his in terms of timeframe. I mentally reordered my priorities, stacking Deborah's report above Adam's, even though I had already started working on Adam's, and it was going to be painful to set it aside and switch gears to a new project before Adam's was finished. I would just have to deal with that. But something was still nagging at the back of my mind.

"Can I tell Adam in email?" I asked, dreading the answer.

I could almost see the exasperated side-smile on Larry's face as he typed back. "Would be better as a quick in-person. He needs to know sooner rather than later to adjust his expectations. And that way he also has a heads-up that Deborah needs more for her meeting tomorrow."

This one was tougher for me to grasp right away. I understood the value of Adam knowing now that I was pushing his timeline back, rather than by five p.m. today when he would finally get through checking all his emails. But that second bit—what use was a "heads-up" that Deborah had asked me for more information? What did that have to do with him? Would it give him some advance notice that she might be coming to him next with another last-minute request? Or would it raise the stakes of Deborah's meeting enough in his mind for him to proactively go make sure she had everything else she needed? As I thought it through, it made more and more sense that Adam would be empowered with the passive information that Deborah was seeking additional support for tomorrow's conversation with a Board member. He and I were both in the position to support her, so him knowing the support she was asking for, even if it wasn't directly from him, put him in a better position to support her, as well.

Larry let me process for a couple of minutes, then finished with the message, "And make a note, for future reference, to get Tanesha trained on this soon when you're not in a time crunch."

"Thanks, love. Will do." Right then and there, knowing I would forget otherwise, I opened my calendar and found an hour block of time the following week to meet with Tanesha. Then I scanned Adam's calendar and saw that he would be between meetings in about fifteen minutes—the perfect time, I had learned, to catch him for a quick in-person heads-up.

This type of five-minute IM session with my husband was a near-daily ritual for me when I first started moving up in the workplace.

You see, I have Asperger's syndrome, or what is now known in the Diagnostic and Statistical Manual of Mental Disorders (DSM-5) of the American Psychiatric Association as part of the broader diagnosis, autism spectrum disorder (ASD). None of the nuances of interpersonal communication come naturally to me as they do to people without ASD.

Now, years later, Larry and I have whittled down our SOS IM conversations to infrequent exchanges—mostly when something new or big happens at work that I don't feel I can handle on my own.

I have learned over the years to differentiate between situations that require a quick in-person meeting or an immediate phone call, and those that will be fine with only an email. I have learned methods for prioritizing my work according to time sensitivity, seniority of the people affected, and the overall value of my time—and my team's time—against our ultimate goals.

But I never would have learned these things—and the many others explored in this book—on my own. There is no class that teaches them and no book that explains the subtleties and complexities of human interaction to the degree that my ASD brain would need it explained. For the most part, the books I have tried to read on the subject of high-level interpersonal communication often rely on metaphor or parable to convey big concepts. Without clear, step-by-step, unambiguous situational application, these mean nothing to me. It's as if I am reading a Communication 201 book without yet having taken Communication 101.

My husband's mentorship—sometimes as literal as a voice in my ear telling me what to say, when to say it, and to whom—has guided me through the "fake it till you make it" phase of navigating professional relationships. I'm now at the point where I only feel like I'm faking it some of the time, instead of all the time. Which, I'm told, is how most people feel anyway.

WHO ARE WE?

I am a thirty-something woman with ASD, and my husband Larry is a forty-something "neurotypical" man. For the sake of simplicity and clarity, I will refer broadly throughout this book to people who don't have autism as "neurotypical," or "NT" for short, though it should be noted that this term is problematic, in that everyone's brain is different. No one is "typical."

Who Is Sarah?

I grew up in a small town, with a single working mother and a younger sister. As a child I was quiet, bookish, and entirely disinterested in things like dolls or dress-up, earning me a reputation as a tomboy. I engaged in a lot of social mimicry to fit in, which of course never really worked because I could never get the context or the mannerisms quite right. As a result, most of my grade-school years were plagued by bullies who preyed on my inability to find a socially acceptable flow. I connected more with my teachers than I ever did with my peers, which of course made the bullying worse.

It wasn't until high school that I finally started fitting in with a similarly nerdy group of outcast band geeks and artsy kids, almost all of them male. I always excelled academically, where rules and instructions and boundaries were clear, and skills like reading, researching, and writing were rewarded. I thank the stars now that I got into the marching band in college, which functioned as my one and only source of social structure there. It gave me a consistent daily schedule (up early every morning for rehearsal, performing at football games every weekend, etc.) and social outlet (all of my friends were fellow band geeks) that made the rest of college manageable for me.

I didn't get to the point of needing to take a step back from life and find answers about what kept me so consistently on the sidelines until much later, when all at once the demands of a career, a marriage, and a child had finally pushed me to my limit. Gaining the knowledge of my autism before that point would of course have been helpful, but up until then I had always just considered myself to be quiet, thoughtful, highly sensitive, and perhaps a little shy. All of which was fine, until I couldn't advocate for myself or my son, I couldn't communicate love as consistently and deeply as I wanted to with my husband, and I couldn't hold all the many threads of my work life together and perform at the level of quality I expected from myself.

I was blessed, however, to have chosen Larry as my counterpart before I received my autism diagnosis, and together we have navigated through a great many of these *couldn'ts*, turning them into *coulds* with a lot of the tools, strategies, and insights we share in this book.

Who Is Larry?

Larry is a boy who never fully grew up, thanks to his godmother's influence of playing video games one minute, then teaching him how to cook in the next.

He is not afraid to admit his failings and flaws, but rather to embrace them, to learn from them. He is a father, a mentor, a kind spirit who makes people feel at ease, especially kids. Though far from a comedian, he still finds ways to bring laughter to those who need it.

He is a geek, a true stay-up-all-night computer nerd who is always searching for ways to not be known as such, but who invariably offers to help sort out any computer problem he encounters.

We Are Professionals in Our Own Fields

Most of my career I have worked in nonprofits, and Larry has had a similarly tracked career in technology. At this point, we are both at a level that requires regular contact with C-suite executives, and we have both run teams of people responsible for various company deliverables.

We Are a Long-Term Couple

We have been together for nearly ten years, and only in the last few have we really begun to experience the particular challenges of an ASD-linked long-term relationship. Certain differences in my brain and the way that I relate to people have become clear only now that we have reached a point together when—if we were both neurotypical—we would have a sort of shorthand: reading each other's minds, anticipating needs, or reciprocating emotions.

We Are Parents

We are parents to a son, who was diagnosed with ASD at three years old, and a daughter who was born while this book was being written.

WHY THIS BOOK?

Ultimately, we wanted to write this book because we have never found another like it. There have been several recent memoirs by authors with ASD that proved very helpful for me in understanding myself, and for Larry to understand me. Two that stand out for me are *Odd Girl Out*, by Laura James, and *Pretending to Be Normal*, by Liane Holliday Willey. Also, several long-term relationship books have been particularly helpful to us in the areas of living and loving and parenting together as an ASD/NT couple. Specifically, Ashley Stanford's *Asperger Syndrome (Autism Spectrum Disorder) and Long-Term Relationships*. I include references to Ashley's book throughout chapter 5, on neurodiverse long-term relationships.

I have also found a few ASD-targeted resources that specifically deal with workplace or employment issues, and were helpful for me in many ways, such as *Asperger's on the Job* by Rudy Simone.

But nowhere have I found a book about navigating the higher levels of professional relationships—the kind of politicking, nonverbal communication, implied messages, and high-context awareness that Larry has judiciously helped me stumble through in real time via SOS-style workplace instant messaging and other support. Until I entered the workforce, I never realized how crucial this awareness of interpersonal communication would be to my professional advancement—at least as important as technical skills and education. I don't think my experience is unique. I know plenty of neurotypical people who also struggle with office politics. But a lot of people, I think, develop these interpersonal skills on their own as they move through life—what I needed was a manual, and I couldn't find one.

Aside from providing what we hope will be a resource to many and will help advance the field of ASD-linked resources, Larry and I also knew that writing down the key factors in what has worked for me/us and why, in various professional, social, and relational situations, would help both of us identify and codify our learning, as much as it would also help other people. The process of writing this book has helped us both to continue to learn more about each other, and about ways to continue growing.

AN IMPORTANT NOTE:
MASKING AND THE AUTHENTIC SELF

I feel it is very important to call out, specifically, the term "masking" or "camouflaging"—which is often used to refer to the coping mechanisms and strategies a lot of autistic people use in order to "pass" in mainstream society. Masking in and of itself is neither a good thing nor a bad thing—it's just a tool—but the way in which we in society try to "normalize" people and make everyone fit into a particular mold of how we think people should be (rather than celebrating our unique individuality), is toxic and harmful for many people who simply don't fit that mold.

I am one of those people. Truthfully, most of us are, and yet each of us shape our behaviors and attitudes throughout the day in order to find our niche in the world.

We did not write this book to propagate that wholly unrealistic and damaging one-size-fits-all mold.

We did write this book to share tools and lived experiences that when combined with maximizing individual strengths, and shoring up individual weaknesses, could help people work around and through the mold in order to accomplish the things they want to in life.

This is a book about ways that I have been able to find my authentic autistic self—shaping myself into the person that I want to be, taking the awareness that my brain works differently and using it to my advantage in interacting with a neurodiverse world.

There is nothing so important as remaining true to yourself. If this book helps you to do that, then we have achieved our goal.

WHO IS THIS BOOK FOR?

When Larry and I first started thinking about writing this book, we were looking at it from an ASD point of view—laying out specific strategies that capitalized on my brain's differences in order to help me grow, and to help us grow together, to fill the hole we'd identified in the literature. But then we began hearing from our friends and family members that much of our experiences applied to them, too, and in turn to many different kinds of people.

Who likes small talk? Nobody. (If you do, lucky you! You probably know somebody who doesn't—hand them this book, will you?) Who agonizes, even just for a minute, about what to wear to the office holiday party? Everybody. Who feels like a fake sometimes? It turns out, quite a lot of people, in fact.[1]

ASD or no, we started thinking about how the ideas and experiences in this book might be helpful to many people who struggle to understand various aspects of office politics, professional communication, emotional intelligence, long-term relationships, social situations, and all the rest of our interconnected, interpersonal communicative world. Analytic thinkers, "introverts," highly sensitive people, people who feel shy or intimidated in social situations, people who are in the business of helping individuals with ASD or similar barriers . . . the challenges and strategies presented through-out this book, while laid out in that clear, step-by-step format that's crucial to an ASD-wired brain, will, we hope, be useful to all kinds of people who haven't found what they need elsewhere.

HOW CAN THIS BOOK BE USED?

In this book, Larry and I lay out the major challenges we have faced—alone and together—and the specific strategies we employed to overcome them. These are our own experiences. They will not apply to everyone, and they are not meant to be depicted as the only way to overcome these specific challenges. We ourselves are still encountering new challenges and learning new strategies all the time. Our hope is simply to provide ideas, insights, and practical advice that might make someone's path easier in the long run.

We have laid out these challenges and solutions in several thematic sec-tions, which can be read in order or out of order, according to your needs and interests.

Chapters 1 and 2 cover the broad topic of communication in general: first the basics of conversational flow, written versus in-person communica-tion, and small talk, followed by more advanced concepts like humor, body language, and how to perceive context.

Chapters 3 and 4 are about communication in the workplace, including topics that have to do with organizing your own work, such as executive functioning (prioritizing, perfectionism, goal setting), as well as common workplace challenges and strengths that accompany ASD. Then details on navigating professional relationships, such as conducting meetings, finding a mentor, and common problem areas for interpersonal professional communication.

In chapter 5 we share some of the specific hurdles and solutions we have encountered together as a long-term ASD/NT romantic couple. We cover topics such as "mind-reading," expressing love, reciprocating emotions, creating external outlets, making space for mistakes, and some specific tools for success together as a household and a family.

Chapter 6 is about our specific experiences learning how to parent together, despite some of my challenges, and some surprising ways in which the ASD brain is a parenting advantage. We share how we learned to work together, to set expectations and boundaries, and to recognize and trust our instincts, as well as some specific tools that work well for our young son, who also has autism.

Chapter 7 includes descriptions of specific and common ASD-linked challenges, like sensory or emotional overload, overanalysis, miscommunication, internalization, and the self-care and partnership solutions we have found work best to address and move past these common barriers, which can occur across many different types of interpersonal communication.

CHAPTER ONE

Communication Basics

"We are here to awaken
from the illusion of our separateness."

—THICH NHAT HANH

WHY IS COMMUNICATION IMPORTANT?

This may seem like a no-brainer, but as those of us with ASD know, better safe than sorry! There are many different reasons why communication is important, often overlapping, and all meriting some exploration for the analytical thinker to truly internalize.

Below are some of the most common reasons for communication, which we will explore in more detail:

Information

- To relay information ("The pharmacy closes at six p.m.")
- To gain information ("What time does the pharmacy close?")
- To arrive at information-creation together via verbal collaboration ("When do you think would be the best time for us to go to the pharmacy today? Probably after lunch?")

Emotion

- To establish or grow _implicit_ emotional connection with others ("Have you seen the new Avengers movie? I loved the part when . . .")
- To _explicitly_ share emotional connection ("I love you.")

Collaboration

- To effectively work together to achieve a common goal

Understanding that this list is not exhaustive, I want to delve a little deeper into each category. First, the informational—to relay information, to gain information, or to collaboratively create the information you need.

Communication for Information

This is the most straightforward reason for communication, and the one that many people with ASD, including me, will automatically assume is the fundamental reason for all communication. I need information, so I communicate with someone or interact with my environment in some way (Google, anyone?) in order to get it. I have information to share (The sky is falling!), so I communicate with another person or people in order to share it. I need information that is not readily available to me to make a decision or perform an action, so I engage in collaborative communication with other decision-makers.

This last one is a little wooly, so let me pull it apart a bit more. Sometimes information is not simple or straightforward, or it may require the input of more than one person to create. This can be a tricky concept for an analytical thinker to grasp; we tend to assume that information is its own pure and un-influenceable construct. But of course, it is subject to the many varied facets of human perception, perspective, and interpretation. It does not simply exist, always, for the taking.

I have found this understanding of information as a fluid concept, rather than as a fundamental truth, to be very freeing, and also unsteadying. Here is a concrete example from my professional life:

Many times, for work, I have been responsible for reviewing and signing a Terms and Conditions document with a new vendor. The first time this happened, I assumed I needed to review it before signing only for the usual reasons that one reads through any document before signing— such as making sure there is nothing egregious hidden in the fine print like "I will give you my firstborn child." I was asked, however, to forward the Terms and Conditions document to our legal counsel for review as well, and they sent back several recommended changes in red ink. That shocked me. Terms and Conditions documents could be changed? They didn't just exist as a pure-and-simple document laying out the information needed to secure a mutually beneficial and legal contractual business relationship between two parties? I forwarded the recommended changes to the vendor, fully expecting them to get back to me with an "Excuse me? Why is there red ink on my informational document?" But instead, they acquiesced to all the changes and sent back a revised version for us to review again and sign.

The contract review, change, and approval process above is a great example of how information as a concept can be complicated. Later, a colleague may require information: "What does it say in our contract about X?" and I might be able to provide that information easily: "On page 5, paragraph 3, it says Y." But that information, while it may be straightforward now, was arrived at via the mutual communication of more than one human being, and may have evolved to be something different from what it originally was, via that process.

Communication is so much more than just information exchange (even when the information is complicated). Of course, if you had told me that even a year ago, I would have looked at you like you had three heads. What I failed to realize is that human beings, with souls and emotions, need much more than information in order to thrive.

This is where the emotional reasons for communication come in.

Communication for Emotion

I find it helpful to approach this from an evolutionary point of view. Initially, humans evolved a socially interdependent nature for survival, to ensure collaboration against natural obstacles and predators, and the efficient sharing of limited resources. Our brains developed a chemical reward system to create positive emotions when we worked together. Now that we are the most dominant predators of our world and have the resources we need to survive (though we are still not so good at sharing them), we no longer need, on a broad scale, the benefits of social interdependency for basic survival. But we still need them to thrive. The human brain—including the ASD brain—is still wired to produce feel-good chemicals such as serotonin and oxytocin when triggered by positive human interaction (it just takes an ASD brain a few more times going through the motions of the trigger in order to produce the chemical payoff, than it does a non-ASD brain).[1]

I want to delve into two distinct areas in which communication is important for emotional reasons: (1) to create implicit emotional connection, and (2) to create explicit emotional connection.

Implicit Emotions

This is perhaps the most difficult concept for an ASD or analytical brain to understand (and implement). In a neurotypical brain, sharing nonessential information verbally with another person—talking about the weather, asking about what they did over the weekend, laughing about a funny moment in a movie you've both seen—releases the feel-good chemicals stimulated by positive social interaction. In an ASD brain, it can take a lot more conversational effort to achieve that same chemical reward. This is one of the reasons why someone with ASD may not respond appropriately to small talk, or initiate it, yet may be perfectly comfortable diving into a deeply thoughtful conversation with a complete stranger. Get someone with ASD onto a topic of conversation that interests them, and it can be hard to get them to *stop* talking (right?), because their brain is now doing the same thing for them (boosting them with serotonin) that a neurotypical brain does in response to surface chatter.

A lot of this implicit emotional communication goes beyond the words conveyed—via body language and vocal inflection. I will go into much more detail about this later in this book, but an ASD brain may not naturally read nonverbal and intonation cues the way a neurotypical brain does, because so much of the implied information meant to be exchanged during "light" or surface-level conversation can be lost on someone with ASD.

Here is a simple example from my personal life—just one of the many times when my husband, who is neurotypical, has tried to grow implicit emotional connection with me as we walked together down the street:

"What a beautiful day," Larry said, looking around. "A little chilly, but I'm glad I didn't wear a jacket. So nice."

My husband and I have been together for just under ten years, but I only recently learned that there is a worthwhile purpose behind his casually commenting on how nice the breeze feels, or how long X construction project seems to be taking, as we walk together down the sidewalk. I used to let comments like this from him pass in silence. Why respond? Yes, the breeze is nice. Does he need me to reaffirm? Is he asking for information about the breeze? What information could I possibly give him?

In fact, his brain is prompting him to engage in positive, casual communication with me because he loves me, and he wants to stimulate the serotonin that will flow through his brain once I start engaging back. And he wants me to feel that too. I have been denying him this simple pleasure for years because I did not know that it existed. My brain does not reward me the same way, so I never learned to engage casually.

Now that I am aware, I can respond more frequently the way he expects, though this is a conscious effort for me rather than automatically-ingrained behavior, so I am far from perfect, or even good at it yet.

On this particular day, I recognized an opportunity for a casual response when he commented on the beautiful day. Consciously, I shut down my instincts to say something about solving the possible lack-of-jacket problem that he already said is not a problem. "Yes," I responded, "it's beautiful."

Both of us walked in silence for a while, probably aided by my lack of any proactive reciprocal casual comment in return.

Larry tried again. "The sun's a little bright," he said. "Probably should've worn one of my baseball caps instead of the fedora."

By that point in our walk, I was slightly distracted by my shoes rubbing in new places, as spring had newly dawned and I was wearing them for the first time in six months. I was also moderately distracted by two distinct birds chirping in two distinct frequencies at two different volumes, and wondering what they might be saying, and whether the two different species of bird could understand each other. At the same time, I was trying to decide whether I should take off my own jacket, because it did feel a little hot, but the wind on my arms might be more distracting. I consciously derailed my train of thought to realize that Larry had said something, and then I replayed what he said, in my head, and recognized it as another opportunity for a casual response. But this time, I lost the battle against my instinct to use communication for a productive purpose, forgetting momentarily the newly learned productive purpose of producing serotonin in my partner's brain. "Uhh," I said uncertainly, "do you want to—should we—go back and change hats?"

Larry sighed. "No," he said. "We shouldn't go back. I'll be fine. Just making conversation."

Realizing my mistake, I felt embarrassed, and sad that he was sad—or at least I thought he might be sad, because he was sighing and his shoulders slumped a little, but I couldn't tell for sure. "Right," I said. "Sorry."

More silence.

I wanted to compensate for lost ground, but I felt like an awkward teenager. I tried to initiate casual communication myself this time. "I'm still thinking about that episode of *Doctor Who* last night . . ." I offered.

Larry seemed to recognize my proactive attempt to repair our stunted exchange, and wanted to encourage me. "Oh?" he said. "What part?"

I then launched into a particularly riveting concept from the TV episode, which gave me plenty of fodder for talking on a semi-casual, semi-deep level where I was more comfortable and still reciprocating in building emotional connection with the man I love.

As you can see, it's a work in progress! I am getting better at this kind of casual communication, with practice. I now have the logical tools and knowledge that I did not before, and I can use them to build strategies which compensate, at least partially, for my brain's lack of auto-process.

The combination of a lack of evolutionarily-developed brain chemical rewards for casual communication (as opposed to communication for the explicit purpose of productive information exchange), and a lack of natural ability to interpret implicit emotions communicated nonverbally, can make this sort of exchange seem entirely useless to someone with ASD. To the rest of the world, of course, it's anything but.

Explicit Emotions

A more clear-cut reason for emotional communication is to create explicit connection. Emotions in general can be tricky for an ASD or analytical brain, whether explicit or implicit. For one thing, many people with ASD may also have alexithymia, a specific neurological difference that renders a person unable to recognize or name their own emotions (people without ASD can have this too). For another, emotions can be very overwhelming on a sensory level, and someone who is already more prone to sensory overload can have a hard time processing them.

Personally, I have lived most of my life in a sort of emotional middle ground. I rarely get overly excited, and I rarely get overly depressed. I used to think this was more of a "nature" thing—a fundamental part of my personality. But after consideration, I believe it may have been a skill I developed early on, realizing that emotions could so easily overwhelm me. I learned to simply not allow myself to get overly emotional about anything, positive or negative. Caregivers or peers perceived me as "emotionless" or aloof. Of course, this balance has been much harder to maintain now that I am a wife of nearly ten years, and the mother of a highly emotional toddler and a new baby—some of the many reasons that I am writing this book now.

"I love you" is perhaps the most common example of a way that communication is used to convey explicit emotion. "I hate you" works too, but let's stay positive.

A simple phrase like "I love you" can mean many different things to many different people.

This inability to be exacting and precise in our language about emotions can cause yet more difficulty for an ASD or analytical brain. Someone with ASD may prefer not to communicate that they are feeling any particular emotion at all, rather than to identify it the wrong way, or use the wrong words to express it. Neurotypical people do this all the time—approximating their emotions with their best guess at the right words—because a neurotypical brain can also make leaps of faith and infer deeper meaning. Someone who is neurotypical may even throw out a series of several words to try to describe how they are feeling, knowing that none of them really do the emotion justice, but hoping that together they may add up to a context greater than the sum of its parts. To someone with ASD, however, this can make for a very confusing melting pot of seemingly unrelated and contradictory emotional states—in other words, a big, scary mess.

One of the most helpful strategies I have found for being able to communicate my own emotions when the words can be so hard to find, is to literally describe what I am thinking, rather than to try to name the emotion. I am much more familiar with my thinking self (my literal thoughts) than my feeling self (my emotions). I might say, "I feel like I can't get anything right," which will more concretely convey my emotional state to a neurotypical person, and to myself, than if I were to try to use more vague terms like helplessness or hopelessness. Or, in another instance, I might say, "I feel like I just walked into a pitch-black room and can't find the light switch," in order to communicate deep confusion, fear, or paralysis.

Another reason for explicitly communicating emotions is to give strong emotions an external outlet and avoid the damaging effects of over-internalization.

Someone with ASD may be intimately familiar with the potentially damaging effects of internalizing emotions. Internalization is a common coping mechanism for people with autism, who may not naturally develop other tools for recognizing, channeling, and expressing strong emotions. But keeping your feelings "bottled up inside," rather than letting them out, done over time and with consistency, can literally cause psychological and physiological damage to your brain and body.

I am often thrown by what I perceive to be emotional outbursts from people around me, when in reality these are often an entirely appropriate externalization of strong emotions that would do more damage, and last longer, if kept inside. If you have ever held a grudge, you know it can grow worse over time if not addressed via mutual communication. There is, of course, a balance—neurotypical people learn how to temper their own emotions so as not to rant and rave all over the place, and plenty of people who are not on the autism spectrum also internalize emotions more than might be considered psychologically healthy. There are also plenty of people with ASD who experience no issues with internalization and are quite adept at expressing any and every emotion as it comes along.

Personally, though, I internalize to the extreme. Not just emotions—everything. Someone is not satisfied with the quality of my work or the outcome of my efforts? It is my fault for not making sure I understood the direction or intentions clearly enough. (Likely partly true, but not the whole truth.) Someone is in a car accident within my visual field? Why didn't I see it about to happen and scream or shout or wave my arms to stop them? (Likely would have made no difference at all, and nothing about the accident is my fault, but that doesn't stop me from internalizing.)

If this sounds familiar, there is more on the tendency for internalization, how ASD traits can make it much worse, and some specific strategies for dealing with it in the Troubleshooting and Self-Care Strategies in chapter 7 of this book. For now, I want to share an example from my life to illustrate the importance of learning how to effectively use communication to externalize strong emotions.

When I was in high school, I developed a physiological condition that corresponded precisely to the times when I felt strongly about something, but instead of voicing it out loud, I swallowed it down and internalized it. After years of having done this since childhood, my body had begun to respond with a painful acid reflux. I developed fairly severe heartburn at the age of fifteen. It even started happening when I knew the answer to a question that a teacher asked during class, and yet I didn't volunteer to respond, paralyzed at the prospect of hearing my own voice out loud in a crowded classroom, afraid I might in fact be wrong, afraid classmates would think of me as a show-off or know-it-all.

It was my mother, always conscious of the body-mind connection, who helped me see that the heartburn and the internalization might be connected. It took several years, but I slowly learned how to speak up when I needed to, recognizing which situations more urgently needed my voice than others, and how I could express myself in a constructive way, and as a result, the acid reflux slowly receded. Since then, the condition has resurfaced only a handful of times, always sparked by an instance of over-internalization.

Communication for Collaboration

Chemicals like serotonin and oxytocin do more than make a person feel good, they pave the neural roadways for other beneficial chemicals that produce other beneficial feelings and actions—a sense of purpose, a sense of community, a sense of courage, honor, duty, passion, love, and selfless-ness. These feelings can be powerful motivators for human behavior and contribute greatly to a sense of overall well-being.

Communicating in order to collaborate with others looks a lot like the "information creation" communication we discussed earlier. But there are distinct elements to collaborative communication that set it apart. In the case of collaboration, you are not just creating information, like a mutually agreeable Terms and Conditions document or the best time to go to the pharmacy. The stakes are higher—you have multiple deliverables to accomplish, multiple steps to complete, multiple perspectives and experiences and ideas and opinions to incorporate, and potentially even multiple cultures, personalities, and communication styles to account for.

This is where you will want to develop skills in professional relationship building and in conducting or participating in meetings. I discuss collaborative communication strategies more deeply in chapters 3 and 4.

WRITTEN COMMUNICATION VERSUS IN-PERSON COMMUNICATION

Throughout my college years, I never perceived any identifiable differences between written communication—texts, emails, books—and in-person verbal communication such as phone calls, talking in-person, seeing live speakers, and so on. In my mind, communication was communication, whatever the method, and its sole purpose was to convey information. Why would it make a difference whether the information was conveyed via email or in-person conversation? But it <u>does</u> make a difference—a big one. We'll get there in a minute.

To me, written communication was preferable, because it limited the potential for confusion and distracting emotions. It was clear and precise, much easier to both express and understand. I thought this was true for most people, unless they liked to talk or were naturally extroverted. Little did I know that most people, unlike myself, gleaned a lot of information from body language and vocal inflection during in-person interactions. It is impossible to read body language in an email. It is very difficult to infer vocal inflection from a text. Even if you have known someone for years, misunderstanding and miscommunication still happens all the time, more often than not (for most people) in writing, rather than in conversation.

Two-Way versus One-Way Communication

Except perhaps for texting or instant messaging, which are very short-form and conducted on platforms designed to facilitate a close approximation of in-person conversation, written communication is a one-way communication flow, whereas in-person communication is usually a two-way flow.

What does this mean? Think of the last time you wrote an email. Likely, it included several separate but related points of information, all of which you conveyed simultaneously *to* someone else. That person is then expected to read all (or most, or sometimes only half, as I have learned) of your words, and then formulate their equally one-way email back to you, adding their own thoughts or questions. This can take anywhere from a few minutes, if someone happens to be checking and responding to emails right then, to a few days (or weeks). Imagine you were to have the same conversation in-person, or even over the phone. Would you have been able to "read" your entire email out loud to them, making three or four separate points, without the other person responding? No. You would cover one of the points, then the other person would add their thoughts related to that first point. Then you would both move to the second point, and so forth. You might even find that after they've added their perspective to your first point, your second and third points become irrelevant, or change in a significant way to reflect the new information.

To an ASD brain, which may take longer to process and communicate thoughts than a non-ASD brain, the pace of two-way communication can at times be overwhelming. For example, I experience a minor audio-processing delay, because I often have to repeat in my own head what I heard someone say before I can actually "hear" and process what they said. This is a common tactic employed by people with ASD in order to participate fully in verbal communication. With thirty-plus years of practice, I have learned how to do this very quickly, almost instantaneously, but it can still interfere with the normal flow of two-way conversation, especially if the topic is confusing or emotional for me.

There are many other reasons why an ASD-brain may experience difficulty with two-way communication, including an inability to listen and form thoughts at the same time (neurotypical brains have difficulty with this, too, which is why people must learn how to "actively listen"), a tendency to be distracted by extraneous details (I can see a piece of white fluff on her shoulder flitting up and down while she is talking to me and it is driving me insane), and simple sensory overload (she is talking to me but the air conditioner is making oddly-timed plunking noises and there is another conversation happening right next to us and I am quickly becoming overwhelmed by too many sounds all at once).

You can see how someone with ASD might prefer one-way communication to the more overwhelming experience of two-way communication. And in many cases, such as in long-form communication like research papers, books, reports, or proposals, one-way written communication is much clearer and easier to understand. But for most neurotypical people, reading a long email about something that could be resolved quickly in conversation can be excruciating.

→ How can you tell if something should really be communicated in person? There are several red flags you can look for before you hit the "send" button on an email instead.

1. <u>Timeliness.</u> Does the person on the other end of this email need to know this information sooner rather than later? Or do you need information back from them immediately? You can still send the email with one of those "high importance" markers, but take into account just how quickly they/you need the information before you put it in an email rather than placing a phone call.

   - Understand that, if you are requesting information from someone else, by putting your request in an email, rather than picking up the phone and calling someone on the spot, you're forfeiting the expectation of an immediate response. An urgent voice mail can be followed up with an urgent email, referencing that you called. But an urgent email can't be followed up (politely) with an urgent call until at least a few hours after the email has been sent, and even then, the situation would have to be dire. Putting your request into email form implies that you don't need the information until at least the next day.

2. <u>Length.</u> If your email is turning into a dissertation—a.k.a. if it takes you more than, say, ten minutes to compose your email—you might need to put it aside into a journal or speaking notes for yourself, and cut your email down to just a request to meet with the person to discuss the topic at hand. If you find yourself going into a lot of details, asking a lot of questions, using a lot of explanatory language, describing your thought process or justifying your actions, then the person you are writing to has a right to respond to your communication in real time, rather than read several pages while sitting alone at their desk. You—if you are an analytical thinker or have ASD—also have a right, however, to get your thoughts out the way that works best for you, so write them all down if you must, and

bring them with you to the meeting so you can refer to them during the two-way conversation. Later in this section, under "Combination Strategies," is a more in-depth exploration of how to do this effectively.

3. <u>Opinions and Assumptions.</u> Are you taking any license in your email/written communication—assuming things you are not 100 percent sure about, or expressing personal opinions? These are often better received in a two-way environment, where your counterpart can immediately course-correct your train of thought if your assumption is wrong, question further to legitimize your opinion, and/or add their own opinions.

4. <u>Emotions.</u> We will get into this in a bit more detail below, but in general, emotions are best kept out of written communications, because neurotypical brains glean so much emotional information from things like body language and vocal inflection. Your own intentions can become lost and muddled if the person reading your communication is attributing the wrong emotional state to your words. Even though emotions can be overwhelming, and two-way communication can be overwhelming, and putting them together is doubly overwhelming, the long-term benefit far outweighs the temporary strife. There are many points throughout the rest of this book where I will lay out specific examples of how an ASD brain can tackle emotional communication with NTs in both written and in-person form.

· · ·

Here is an example from my personal life of how one-sided communication can go awry very quickly, and a strategy for mitigating the potential damage:

Early in my romantic relationship with Larry, we would have what appeared to me to be a confusing or negative interaction, often quite brief, that would induce hours of mental gymnastics as I tried to unravel what had gone wrong. I was also formulating my own thoughts about what I should have said, or wanted to say now that I couldn't think of it in the moment, until after I had been able to process his words more fully in the quiet of my own mind. To me, our in-person two-way interaction had been much more of a one-way interaction, because his neurotypical brain had communicated toward me in real time, while my ASD brain was not able to reciprocate a two-way response. Often when this happened, it would result in my sending Larry an email, hours later, sometimes in the middle of the work day, with what constituted my two-way response back to his one-way communication from earlier in the day. Imagine getting an email, seemingly out of the blue, about something that happened hours ago that you had already forgotten, with an entirely one-sided response to what you had said earlier that you might not even really remember saying. Frustrating, yes? But for me, it felt like the natural next step in the interaction. He'd gotten his thoughts out about whatever particular topic, and now it was my turn.

Neurotypical communication does not work like that. Before learning more about my communication style, Larry may have assumed that our earlier in-person interaction was as two-way as it was going to get, and to suddenly get a retroactive one-way communication that changed that was jarring and ineffective.

Today, we have both learned several strategies to address the gap in our communication styles. Larry understands that, in the heat of the moment, I might not be able to say what I need to or intend to convey in real time, so he tries to give me space to process and respond. I have learned that some negative interactions are not a big deal, and don't require analysis or fixing, so it's better to just let them go. If something particularly sticky comes up, I can still write an email with my longer-form thoughts, but I put "journal" in the subject line before I send it to Larry, so that Larry knows this is an intentionally one-sided journaling of my thoughts, which I want to share with him, but that I don't expect an immediate response from him. These missives are more therapeutic for me than they are intended to actually continue the conversation.

Emotional Reciprocity

Another subtle way that in-person communication differs from written communication is emotional reciprocity, inferred from body language and tone of voice. Now that I have learned about the most common forms of body language and vocal inflection, explored later in this chapter, I can glean much more from my in-person encounters by actively reading body language and interpreting tone while listening to the person's words at the same time. It takes a lot of conscious effort, but the results are well worth it.

For a neurotypical brain, for example, someone crossing their arms over their chest generally communicates defensiveness, frustration, confusion, and in some cases, the beginnings of anger. Exactly which of these emotions is indicated will depend on the person and the context. For example, I once had a boss who crossed his arms when he was confused and thinking deeply about what to say next. Often the gesture was accompanied by a furrowed brow or drawing in of his eyebrows. I learned this over the course of many interactions, observing and noting the specific ways in which he used body language (probably unconsciously most of the time) to convey information about his mental and emotional state.

Another person might cross their arms when they feel under attack, because your words are striking on a deeper level than you perhaps intended. Interpreting body language manually will take a lot of practice—both to learn the quirks of specific people, and the larger commonalities of body language in your culture. But you can see how realizing, in real time, that the person you are communicating with might be becoming confused or defensive can (and should) change the way you approach the moment.

When my boss crossed his arms, I learned to finish my current thought and wait, so he had time to process whatever he was confused about. I braced myself for probing questions or pushback. Once he had worked through it, he would uncross his arms, and the conversation would continue. Such immediate emotional reciprocity would be impossible over email.

I go into more detail about various common forms of body language and what they generally mean, in chapter 2. But even if you don't know exactly what someone's body language means, you can recognize when something is amiss and change your interaction to match. "Does that make sense?" is something you might ask to determine whether someone is confused. Or you might pause and say, "What do you think?" to give the other person a chance to respond.

Combination Strategies

Earlier, I mentioned that I would share some specific examples and strategies for combining written and in-person communication to ease the interaction between an ASD-brain and a neurotypical brain.

The key here is to recognize that while a neurotypical brain generally experiences in-person communication as two-way, and written communication as one-way, an ASD brain might feel differently. For me, most communication, whether spoken or written, feels one-way. I find it very challenging both to process input and formulate and execute a response in real time. This is why, before heading to someone's desk to chat, I prepare several pre-mapped pathways for where the conversation might lead, and responses I have already vetted. I share more of these specific strategies throughout this book.

Occasionally, when I know the in-person interaction will be emotionally taxing, I use a relatively unorthodox yet highly effective combination of both written and in-person communication, to participate in the way I need to.

My workload had become too overwhelming.

This was difficult for me to recognize and admit, given how much I internalize and take responsibility for everything. I asked myself all the usual questions: Were my priorities not aligned properly? Was I not using my time effectively? Was my work pace too slow? But the fact was, I simply did not have enough work hours—or hours, period—in the day to complete what needed to be done.

I had gotten into this situation mostly due to a mismatch of planning and execution. The way I had planned for things to go (hiring staff and other resource support, the pace at which growth would take place, etc.) was not the way that they were going in reality, and it was time to reassess the original plan and course-correct.

But how do you walk into your boss's office and say, "I have too much work to do"? That's not something most bosses will appreciate hearing. Everyone has too much work to do, right? Some people may have the kind of relationship with their manager that would allow for it, but I knew I didn't. I needed to put together solid evidence, identify key problems that were blocking progress, and lay out vetted, strategic solutions he could evaluate.

I also knew that, because I can't naturally regulate my own body language or tone of voice, if I walked into my boss's office and launched into a long-winded explanation of all the evidence that had led me to the conclusion that my workload was too much, it would come across like a string of excuses. I needed to present some of my argument in written form, to avoid the miscommunication, and the inevitable pushback, that would follow.

• • •

So, I wrote out my key thoughts in advance and cut them down to a single page of short bullet points.

I made sure that no more than half-to-three-quarters of my one-pager focused on the fact-based "problems," and the rest laid out, in bullet-point

AN IMPORTANT NOTE:
WRITTEN AND VERBAL COMMUNICATION

In order for a combination written/verbal communication strategy like this to work, the written portion must be exceedingly brief and to the point. Some emotional expression in the written portion is okay, but only to illustrate the importance and passion that you attribute to the subject. Avoid derisive or cutting language, attributing blame, or sarcasm in the written portion of your problem identification, as these devices can cause defenses to go up in your reader.

form, the solutions I had already identified. A solutions-focused conversation is much easier (for me, and I think for many people, ASD or no) to have in person than a problems-focused conversation. For one, the overall emotional tone of a solutions-based conversation is positive and constructive, which allows for smoother interaction all around, rather than the more negative overtone of a problems-focused conversation.

So instead of walking into my boss's office and saying, "I have too much work to do," I was able to walk in and say, "I have run into some issues that are impeding progress toward our goals. I know this is a little unusual, but I've laid out some key thoughts in this one-pager, which I'd like for you to take a minute to read before we talk them through, and then I want to focus on the potential solutions and how we can execute a better strategy." I then handed my boss the written document and retained a copy myself, so we could both sit in the room together reading the document. The fact that I plainly acknowledged, when I handed him the paper, that this was a little out of the ordinary, made things less awkward. The fact that I also looked down at my own paper and read, rather than watch him while he read, helped remove any time pressure he might have felt as a neurotypical person, "rudely" reading a document rather than talking directly to the person in front of him.

In the end, the single page of written, one-way communication from me served its purpose beautifully, putting my voice into the room in a way that best suited my communication style, and empowering both of our voices to then come together and address the positive, forward momentum of solutions-building in a subsequent two-way interaction.

This strategy worked well for me in this case, but there are situations where it might not work as well.

For one thing, the other person in the equation needs to be at least partially receptive to the use of uncommon or unorthodox communication methods, and demonstrate at least a somewhat individualized approach in their interactions with other people. In the above instance, my boss was a highly analytical thinker himself, and could probably relate personally on some level with my need to share logically organized thoughts in a written form. It also helps, I think, that an office environment already lends itself to the use of memos and emails and other forms of written communication that act as precursors to in-person communication. But as the world grows ever more digital, there is likely a way to apply at least part of this strategy in any kind of workplace.

THE DREADED SMALL TALK

Why Is It Important?

We all know it. Most of us hate it. And yet we do it. Why? There are, in fact, many reasons that small talk is an important part of human communication:

1. It establishes common ground. People use small talk to gauge, on a safe, superficial level, where the other person is at emotionally and mentally. Most of the time, you will find

that the person you are interacting with is close enough to your wavelength that you can move fairly quickly onto more substantive topics. It is essential, however, if you want to have a productive conversation, to take a minute or several to establish this common ground. If someone was just at a funeral, or had a big fight with their spouse, their mind might be elsewhere. Without some innocent small talk to clear the air or reset that person's mind toward the matter at hand, they might spend your entire conversation being mentally distracted or emotionally distant. They likely won't share with you exactly what did happen that morning, but by reading body language and tone of voice as you talk about the weather or ask about their weekend, you can gauge whether they are energetic or drained, engaged or preoccupied, motivated or unmotivated, and alter the remainder of your interaction in order to match or account for the other person's emotional and mental state. Or just come back later!

2. It gives you a chance to "warm up." Most people resist jumping from one state to another too quickly, or from one topic to another without transition. Someone just coming out of a meeting that was about an entirely different subject than your meeting is going to be, or someone you run into on the street or in the office pantry, is likely to benefit from a minute or two of "warming up" to your presence and your topic of conversation. Mentally, they are transitioning from a previous state into a new one. In the back of their mind they may be wrapping up thoughts from their previous interaction, even on a subconscious level, while they engage in surface-level chitchat. You can think of it like taking a minute to clear off a section of your desk in order to work more effi-

ciently, or filing away notes from one meeting before going to the next one.

3. It builds implicit emotional connection. One of the reasons that I always hated small talk was my perception that nobody asking me lightly how I was that day or what I did that weekend, really and truly wanted to know. I always felt forced to give a static, superficial answer, no matter how I was feeling or what I had done. What I failed to recognize was that it mattered very little what I actually said; more important was the <u>way</u> I said it. If I said my weekend was great, but sighed and shrugged my shoulders while I said it, the other person would intuit that maybe it hadn't been so great and that I didn't feel much like sharing beyond that in the moment, and they might give me a few more minutes of light talk to clear the air a bit more before moving gently into the topic at hand. On the contrary, if I said my weekend was great, with enthusiasm and volume in my voice, leaning forward in my chair and making eye contact, the other person might feel free to ask for more details about what I did that was so great, so they could share in my success and reciprocate my enthusiasm. I have never experienced the emotional connection that a neurotypical brain gains from superficial interaction like this. But I recognized the value in making the other person feel emotionally recognized, validated, and included. By engaging someone in small talk before diving into the meat of your conversation, you are essentially letting that person know that you care about their well-being (even if you don't have time to hear their life story right now), and that if ever there was something major bothering them or something crazy going on in their life, you would be understanding and accommodating.

How to Use Small Talk Effectively

If you think of small talk as one of many tools at your disposal for interacting productively with the world, it should become much less of a burdensome mystery. You won't need to use small talk in every situation, and you needn't let it go on too long or take you past your comfort zone. Below are some of the more concrete things I have learned about small talk that might be helpful as you learn your own strategies for success.

In What Situations?

You needn't use small talk in every situation. There are certain settings, certain types of people, and certain circumstances in which small talk can be useful, and there are those where it's unnecessary. In general, I have found small talk to be very useful in the following situations:

Settings

- Work (meetings, passing in the hallway, getting food in the shared pantry, eating lunch in a shared cafeteria space)
- Work-related social events (holiday parties, happy hours, etc.)
- Public transportation (bus, train, etc.)
- Public waiting areas (doctors' offices, Department of Motor Vehicles, etc.)
- Other public institutions (grocery stores, restaurants, local playgrounds, post office, etc.)
- School functions (school plays/shows, field trips, graduations/assemblies, etc.)
- House parties (gathering at a friend's home—or your own—with other people of varying familiarity)

Types of People

- Strangers (people you have never met before who engage you in a public setting)
- Acquaintances (other parents from your kid's school, a friend of a friend, etc.)
- Colleagues (until perhaps you have built enough of a relationship with a colleague to consider them a friend)
- Distant relatives (cousins you see every few years or folks you only interact with at family reunions, etc.)

Circumstances

- Upon first seeing or speaking with an acquaintance or distant relative again after time apart
- When trying to determine the purpose or intention behind a stranger's interaction (do they need directions, do they just need someone to talk to, do they in fact have ill intent, are they just being friendly, did something about you or what you were doing bring up an intense interest or need to connect, etc.)
- When trying to establish a baseline emotional connection with a service provider from whom you need a particular service (chatting with the waiter to build emotional reciprocity and cache that you may need to use later when your toddler makes an inconceivable mess with his ketchup—my husband is much better at this one than I ever will be)

And, in general, I have found that small talk is usually not as necessary with the following:

Settings

- Home
- A close family member's or friend's home (without the presence of any unfamiliar people)

Types of People

- Close family (family members you live with or have known most of your life, etc.)
- Close friends
- Friends of close friends with whom you have become familiar
- Friends you have known for a long time, regardless of "closeness"
- People you share other common ground with and have known in the context of that common ground for a long time. The best example I have of this is the few fellow parents from my son's school with whom I have interacted on many occasions throughout the course of a school year, and with whom I have had many in-depth conversations about various topics. I would not necessarily consider them to be "friends" yet, but we have become friendly enough, and we have enough common ground in our children's experiences that we can often skip the small talk portion at the beginning of an interaction and jump right into kid- or school-related topics.
- Children—whether your own or someone else's—rarely require small talk, as they are still learning the "social graces" themselves, and tend to favor more direct conversation as they take in new details about the world around them.

Circumstances

- Interacting with close family members while on vacation or visiting. This will often require a different kind of small talk in the beginning as you first settle into your visit, more like catching up on the lives you have lived away from each other for the past year, or however long it has been, and tends to be much easier to tackle spontaneously because there is more room for you to talk about whatever you wish in this context.
- At a gathering of close friends, like a hobby meet-up group (book club, wine club, etc.) or a night out together (drinks, movie, etc.)
- Interacting directly with children, your own or others, wherever that might take place: at home, at a park, at school, etc.

For the most part, the above bullets lay out a basic structure: Small talk is most useful when interacting with people who are less familiar to you, and becomes less useful as you get to know a person more deeply. Your brain (and that person's) will have built enough of a pathway and foundation of emotional connection that the small talk becomes unnecessary.

Creating a Quick-Reference Mental "File" for People Important to You

That said, one of the reasons that the specific tool of small talk may not be needed when you are interacting with someone you have built emotional common ground with already is that you will be expected to notice, more easily than you would when interacting with a stranger, how that person is feeling. In neurotypical relationships (friends, colleagues, partners), people who know each other fairly well are expected to be able to gauge the main underlying emotions of the other person without need of a superficial small talk warm-up.

In my experience with an ASD brain, however, it can be hard to parse out the unspoken emotional landscape of another person while I am also actively engaged in conversation (as opposed to just lightly returning surface-level small talk). While using small talk still takes more conscious effort for me than most people, it does allow me the mental space to actively read body language and tone of voice, cues I may miss if more of my brain space is taken up by the actual content of a substantive conversation. It was for this reason, and also because of my inability to naturally adapt different skills to different contexts (something I will get to in more detail later), that up through my midtwenties, I would continue the use of small talk far longer into the cultivation of a relationship than a neurotypical person would have. Often, people told me I came across as too formal, or people would appear confused or thrown off by my asking seemingly inane questions upon a third or fourth meeting—trying to make small talk when it was no longer necessary.

Now I have learned how to use a form of "small talk 2.0," where I still give myself a chance to read and react to a familiar person emotionally, without appearing to be stuck in an overly formal or superficial mode. Instead of engaging a friend or acquaintance about something superficial like the weather when I first see them again after some time apart, I keep a mental file of specific things that interest that person or that are happening in that person's life, so I can engage them about something more substantive to their life, while retaining enough brainpower to read and interpret body language and vocal cues. I might ask one of my husband's friends about a movie I know they just saw, or I might engage a fellow parent about an event that I know is coming up at our kids' school. This gives me the minute or so that I need to actively read their tone of voice and nonverbal cues to determine, in general, if they are in an emotionally positive, negative, or neutral place, if they are in a hurry to get somewhere, or if they are feeling friendly or preoccupied. And then I am more prepared to react and respond to them appropriately as our conversation might shift into deeper waters.

It can be very helpful to spend a little bit of your own free time creating "quick-reference mental files" for the people in your life who you are closest to in order to facilitate this ability to use "small talk 2.0" as a tool for giving yourself time to read the other person's emotional cues at the beginning of your next interaction. When I learn something new about a person I have known for a while—like their sibling has chronic asthma, or they are going on a trip to another country next month, or they have a specific hobby or extracurricular they engage in like kayaking or volunteering at their church—I take a moment to consciously file this information away for future use. The next time I see them, I am then empowered to ask how their trip went, how their sibling is doing, or whether they've been kayaking recently, or even just what they like most about kayaking, as a form of more engaged small talk that can lead quickly into other subjects of interest for us both. This also has the obvious benefit of making people feel known and remembered, ensuring they will think of you fondly in the future.

There is no need to catalog and mentally file every single thing you learn about every person you meet—don't go down that rabbit hole. Just choose a few things about a person that perhaps also hold a certain level of interest for you, or perhaps that you truly don't understand (why there are so many people who love to cook is still a mystery to me), so that you can remember them more easily and fall into conversation when you meet again.

How Long

Because small talk is a tool people use to warm up or clear the air or establish common ground, it need not go on forever.

In general, a few minutes of small talk is all you need before you can actively shift the conversation to the next level. Sometimes, especially if I am interacting with a colleague at work whom I know well, or someone who has a similarly productivity-focused mindset, I can get away with only about sixty seconds of back-and-forth small talk before diving into the forward motion. Other times, regardless of how well I might know a person, one or both of us may need up to five minutes to really clear our minds and set an emotionally level playing field. Any more than five minutes, however, and I start to get antsy.

If you find yourself in a situation where the small talk seems to be going on for ages, you may have slipped past the use of small talk as a tool and entered into idle conversation that may or may not be productive for you. The other person might just need to get some things off their chest, or be starving for interaction after being alone all day, or might be genuinely interested in hearing more about your life than you are particularly interested or inclined to share. It is not considered impolite, in general, to gently extricate yourself from these situations or move the conversation into the realm of productivity.

There are times when people will engage in small talk just in passing, as a way to build emotional reciprocity with another person, rather than as a tool for warming up to more substantive conversation.

After engaging for a few minutes in this type of casual conversation, here are some specific strategies I have found most useful in removing myself, politely, from passing small talk that has gone on for too long:

If at work:

- Apologize and say you have to run to a meeting, or that you are late for your next call.
  - If you don't in fact have a meeting to get to right at that moment, this is still a perfectly acceptable

white lie to tell—even if it's not specifically a meeting you are getting to, you undoubtedly have enough work to do that the intention of "getting back to work" trumps exactly how you say you are doing it.

- Use a softener as you leave, like "talk more later" or "good luck," or something short and polite that acknowledges the context the other person just shared with you, but makes it clear that these are your last words for now.

  - AVOID saying anything more directly along the lines of "I have to get back to work," even if that is the truth, because this type of language—unless you know someone well enough that you can spin it as a joke by making it seem like a small inconvenience—inevitably carries with it an implication (intentional or not) that the other person is (a) purposely keeping you from your work, and (b) not getting back to their own work, both of which are not generally helpful or socially acceptable implications to make in the workplace, even if true.

If in a social setting:

- Meeting someone on the street and engaging in small talk as you pass.

  - Again, apologize and say that you are running late for something. You might even be truthful here, letting the person know that you are in fact running late picking up your kid from school, or running late to an appointment, or running late to get to the grocery store to pick up what you need for dinner that night, even if you aren't exactly running "late" yet. If you are not in fact running late for anything but just want to get out of the conversation, avoid making up a specific excuse beyond "Sorry, I'm running late, but we'll talk soon!" Usually, if you do this while you start to walk away, the other person will understand and not badger you.

- Meeting someone in a store or park or other public place where you are "stuck" for a while (not simply walking by on your way to somewhere else).

  - It is often acceptable to turn the need to exit small talk into something that appears as a courtesy to the other person, such as "Well, I'll let you get back to your shopping." An NT person, reading between the lines, will know that you are done talking and ready to move on with your own shopping, and recognize that you politely acknowledged their needs rather than making it only about your own. You can use this in a variety of settings, such as at the playground when you run into another parent from your kid's school: "Well, I'll let you get back to your kid." This way, you don't have to try to run out of the store or park in order to get away, you can just move on to the next aisle or go engage more fully with your own kid for a few minutes.

- Meeting someone while on public transit.

  - This is perhaps the trickiest of casual social settings in which to gracefully exit small talk. It's highly inconvenient to make up the excuse that "This is my stop," when it really isn't, and get off the train or bus at the wrong stop just to get away from casual interaction with an acquaintance. (I have done this. Trust me, you really don't need to.) Often, you might have to just grit your teeth and sit it out. What I will do, if I have the energy in these situations, is use the time as an excuse to really try to get to know the person better, and move the conversation as quickly as possible beyond the small-talk stage and into a deeper connection. I will try to find a mutually invigorating topic that we both seem to enjoy, like a particular hobby or TV show or current event. This helps me move to a place where I am more comfortable interacting—talking about something that interests me and the other person—rather than trying to come up with polite surface-level things to say for the rest of the bus ride.

- If you had been counting on your commute for some quiet alone time with your book or music or your own thoughts, this can be difficult to give up. If you can, remember to block off another time not too long afterward to give yourself a few "me" minutes back. Sometimes I will find a coffee shop or even just a bench on the sidewalk to sit by myself for a few minutes and listen to music or do a little bit of what I had intended to do with my commute time, so that I can still be rejuvenated even though my plans had to change.

There are also socially acceptable ways for moving a conversation out of the small talk phase and into the content phase. Sometimes this is in fact the most appropriate thing to do, like at the start of a meeting, when small talk is eating into the short window you have.

If at work:

- After allowing for up to five minutes of small talk, you can use nonverbal cues to indicate that you are ready to move the conversation along. These might include shifting in your chair and inhaling deeply, as if you are gently waking your body up and getting it ready to engage in a more challenging activity; picking up your pen and getting it ready to start taking notes on your notepad; or moving to the front edge of your chair and taking up more space with your arms or elbows on the table in front of you, as if to indicate you'll be using the table to support you in the next, more taxing part of the conversation.

- After engaging in one or more nonverbal tactics, if the small talk still has not shifted into substantive conversation, you can start to employ gentle verbal cues, such as truncated responses. Instead of responding with apparent interest and asking for more details about their plans for the weekend, nod politely and say, succinctly, "Right." Or "Cool." Or "Uh-huh."

  - If you do this, be sure to use a FLAT monotone to avoid inadvertently communicating any overt annoyance, sarcasm, or actual disinterest.

  - After employing at least one of the above subtler cues, it is acceptable to directly move the conversation into the business of the meeting by gently interrupting the flow (but don't cut someone off in midsentence!) to say something like, "Okay, so, to be respectful of everyone's time, let's start talking about X" or "All right, should we go ahead and get started?"

- These kinds of direct shifts are best said slowly, with a second or two pause between words, with obvious room for the other person/people in the room to register that a shift is being made and to allow enough space for someone to object, if they really want to.

- If you do this at more than one meeting, you may gain a reputation, as I have, for being someone who likes to "get down to business"—but this is not necessarily a bad thing, and may in fact gain you some reprieve in having to engage in longer small-talk phases in the future. Win-win!

Subjects to Keep in Your Back Pocket

It can be extremely helpful, especially when in a setting where the need for small talk can come up at any random unpredictable time, to keep a few key, relevant, interesting small-talk subjects "in your back pocket," to pull out on short notice.

This is different from the "quick-reference mental files" you might maintain for specific people who are closer to you. These back-pocket small-talk subjects are your own personal file to pull out when you need to engage in small talk with someone who is less familiar. These are topics that interest you, to some degree, and that are also socially acceptable as topics for light, superficial conversation.

Some good options include:

Sports. If you are an avid sports fan or follow one or a few particular sports or teams closely.

Weekend Plans. If you happen to have some specific plans coming up, like a movie you are planning to see, or a local carnival you are taking your kids to, keep them in mind to bring up as a positive "I'm doing something fun this weekend, how about you?" kind of small talk option.

- This also works in short-term past tense: If you went somewhere cool or did something noteworthy last weekend, you can use that as a topic for small talk that engages the other person in what they did last weekend or what they are planning to do this coming weekend. But don't reach back too far—this works best if it's just one weekend prior, not something cool you did last month or last year.

Kids. There was a time, perhaps, when (especially as a woman), actively bringing up kids or family life in the workplace was not the best idea. And I am sure, unfortunately, that there are still work situations where this remains the case. For the most part, however, in the majority of working environments today, what your kid/s have been doing recently, or a funny, quick, recent story about them, can be a very safe, engaging, surface-level topic for small talk, especially with coworkers who are also parents.

Movies / TV Shows / Books. If you don't watch any TV or haven't seen a recent movie in years (or you read the same books over and over again . . . Harry Potter, anyone?), then this is not the best casual subject matter for you. But if you have seen a movie or read a book that has come out in the last year, or watched a currently running TV show, you can easily create a minute or so of small talk by asking the other person if they've seen/read it, and commiserating together over what you each thought of it. Even if they haven't seen the show/movie or read the book, you can still recount a particularly funny or engaging moment from the content that you think the other person might like. Be careful, though, not to go into too much detail, and to keep your brief retelling to no more than sixty seconds—you're just offering a glimpse of content, not recounting the entire plot line.

CONVERSATION FLOW

Now that we've covered the basics, and the "why" of small talk, I want to share some of the fundamental aspects of two-way conversation flow that I have found hugely helpful in facilitating in-person, real-time communication with a largely neurotypical world. These tactics are relevant in both small talk and in "longer" talk—any kind of verbal interaction with another person.

Remember the example I shared in an earlier section of Larry and I walking down the street, and me failing to recognize opportunities for casual interaction in order to build implicit emotional connection? One of the issues that arises from not realizing this use of communication, nor therefore having much practice in using it, is that I never learned, the way neurotypical people do, the best way to simply "make conversation." I can talk effusively about subjects of shared interest—Harry Potter, international peace development efforts, or multicultural communication. But even then I struggle to find a natural balance in conversation that creates a "flow" between me and the other person/people, rather than one or the other of us doing all the talking. And I find it even harder to strike the right balance about more surface-level, banal topics.

"Making a Sandwich"

One way you can approach establishing and maintaining effective conversational flow is by thinking of it as if you are "making a sandwich" together with the other person, in a verbal sense. Another phrase used to describe this strategy is "give-and-take."

Daniel Wendler first introduced me to this concept in his book *Level Up Your Social Life*. At the beginning of the conversation, perhaps the person you are interacting with (metaphorically) supplies the first slice of bread. To reciprocate, you then spread on the mayonnaise. But that's it. Leave it at the mayonnaise. That gives the other person room to then put on a piece of cheese. Then you put on a piece of ham. They put on a piece of lettuce, and so forth (imagine you are both wearing latex gloves, if this helps you accept the metaphor). Each of you is adding a short, substantive, useful thought, observation, question, idea, or piece of information to the "sandwich"—the conversation.[2] Making a sandwich together wouldn't work if you just stood and watched the other person making the whole sandwich—that's not making it together, that's just you being present while the other person does all the work. And vice versa—if you start making the sandwich your own way, and don't allow room for the other person to add in their lettuce and meat in between yours, you are no longer flowing together. A conversation can feel very one-sided if one person is doing all the talking, and the other person is just standing there.

One key strategy is to find things that you feel are genuinely worth contributing to what you might consider an otherwise mundane or unnecessary conversation. Remember, it's not actually unnecessary—it's producing feel-good chemicals in the brain of the person you are interacting with, and if you go along, it will do the same in your brain after a while. If you genuinely can't think of something you would like to add, ask a question to solicit more information from the other person. Make sure your question is relevant, not too probing, and not something that you already know about the person. It's okay to take a little time selecting the right slice of ham to add to the sandwich. You are trying to make a quality sandwich, not just throw something together.

Another key is remembering that you are making the sandwich together—you don't need to start piling on all the meat and cheese and lettuce in order to fill the space, going into tremendous detail. Restrict yourself to one piece at a time, letting the other person add their own piece after yours. This helps you keep to a relatively normal "flow" or pace of conversation, which automatically facilitates two-way interaction.

Here is an example from my work life of when I consciously used this strategy to comfortably make conversation with a colleague:

I was standing at the sink in the office pantry, rinsing the cherries I had planned to eat along with a Babybel Cheese for an afternoon snack.

It was a Monday, so I already knew that a good topic for casual office conversation was what I or the other person did over the past weekend. I'd already thought through a few light, fun things that I might share from my weekend, if needed.

Lo and behold, in walked a colleague, looking to make his 2:30 p.m. cup of coffee on the shared Keurig machine.

"Hi, Sarah," he said brightly.

"Hi, Craig," I replied, turning slightly from my position at the sink in order to make brief, acknowledging eye contact. He returned the smile and then busied himself looking for the flavor of coffee he wanted to make.

"Have a good weekend?" he asked as he searched.

I was ready for the question, and knew that if he hadn't asked it within the next twenty seconds, I would have prompted him the same way, to promote a comfortable atmosphere and avoid him thinking I was standoffish or feeling awkward about the silence. Silence doesn't bother me, but I know it bothers a lot of other people.

"Yeah, it was nice," I started to respond, deliberately pausing for two seconds to make it appear as if I were just coming up with my response, rather than having thought it out previously. "We took my son to the Central Park Zoo! Our first time there." I purposely stopped there, although I had more details prepared in case Craig showed signs of wanting to move the conversation further down that path by asking questions.

"Oh, excellent," Craig responded, appropriately pleased at the idea of a child having fun at a zoo. "How old is your son?" he asked.

"He's three," I said, smiling. I knew Craig was now forming a mental picture of a three-year-old jumping around at the zoo. Again I stopped, because he only asked about my son's age and nothing else, though depending on his next response, I might offer other information.

"Oh, great age for the zoo," Craig said, fitting his chosen coffee pod into the Keurig and placing his mug underneath. "We took my daughter there a lot when she was younger. She used to love the monkeys." He smiled to himself in nostalgia, and I made a mental note to remember that Craig had a daughter, a new piece of information about him.

"How old is your daughter now?" I asked, naturally gravitating toward the balance of asking him the same question he asked me and seeing by the smile on his face that he enjoyed talking about his daughter.

He grinned as his coffee spluttered to a finish. "Oh, she's in college now—nearly nineteen. It goes by fast!"

"Yes, it does!" I agreed enthusiastically, recognizing a common platitude that people with older children use when talking to people with younger children.

I started to panic a little bit, not sure where to take the conversation from there, and wondered whether I should ask him about his weekend, but thinking that, at this point, it probably would prolong this conversation more than necessary. Luckily, Craig now had his coffee and I'd finished washing my cherries, and so we'd reached a natural ending.

"Enjoy it while it lasts," Craig said, referring to my still-young son and mock toasting me with his freshly made cup of coffee as he moved toward the pantry door.

"For sure," I agreed. Then, recognizing that he was leaving, I added, "Have a good one!" I have cultivated this phrase for automatic use, because it does not imply a specific time of day (a.k.a. "Have a good day" or "Have a good afternoon"), so I can use it whenever and not have to add in an extra process step of remembering what time of day it is so that my social platitude matches. "Have a good one" can be used any day, at any time.

"You too," he replied, and then he was gone.

• • •

You can see in the above exchange how the "one piece of the sandwich at a time" pace is helpful for maintaining appropriate conversation flow. I still talked less than Craig did, just by my nature, and that is okay. I was still an active participant in a two-way exchange that remained light, flowing, and relevant. I gained new information about a colleague and succeeded in avoiding a relatively silent or one-sided interaction that would have left Craig feeling awkward. Instead, he walked away (I hope, anyway) feeling like he'd had a perfectly normal, load-lightening conversation with an acquaintance, a nice mental break from work, now with a fresh cup of coffee to help him refocus, and I walked away feeling like I had successfully navigated a casual, "unstructured" conversation.

Listening and Asking

Once the "making a sandwich" or "give-and-take" flow of casual conversation becomes a familiar tool, it can be helpful to start augmenting this structural framework with other key strategies for making conversation. One of these key deepening strategies is actively listening, and asking relevant questions to stimulate further, deeper conversation.

You can use this strategy when a conversation has moved past the initial small-talk stage and is naturally going on for longer than a few minutes. I generally don't go this far with casual work conversations because I don't like to spend more than a few minutes in casual conversation with most colleagues, especially within a work setting.

Instead, I end up using this strategy more with friends and acquaintances outside of the office—parents of other children in my son's school, my husband's friends, or local acquaintances from bars and other frequented establishments.

Had the above example of a conversation in the office with Craig happened instead with an acquaintance outside of work, say at the playground with another parent, we may not have had the easy natural ending of finishing up our respective tasks in the pantry. We might have found a similar natural ending in one or the other of our kids needing us, but we also might have needed to keep the conversation going past that panic moment I had in the above example with Craig. In that moment, as it became clear that the small-talk portion of our interaction was coming to a close, if I had wanted to continue the interaction, I would have transitioned to a listening-and-asking strategy, maintaining the framework of "making a sandwich" to keep the flow going.

For example, I'm standing off to the side at the playground, watching my son run around with the other kids, climbing on the playground equipment.

It's the weekend, so I know there's a good chance we will run into a familiar family, either with kids who go to my son's school, or simply whom we have seen multiple times at the park before, since we all live in the same neighborhood. I've already thought through a few light, fun things that my son did this week and last weekend, to share as potential topics during conversation. Unlike in a weekday office setting, talking about what you did the previous weekend during the current weekend is acceptable conversation outside of the workplace, where the people you are interacting with are in a "weekend" frame of mind to begin with.

Lo and behold, a familiar face approaches—the father of one of my son's classmates from school.

"Hi, Sarah," he says brightly.

"Hi, Jeremy," I reply, matching his brightness, and reciprocating with brief, smiling eye contact.

"How's your son?" he asks as he takes up a position standing next to me and turns his body toward our kids on the playground. This body language indicates to me, now that I have learned how to read it, that he is intending to engage in surface-level conversation, while we both keep our eyes on the kids, rather than engage more deeply. If he wanted to talk on a less superficial level about something specific, he would not have turned his body to the side but remained facing me directly.

I'm ready for the question, and know that if Jeremy hadn't asked me about my kid within the first twenty seconds of coming over, I would have asked him about his kid instead, to promote a comfortable, chatty atmosphere.

"He's great," I start to respond, deliberately pausing for two seconds to make it appear as if I am just now coming up with my response, rather than having thought it out previously. "We took him to the Central Park Zoo last weekend! Our first time there." I purposely stop there, although I have more details prepared in case Jeremy shows signs of wanting to move the conversation further down that path by asking questions.

"Oh, excellent," Jeremy responds. "Jessie loves the zoo, especially the monkeys. Does your son have a favorite?"

Why yes, he does, Jeremy, and I thought you might ask, so I already know that I'm going to say, "Yeah! He loves the bears. I think it kind of blows his mind to actually see how big they are in real life." Mentally, I make a note that I could ask more about why Jessie likes the monkeys, if I need a conversation deepener.

"Yeah, it's great for them to be able to see the animals," Jeremy says. "Central Park has that petting zoo, too, right? Where they can actually touch and feed the goats and stuff?"

"It does." I'm not quite sure where to go from here, as I dislike the overwhelming smells and sounds and sensations of petting zoos, and therefore didn't spend much time taking my son there. I decide to ask the deepening question I had made note of earlier. "Jessie likes the monkeys, you said?"

"Oh yeah, the way they move and climb through the trees. She loves mimicking their sounds, you know, and sometimes it's almost like they hear and respond to her."

"Oh cool." I can tell by the length of his response that this is a good topic to keep deepening. "Does she know about some of the different kinds of monkeys?"

"Yes! She knows, you know, that orangutans are the orange kind, and that gorillas are the really big ones, you know . . ."

"Oh, that's great!" Mentally I had already started culling back through what I had heard from our earlier conversation, to look for more questions I could ask, knowing we could only talk about monkeys for so long, and I hit back on Jeremy's mention of the petting zoo. I'm struck by a quirky idea that may or may not get a laugh from him, so I try it, suggesting laughter in my tone of voice to indicate that this is a kind of joke. "Wouldn't that be fun, if there was a monkey petting zoo? Where the kids could have monkeys climbing all over them?"

Jeremy laughs obligingly. "Oh man, yeah, Jessie would love that. Wouldn't go so great with the bears, though, for your son . . ."

Thankfully I recognize that as an authentically funny follow-up, and we're both laughing genuinely now, eyes on our kids as they swing around the jungle gym.

LARRY'S TWO CENTS

Reading through Sarah's wonderfully structured and introspective accounting, I could not help but remember how our relationship began, and more
important, how it almost ended before it ever got going.

I met Sarah in Penn Station, New York City, on a cold February in 2011,
while she was on a grad school trip. We were in line at a busy Starbucks, full
of strangers chatting about the snow and their resulting travel frustrations.
Years later, I can fully appreciate how overwhelmed and exhausted Sarah
must have been listening to it. I can imagine Sarah's inner monologue, how
she would want to lecture everyone on how Vermont or Michigan handles
snow, and that life will go on, so maybe everyone should just go find a good
book to pass the time.

But at the moment, all I could see was that she had an old-school flip
phone and obviously wished she could just get her drink. Fortunately for her, I
decided to strike up a conversation about the inanity of our present company.
I probably also made some comment about her museum-worthy phone.

Twenty minutes later, we were sitting at a table chatting about interests, New York, her degree in conflict transformation, totally indifferent to
the hundreds of people who coveted our chairs. As our impromptu first
meeting wound down, we had that wonderful moment of swapping phone
numbers . . . and, as we did back then, Yahoo! IM handles.

Then Sarah traveled back to Vermont to finish her degree, and I stayed
put.

Over the next few weeks, we continued to chat and flirt over IM as we
got to know each other. I was fascinated by Sarah's studies about how humans communicate, especially during times of conflict, and she loved that
we had something tangible to talk about. Soon though, I began to crave
hearing her actual voice. As we IM'd, I wasn't sure when she was joking or

wanted to emphasize a point. Sarah obliged me as best she could, and we started to talk for five or ten minutes on the phone, but the conversations seemed to stall, and I found myself talking for the majority of the time. Later in the evenings, we would wind up back on IM, where it flowed much more naturally. I didn't think that much of it at the time—after all, she was at school all day, so maybe she was just "talked out."

Fast-forward a couple months, including a couple in-person dates later (remember the three-hour driving distance between Vermont and New York?), when Sarah dropped a bombshell—her upcoming two-year postgraduate Peace Corps commitment.

Given that this implied a two-year break from our budding relationship, there was a lot to talk about—or at least I thought there was. Each time it came up over IM, Sarah shared basic details, but the bigger question—the "us" part—never seemed to get going. As much as I enjoyed our IMs, and though we both agreed we liked each other enough to keep in touch, I needed more (or any) emotion from Sarah. I wasn't expecting the "L-word," necessarily, but before I invested much more, I needed her to acknowledge some skin in the game.

I started pushing for more phone calls, but they played out the same way as before. I did most of the talking, and Sarah was quiet. It felt like she was thinking, constructing her response. Of course, now I realize that is exactly what she was doing—not because she was deliberately withholding, but because that was how her brain worked.

Especially exasperated after one of these "conversations," I confronted Sarah about it over IM. This led to an emotional three-hour exchange that changed everything.

Sarah painstakingly broke down how it was easier for her to type responses, how it was easier to use the normal sense of delay in typed conversation to organize her thoughts, while I read and processed. I thought back to our in-person meetings, how I always seemed to drive the conversation, but Sarah was the one who invariably said a profound thing that moved it to the next level. How time would fly by when we were together in person, because it always felt like we both enjoyed the conversation.

By the end of those three hours, I had learned more about Sarah then I had in the three months prior. I did express why talking on the phone was important to me, for the sake of conveying emotions, which Sarah readily agreed to. We devised a plan to intermix phone conversations and IM conversations. Skype was not reliable enough at the time, and Sarah didn't care much for technology, so I figured, why fight that battle?

What we didn't know just then, but would learn soon after, is that owing to a surfeit of applicants, Sarah would be presented with a long delay before being able to start her two years of Peace Corps service. Suddenly she had to choose between moving back home to wait, or doing something crazy like moving in with this guy she met at Starbucks only four months prior.

Spoiler alert: She did the crazy thing, and the rest is history!

Our origin story speaks to the power of communication styles, and how important it is to understand where someone is coming from during any engagement. As much as the person and the topic matter, *how* the information is presented may matter even more. This is a truth all communicators have learned.

Personally, I don't have a degree in communication, but I have spent my entire professional life building technology-based solutions to help people and businesses communicate effectively. In many ways, much of my professional life is about getting rid of the small talk and making sure the things we often wrongly take for granted can be better managed using computers. Through my relationship with Sarah, I have discovered that these efficiencies can be just as valuable in interpersonal conversations as they are in programming.

In the end, we all want to be heard and understood. For Sarah, having IM as a tool—to ask a question, to seek clarification without emotion—has been profoundly important both professionally and personally. ASD or otherwise, everyone has a style, and when we try to understand what drives those preferences—and better yet, meet people halfway—amazing things can happen.

CHAPTER TWO

Communication 201

"If you talk to a man in a language he understands,
that goes to his head. If you talk to him in his language,
that goes to his heart."

—NELSON MANDELA

UNDERSTANDING AND USING HUMOR

Humor is a highly versatile device in interpersonal communication. Both neurotypical and neurodiverse people use it all the time, so it is well worth at least a quick review of why it is used, how it can be used, and to some extent how to recognize and use it yourself, if you are so inclined.

Some of the most common reasons to use humor include:

- To lighten the mood of a difficult or strenuous conversation
- To help deliver a difficult message that might not otherwise land, by putting the other person at ease
- To imply confidence and demonstrate command or control of a situation
- To intentionally reverse or lessen an imbalanced power dynamic (someone with more power using humor—self-depreciating or otherwise—to temporarily lower their place in a perceived hierarchy while at the same time elevating the person with less perceived power)
- To implicitly include or invite another person into active participation
- To implicitly exclude or alienate another person from participation
- To engage an audience (as a public speaker) and assure that their attention will be rewarded

AN IMPORTANT NOTE:
USING HUMOR TO ALIENATE

I would strongly recommend against ever using humor for the purposes of alienation, or in a way that might inadvertently alienate someone or a group of people/type of person. Any jokes that make fun of a particular person ("Judy's sweater is so ugly"), type of person ("New Yorkers are _____"), or a trait of personhood (being blonde, being a certain race, ethnicity, gender, or ability) will almost always come across as offensive and inappropriate. You can just as easily use humor to lift a person up, rather than make fun of them or put them down. Use humor for the powers of good, not evil!

• • •

A great example I witnessed of humor being used for the purposes of good (inclusion) as opposed to evil (exclusion), was during a work meeting:

We were deep in the throes of our monthly departmental strategy meeting, led by our executive leader, Adam. This was everyone's chance to hear directly from him about the larger strategic direction of the organization, and to bring forward their questions or contributions.

These meetings always took place in the shared office space that our department occupied, separated from other areas of the building by a door. Adam would come over to our space from his office in the executive area— one of the rare occasions that he came our way, rather than vice versa.

Just as Adam was explaining something happening in another vertical of the organization (led by a different executive), that very executive, Magnus, opened the door.

If it was rare to see Adam in our offices, it was even rarer to see Magnus. The fact that he had taken the time to come over meant that he had something fairly important to share.

Normally, Magnus would not be concerned about interrupting us. He would have been polite about it, sure, but as the leader of another whole branch of the organization, with very little time on his hands, he held enough power to interrupt. We all understood contextually that, even though we were all busy and contributing to the success of the organization, his time was more precious than ours.

In this case, however, he saw that his peer, Adam, was part of our meeting, and therefore the power dynamic warranted more deference on his part. Suddenly Magnus was intruding on the territory of his equal, rather than dropping in quickly to get something he needed.

"Oh," Magnus said, half-in and half-out of our door, looking straight at Adam. "I see you're in a meeting. Sorry about that. I'll come back later."

Adam, immediately understanding the power dynamic, interjected a bit of humor that both reinforced his position of power within our department, while at the same time inviting Magnus, as an outsider, to come inside that circle of power and get what he needed.

"Magnus—the man of the hour," Adam said, leaning back in his seat. "Were your ears ringing? We were just talking about you." This small but effective joke served to let Magnus know that he didn't have to jet away, that his needs were important, and that Adam still held the power in the room.

If instead Adam had said something more direct like, "No, it's okay, Magnus, what do you need?" it would have accomplished letting Magnus know it was okay to interrupt, but it also would have made the whole interaction feel awkward and forced, because now Adam would have been deferring to Magnus in what was supposed to be Adam's department, which would have made Magnus feel uncomfortable, and everyone else feel unsteady.

Learning to Bypass Literal Interpretation

One of the main challenges I experience with humor is that I have a natural tendency toward literal interpretation of people's words. This is a common ASD-linked trait and can be problematic in many different situations.

Often when someone is using humor, they will say or imply something that is meant to be absurd, like: "I mean, unless pigs start falling from the sky . . ."

Even with such an obvious absurdity, my brain needs a few extra seconds to bypass its reflex for literal interpretation. I have learned to think of it like switching tracks on a railroad. My brain is a train going down one track, a joke comes along, and my train misses the switch and keeps trundling down the literal track. "Pigs?" I might think. "Why are we talking about pigs? Falling? Like, with parachutes? Or from a plane? Oh wait, the pigs are not the point of this exchange." I have to actively imagine putting the brakes on my brain-train, backing up, switching to the metaphorical track, and heading down that one instead. Then I can disregard the physical improbabilities involved with pigs falling from the sky, and realize that the person is implying that whatever we might have been talking about is never going to happen.

With some practice on the tracks, so to speak, I have learned that there are times when I can see a joke coming and therefore make the switch in real time. I look for nonverbal signs, like the person starting to smile or laugh a little, or using more expansive body language like leaning back or moving their arms more. Slowly rising eyebrows, when coupled with other positive nonverbal cues (as opposed to angry cues) is another sign that someone is building up to a joke. Often, absurdity humor is prefaced with the phrase "I mean . . ." or "Well, unless . . ." Other times, it takes someone long enough to get the whole joke out that somewhere in the middle of the joke I have time to back up my train and switch over before they get to the punch line.

Another obvious barrier caused by literal interpretation is in recognizing and understanding <u>sarcasm</u>. Unless someone is being extremely overt in their sarcastic body language and intonation, I may not realize that some-one is trying to imply the exact opposite of what they are saying. For exam-ple, "Oh, no, he *definitely* read that email," when they really mean to imply that he didn't read it, which is meant to be funny because it hints at a shared contextual knowledge of a coworker's working style.

With sarcasm, I have found that manual track-switching is not as effec-tive, because a sarcastic comment is often much quicker, and requires a more immediate response, than a joke. If I'm 80 percent sure that someone is being sarcastic, I have learned to be okay with letting go of that 20 percent uncertainty and responding accordingly. When I'm wrong—and sometimes I am—I can read the other person's response that they were actually being serious (they don't laugh along with me, they quickly raise their eyebrows and tilt their head down slightly, they seem surprised by my reaction, etc.), and all I have to do to save face is to lightheartedly apologize with a hint of surprise: "Oh! Wow, I'm sorry, I thought you were being sarcastic. Are you serious!?" And then act earnestly interested in the seriousness of what they are saying. If I'm less than 80 percent sure that someone is being sarcas-tic, I have found that it is okay, in most situations, to just ask. Most people will not begrudge the double-check, especially if you deliver it with some deference—smile and lower your voice a little when you ask, and it won't come across as rude or accusatory.

Playing to Your Strengths When Using Humor

When it comes to using humor yourself, I have found success when I play to my own brain's strengths, using tools such as:

Play on Words, or Puns

Puns are jokes that use juxtaposed words or phrases which have multiple meanings or that sound like other words, to form content that is surprising because you wouldn't normally think of using language that way.

For example: "I was wondering why the ball was getting bigger. Then it hit me."

These are probably the least popular of jokes (most people groan when they hear a bad pun joke), so I don't use them often, but they are one of the easiest for me to understand and deliver, as they have to do with words. The best times to use them, I have found, are just for a little boost of positive energy (not a full belly laugh) when you can find a word or phrase with double meaning relevant to the current conversation. So, for example:

We were at the start-of-year barbecue for our son's school, where teachers, parents, and kids come together for hot dogs and hamburgers in the outside play area behind the school building. Families are asked to bring a dessert to share, and the school usually provides the food for the grill, along with chips and fruit.

Every year there's also a family that brings an enormous plate of empanadas, which are great for the little kids running around because they are a quick, protein- or veggie-filled, handheld food item that they can grab and go, playing and eating at the same time. And every year, the empanadas are the first things to disappear, as ravenous kids and parents descend upon them.

This year, there were two giant platters of empanadas. *Eureka!* we all thought. *Enough for everyone! But wait . . . What is that smell?*

The mother of one of my son's friends braved the first bite of the mysterious second plate of empanadas. "Yup," she confirmed. "Tuna!"

"Ah," I said, laughing. "Thank you for trying that! I was like . . . something *fishy* is going on here."

And everyone in the vicinity chuckled at the use of the double meaning in the word "fishy" to describe both the smell, and the fact that something new and different and a little suspicious was afoot with the extra platter of coveted food.

Slow-Burn Humor

This is the type of humor that I have found produces the widest and deepest effect, in terms of inviting people to laugh. It also works well for me because it gives me the time that I need to ruminate on a joke in the back of my mind before delivering it. It can also work equally well in a one-to-one situation or a room full of people.

Here's how this usually plays out:

1. Something funny or unexpected will happen early on in an interaction:

    - One of the overhead lights flickers out at the beginning of a meeting, plunging half the group into darkness, or
    - While everyone is still coming in and getting settled before a meeting, Don comments ruefully on the fact that he hasn't had lunch yet today and the rest of the room commiserates, or
    - I'm chilling with another parent at the playground while our kids play, and they drop their phone, but it doesn't break or anything, or
    - It doesn't have to be anything big or even anything overly funny in that moment, just something lighthearted and out of the ordinary that the other person—or in the case of a group, most of the room—notices or acknowledges.

2. I let that moment simmer in the back of my mind while the meeting proceeds, focusing my conscious attention on the work of the meeting or the substance of the interaction.

3. At some point later—it could be a few minutes, or it could be as much as half an hour (though probably not a full hour,

as then whatever happened is likely too far forgotten)—I will spot an occasion to resurface the unexpected or funny moment in a way that ties the two moments together, and yet is surprising and therefore humorous:

- After the lighting situation is fixed, say we happen to be in a meeting where financials or budget items are being discussed and we're having to decide where we can cut down or move around expenses, which can be a stressful conversation. To loosen some tension, I might find an occasion to chime in with, "Oh, well, we clearly don't need lights, so take that out . . ." or

- Say Don makes a minor mistake while talking in the meeting, but he is good-natured about it and the room is forgiving, I might pipe up with "Well, Don, if you'd had lunch today . . ." Therefore implying that he would be in better form with proper nourishment—a positive comment on his capability, which also acknowledges the less-than-ideal and slightly tense situation of having no time for lunch, or

- After initially showing concern and making sure the other parent's phone is in fact perfectly fine, sometime later, say we see one or the other of our kids send some object hurtling down the slide and crashing at high velocity onto the ground—like a twig or a toy car. We both might pretend-cringe for the benefit of our kids: "Ohh, good one," and then I might turn to the other parent and say, smiling, "Just as long as it's not your phone . . ." as a way to release some of the earlier tension we both felt when they dropped it.

Building on Someone Else's Humor
(Be Very Careful Whom You Emulate!)

A quick note on when and how you choose to build on someone else's humor. This can be very tricky, especially if you don't fully understand what made the other person's joke funny. A lot of humor is contextual—meaning it can be funny in one instance, but crass or awkward in another.

If someone you know is very funny or always makes people laugh, think twice before you repeat one of their jokes to another audience or in another setting.

To this day I could die of shame when I recall the multiple times I have tried to repeat or build on a joke I heard used to great effect, only to realize too late that it was actually derogatory to someone else, or that it made absolutely no sense when taken out of context.

Save yourself time and energy spent wishing it never happened, and try not to resort to repeating a joke, unless you know exactly why it was funny and have 100 percent confidence that you are using it in the right context.

COMMON FORMS OF BODY LANGUAGE

Learning how to notice, interpret, and effectively use body language and nonverbal cues will help you feel more confident and in control—and probably less confused—during in-person interactions.

Common Body Language Cues

There are a ton of resources out there on how to read and interpret body language. For the purposes of this book, I'll touch on just a few of the most common forms. Note that any one of these taken on their own may or may not provide an accurate reading of a person's mood/underlying nonverbal communication—the more you can learn to recognize and combine various indicators into a fuller picture, the better.

Eye Contact

Perhaps the most important form of body language is eye contact. As you may know, eye contact can be a particular problem for people with autism.

For me, it's difficult because I get easily overwhelmed with the amount of information coming at me from looking into someone's eyes. I am barraged with every emotion—and each variation thereof—flitting through the other person's gaze. Every thought that flickers from their eyes goes straight into my brain, and becomes *my* thought, as I try to interpret it all at lightning speed. It's very hard for me to listen to what another person is saying while I am making eye contact, and next to impossible for me to talk to them as I try to think about what I am saying and say it at the same time, and I am already distracted by the sound of my own voice and my own self-consciousness. It's almost as if you were listening to a podcast and you accidentally held down the "volume up" button—that moment when the sound suddenly blasts your ears off is what it feels like for me when I make eye contact with someone.

Others with ASD may in fact glean nothing at all from eye contact (no sense of trust, no emotions), and therefore just never learned to do it habitually. If an ASD brain does not reward a person for making eye contact the way a neurotypical brain does, the behavior may need to be learned deliberately (if desired).

As humans, we *depend* on eye contact. It's one of our most fundamental means of connection. Most kids with ASD learn very quickly that eye contact is *required* of them—by parents, teachers, and friends. Eye contact is how people tell each other that they're listening, they're present, and they appreciate each other's experiences.

If you want the person you are communicating with to trust you, at least some eye contact is essential. Here are a few tactics for balancing eye contact that I've found useful, and some that I know have worked for others:

Steady Gaze. When you are deliberately not looking in the other person's eyes when it would be preferable to make eye contact (whenever you are engaged in an in-person one-to-one exchange), don't let your eyes travel all over the place. This gives the unconscious impression that you are distracted and not listening to the other person or fully participating in the conversation. Instead, find a fixed point to look at, and make sure the rest of your body language communicates interest and engagement (leaning forward, not overly fidgeting, nodding your head). This way you show that you are at least concentrating on the conversation and the other person's words, as opposed to not paying attention at all.

Half and Half. Try giving eye contact during half of the conversation—if it's easier to make eye contact while listening to the other person, do it then, and look away when it's your turn to talk, or vice versa. Remember to find one fixed spot to look at if you look away while the other person is talking.

Close Enough. If you get overloaded by eye contact, try directing your gaze to the person's eyebrows, or to the bridge of their nose—very near to the eyes but not quite right on, so that you can avoid that zing of too much information. You can then move your gaze slightly to make eye contact briefly every minute or so. The other person will know you are not fully making eye contact, but they will recognize that you are still attuned and authentic.

Step-by-Step. If you get no information from looking into someone's eyes and need a reminder to give eye contact during a conversation, break it down into small steps. Try starting with always
making a point of turning your face toward the person with whom
you are communicating. This is a polite indicator that you are paying
attention to what the other person is saying. Once you get that habit
down, take the next step of always directing your eyes to theirs.

"Interested" versus "Bored" Stances

There are a couple of generalized pieces of knowledge about body language that can give you a lot to go on, even without knowing exactly what
another person's nonverbal cues are telling you. One is being able to discern when someone is most likely "interested" in the interaction, as opposed to when someone is most likely "bored," or ready to move on to
something else.

Here are some broad nonverbal cues to keep an eye out for when you
are engaged one-on-one with someone:

"INTERESTED" CUES	"BORED" CUES
Making (or trying to make) eye contact with you	Looking around the room or at their computer/phone
Face and/or body turned toward you	Face and/or body turned or turning away from you
Body relatively still and relaxed	Body fidgeting, tense, and/or rigid
Thoughtful exchange of words/ideas	Responding mainly in grunts or "hms"

"Closed" versus "Open" Stances

Another very helpful general skill is being able to tell the difference between "open" stances and "closed" stances. If someone is giving you "closed" body language, it might mean that they are no longer amenable to the current direction of the conversation; they're distracted by something else; the conversation has gone on longer than they would have liked; or they don't necessarily agree with what you're saying. "Closed" body language usually indicates that it's time to wrap it up, or shift to a new topic.

If someone is giving you "open" body language, it's a good indicator that they are enjoying or engaged by the topic of conversation, that they feel they have more to contribute and/or want to hear more of what you have to contribute. "Open" body language usually indicates that the conversation can continue down its current path, and the emotional exchange underneath the words is positive.

Some common forms of "closed" body language include:

- Arms crossed in front of the chest
- Hands together or crossed at wrists in front of torso
- Hand touching the face (touching the mouth, rubbing the forehead, covering the neck, etc.)
- Front of the body turned slightly away or at an angle, as opposed to facing you straight on
- Eyebrows drawn in and down
- Eyes perhaps partially closed or blinking for longer than usual
- Mouth and/or jaw tight or clenched, lips pursed or drawn in a thin line

AN IMPORTANT NOTE:
"CLOSED" BODY LANGUAGE

While a lot of this applies to a lot of people, I have found that some people may exhibit what is typically thought of as "closed" body language when in fact they are intensely interested in the conversation, and are simply thinking hard about the content. For example, sometimes a hand on one's mouth or touching the lower half of the face might be more of an indicator that they are highly engaged, thinking hard, have something to say, and rather than interrupting, they are subconsciously trying to keep their thoughts to themselves until the appropriate time for them to interject. If a hand on the mouth or face is accompanied by the rest of the body leaning forward, focused eye contact, and/or body stillness, it may be an indicator of intense interest as opposed to an indicator to shift the conversation elsewhere.

Conversely, some common forms of "open" body language include:

- Hands/arms apart—wherever the hands may be (in pockets, crossed behind back, loose at sides, on hips, etc.)
- Leaning back, but still with body turned toward you
- Eyebrows slightly raised or else just relaxed
- Eyes open and focused for the most part on you
- Facial muscles overall relaxed, particularly the mouth and jaw

When to Stop Analyzing and Start Reacting

At some point, and especially if you are learning to recognize and interpret some of these cues for the first time, there comes a moment in a conversation when you need to start reacting, as best you can. You may be wrong in your interpretation and therefore react in a way that confuses the other person, or conveys something you didn't intend. That's okay. You're learning—just be sure to make note of the experience so you can learn from it later.

People will usually forgive mild social faux pas much more easily than stony silence—even if you say something odd, at least you said something. The other person will most often react graciously as long as they know you are trying to play an active part in the interaction. In the long run, it's more important to keep some approximation of natural flow than to interpret every single nonverbal cue correctly.

As you gain more experience with body language, you will be able to interpret cues faster and with greater accuracy and have fewer misunderstandings and awkward exchanges.

Staying Attuned to Your Own Body Language and What It Communicates

You might find that, as you practice interpreting the nonverbal cues of others, you begin to notice your own body language, and what you may be conveying to others, consciously or otherwise.

It's a good idea to spend some time deepening this knowledge and learning to control your own body language, if you are so inclined.

I have found that this awareness of my own nonverbal cues makes a big difference in getting a desired reaction from people. If I want someone to know that I enjoy spending time with them and am interested in what they are saying, I will consciously give "open" and "interested" body language cues. If I'm ready to move on from the conversation and want to be polite about ending the interaction, I will start giving "bored" body language cues. Usually it works! The other person picks up on my cues and moves in the direction I had hoped.

AN IMPORTANT NOTE:
SELF-AWARENESS
WITHOUT SELF-ABSORPTION

One note on this: It's easy to quickly get too absorbed in—and therefore distracted by—your own body language. Yes, you want to communicate your intent and underlying emotion as effectively as other people do, but be careful not to sacrifice too much of your brain space to self-regulation.

As you can probably guess, I have experienced this more than once. I will be talking to someone, and I will get to a point where I am trying so hard to maintain eye contact that I start to lose track of what they are saying. In my head I will be telling myself, "Eye contact, keep eye contact, but don't stare, keep my eyes gentle, eyebrows relaxed, stay with the eyes, don't stare, you're staring now, stop staring, okay maybe try flitting back and forth between one eye and the next, but not too fast, stay relaxed . . ." And soon there's no other room in my head for their words.

If you find yourself having this kind of intensely distracting internal monologue while you try to manually control your nonverbal cues, give yourself a break.

Look away for a minute, relax your body for a minute—whatever that breather is, to refocus your attention away from yourself, and turn it back toward the other person.

HIGH CONTEXT VERSUS LOW CONTEXT

I first learned about the concept of "high context" and "low context" in graduate school, while studying Dutch psychologist Geert Hofstede's pioneering work on cross-cultural groups and organizations. Hofstede postulated that cultures, in general, find balance along six different spectrums, one of which is whether the culture is generally lower context, like most Western cultures, or higher context, like most Eastern cultures.[1] American anthropologist Edward T. Hall also wrote extensively on this model of contextual cultures.

The higher the context, the more the people in that culture retain and use unspoken, tacit, or underlying knowledge in their interactions with each other. For example, the unspoken knowledge that a prearranged meeting time of 2:00 p.m. actually means anywhere between 1:50 p.m. and 2:15 p.m., due to any number of cultural subtleties like:

- Generally accepted unpredictable travel conditions
- A cultural emphasis on meaningful personal interactions over punctuality, which may make either party late depending on how their familial or other interactions play out that day
- The unstated social status of the people who are meeting (a person of lower social status—less perceived power—might need to arrive earlier, while a person of higher social status—more perceived power—might be expected to arrive later)

The lower the context, the more explicit this knowledge is: If I say we're meeting at 2:00 p.m., don't arrive at 2:05 p.m. unless you want me to think you are rude, regardless of whatever other context may be at play (if the roads were bad, if your kid needed extra time for lunch, etc.). It doesn't matter, because we said we'd meet at 2:00 p.m.

If we apply this concept on a smaller scale, for everyday interpersonal interaction, it would dictate that the higher the context, the more unspoken knowledge about the other person, their situation, and the surrounding circumstances you are expected to have. This can be particularly difficult for a person with ASD, who may function much more successfully in lower-context environments due to lack of awareness of nonverbal cues (implied rather than explicit, and therefore high context), inability to see the bigger picture through the details (including a tendency to get too caught up in all manner of extraneous "what ifs," which in the moment seem relevant but in fact are not, and make extrapolating real meaning much harder to do), and rigidity of thinking (seeing everything as black or white, no gray areas).

I experienced a very concrete example of high context versus low context communication one morning after I dropped off a bag of dirty clothes at our local laundromat on my way to work.

While walking away from Magic Laundry, newly divested of the hefty clothing bag I had carried in my arms for three blocks, I took out my phone to text Larry an update.

He had long since headed off to work. His commute into the city, compared with my commute down the block, meant that it was much more convenient for me to handle laundry drop-off on busy weekdays when neither of us had the time to spend hanging around at the laundromat doing our own washing. It was an expense—one we tried to indulge in rarely—but with a hectic city lifestyle, one that made all the difference when we needed it.

In this particular instance, the weekend had taken all of our time and energy handling a rowdy toddler, while at the same time transitioning the apartment over from "winter" mode to "spring" mode—vacuum-packing and storing all of our winter coats and boots, making room in our closets for the warmer-weather clothes we had put away as the temperature dropped.

Our original intention of fitting in a few hours of laundry time had turned into a plan to drop off our week's load on Monday morning, and pick it up, clean and ready to go, that same night.

I started typing into my phone:

> Dropped off the laundry. It was 18 pounds, so $16.20 plus tip. Heading to office now.

Then, before I hit send, I realized that I didn't need to be so low context. Staring at my three-sentence-long message, it dawned on me (after a few years of learning how to communicate with my husband), that all I really needed to say was:

> 18 lbs—$16

From that simple text, my husband would be able to infer the rest of the context—that I had dropped off the laundry (which I didn't need to say, because it was already obvious by the fact that I knew the poundage), and that I was on my way to the office (which I also didn't need to say, because that was where I was always going to go after dropping off the laundry, so the fact that I was texting the pounds and cost of the laundry therefore meant that I was now on my way to work). I also didn't need to say anything about a tip, because I knew my husband would assume that I had not factored a tip into my calculations, as he knew I was no good at mental math, and that I was much less adept than him at reading the underlying social dynamics that help determine how much or how little of a tip to leave in various circumstances.

The first message I had typed, explaining each detail of what had happened and what was happening now, was *low context*. The second message—which is ultimately what I ended up sending—sharing just the number of pounds and subsequent cost, was *high context*. The second message assumed that the person receiving the message would be able to extrapolate other important things from known context without needing them explicitly spelled out.

How to "Read the Room" or "Gauge the Temperature" of a Group Interaction

One of the most useful applications of high-context interaction—both in work situations and elsewhere—is the ability to "read the room" or "gauge the temperature" of a group interaction, either before you enter, or while it is happening. This can head off awkward moments or social faux pas before they happen.

On the obvious level, you wouldn't want to appear frivolous or jovial at a funeral. The "temperature" is muted and serious—not the right time or place for playful behavior (unless you ever come to my funeral, which will be a party, as I have expressly instructed all loved ones).

But in everyday life, reading a room is a much subtler exercise. Most atmospheres are not so clear-cut.

There are several key factors I often look for when I am in a room—or entering a room—full of other people, which help me determine the appropriate behavior to exhibit:

- Who is there?
  - If it's a social setting, is it mostly friends, or mostly strangers?
    - Friends: You might feel comfortable enough that you don't have to think so much about each interaction you have or how to integrate yourself into the room. You know these people, they know you.

- Strangers: Find someone you know, even if just as an acquaintance, establish a warm connection with them (tiny bit of small talk), and then ask them to introduce you to people they know.
- If it's a work setting, are there higher-ranking people in the room, or only peers?
  - Peers: With peers, you might be able to let your guard down a little easier and respond more freely than if there are higher-ranking people in the room.
  - One or more people with higher-ranking titles: People with more experience, higher titles, and more wide-spread responsibility tend to know and notice more context than others, so if anyone like that is in the room, you might put a few extra thinking steps into any interaction that you have, even if it's not directly with them. They may or may not notice who you are talking to, and how you are interacting—not in any kind of creepy big brother-ish type of way, but just in the passive, almost subconscious landscape of adding more contextual background knowledge about you and how you conduct yourself in various situations. Information that can be useful to them if they were ever called upon to participate in deciding whether you should receive a promotion, or what type of assignment you should be working on next.
- What is the noise and activity level?
  - Are people moving around a lot or talking so much that it's a bit hard to hear?

- Make decisions that allow you to be successful in an active environment, like finding a corner to safely stow your bag so you're not accidentally knocking into people, or if you are noise-sensitive, putting in earplugs.
- Are people mostly still, or not talking much?
  - Try to match your energy to that of the room, at least at first. A quieter room might be waiting for something to happen (a planned piece of entertainment to start, or a certain guest or host to arrive), or perhaps something unexpected happened just before you arrived and the room is still recovering. Find a comfortable place to be, and maybe occupy yourself with your phone for a bit until you can feel it out or find someone you know.
- If there is a higher activity level, is the activity mostly positive and loose (people laughing and smiling), or mostly tense (people conversing seriously or debating with each other)?
  - Positive/Loose interactions: People are more interested in enjoying themselves than the actual content of their conversations. Match other peoples' smiles, and offer polite laughter when others are laughing, even if you don't know exactly why they are laughing yet. Emotional matching is more important in this context than content-matching.
  - Serious/Tense interactions: Perhaps people are having work- or politics-related conversations,

or the atmosphere is one of learning or debate rather than social fun. Spend a bit more time listening intently to a conversation before jumping in with your own contribution, as opposed to entering with an easy smile and polite laughter. People who are more seriously engaged will be more interested in what you have to say about a particular subject, than whether or not you are on the same emotional wavelength.

- What is the overall body language of the room?
  - Are most people in "closed" or "bored" stances, or are most people in "open" or "interested" stances?
    - Closed/Bored: Again, this type of room might be waiting for something else to happen or might have just experienced something unpleasant or unexpected. Maybe it's a room full of people who don't really know each other very well. It's okay to enter into conversations cautiously, without assuming much, and be very sensitive to the energy others are giving off. People might not reciprocate with much small talk, and conversations may end quickly, and that's okay—it has to do with the energy of the room, not you.
    - Open/Interested: Be ready to dive in. People will likely be quick to respond and eager to welcome new voices, but in turn, may forget about you if you aren't ready to contribute soon enough. This type of room might also be more willing to entertain a change of subject or a

deepening of subject matter if you are having trouble interjecting with the current subject or superficial level of conversation.

- Are people positioned close to one another, or is everybody kind of far apart from everyone else?
  - Close together: Similar to a high-activity room, make sure you don't have extraneous personal items in the way like bags that might make closer physical interaction awkward or more difficult. Scope out areas of the room that seem to have more space, or a natural break like an alcove or hallway, so that if you need to step away for a few minutes, you already know where to go and don't end up feeling trapped.
  - Far apart: This is another situation where finding someone you know can be a big advantage to navigating the room. You can establish a connection with that person, and then find out from them what may be making people nervous or keeping them from interacting. If there is no one you know, treat it like the quieter room above, and try to find a niche where you can hang out on your own with your phone for a bit until something changes or someone approaches you.

After I have established the answers to these basic questions—which can be done relatively quickly by a minute or less observation of the room—then I can make some fundamental decisions about how I conduct myself as I enter into the group interaction, as described above.

Once engaged in a group interaction, it can be very helpful to take a moment every now and then (every ten minutes or so, unless an obvious change happens sooner) to reassess the "temperature" of the room. You can do this by going through a quick mental checklist of the above basic questions—has anyone new entered the room? Peer or higher-up? Friend or stranger? Has the activity level in the room shifted? Have the overall conversations in the room become more intense, or died down a bit? This way you can keep tabs on the overall energy of the people in the room in real time, and be more prepared to shift your own interaction to match that of the group.

You can also use a lot of the above techniques to "gauge the temperature" of a one-on-one interaction in real time—running through a quick mental checklist of assessing the openness or closedness of the other person's body language, the seriousness or lightheartedness of the content they are offering, etc. I like to try to do this every five minutes or so when interacting one-on-one with someone, to check in on whether they are still interested in the conversation, or ready for a change.

Deciphering Hidden Meanings— "Reading Between the Lines"

In many situations, being low context, or more direct, and saying exactly what you mean, can be interpreted by the other person as rude or combative. If you don't mind coming off as rude, that's fine—but if you want someone to listen to you, to internalize your contribution and not just shove you off, then sometimes you need to verbally dance around what you're really trying to say rather than saying it outright. Often, this is referred to as "tact." Other people will do this to you, too, when they think that what they have to say might hurt your feelings, or might put you on your guard and therefore make you not want to listen to them. As a result, their real meaning is slightly hidden by diplomatic or deferential language. This is what people mean when they refer to "reading between the lines" of a conversation.

A classic example is when someone offers you a breath mint. Usually this happens after they have just taken out their mints to use one themselves, and then they casually offer one to you as well. Maybe they are just being nice and sharing their wealth with the nearest person, but more likely, they didn't really need or want the mint themselves, they just wanted to give you one because you just ate an onion bagel or something and your breath smells. But how rude would that be if they just outright said, "Girl, your breath stinks. Go brush your teeth." Instead, they are being diplomatic. But if you don't "read between the lines," you might refuse the mint because you don't like them, or you don't think you need one. Then the person you are with will either find a way to exit the interaction more quickly, or will have to suffer through something you didn't intend to put on them. As a general rule, if anyone ever offers you a breath freshener of any kind, don't refuse. Take it. They are probably trying to tactfully let you know that your breath needs freshening.

Reading between the lines successfully takes practice, and time. Unlike the breath mint example, you'll usually be able to suss out the hidden meanings of a given interaction later, rather than having to do it in real time.

One of the best examples I have experienced of tactfully hidden messages—and of deciphering them later—was an interaction I had one afternoon with my boss:

I was one of the youngest people in the room. That didn't bother me in and of itself—I was usually one of the youngest people in the room, ever since grade school, where I was a year younger than most of my classmates. But this particular room was full of executives, vice presidents, and senior directors. Essentially, it was a meeting of the board-level leadership team of the organization—the executives and their direct reports.

My boss at the time, Adam, was there along with the rest of his peers from the C-suite. This was our monthly strategy meeting, where the leaders of various departments reported on the last month's progress against goals and set plans for the coming month. It was important for people from across the organization to come together like this and share their main strategic priorities, so that interdependencies could be identified, and all of us could make sure we were collectively working toward the same goals, holding each other accountable.

This meeting also happened to be one of the first for a new C-suite executive, Louise, who had joined the organization a few weeks prior. Louise had expertise in my area, as well as the area she had been hired to oversee.

It was my turn to report out. I had prepared in advance, both on my own and with Adam, so I knew what to say and how to say it. While I reported on the plans Adam and I had agreed to set in motion for the coming month, however, Louise started shaking her head.

By then I was adept enough at seeing and reading body language that I knew Louise's head shaking to be a sign of negative emotion. Paired with her pursed and down-turned lips, and one eyebrow up, one eyebrow down asymmetry, I knew she wasn't just experiencing any old negative emotion— there was a certain level of disdain, even contempt behind her gaze.

Of course, these were the very last feelings that I wanted to be eliciting from one of my boss's peers in this meeting. Louise was in a position of higher power, more experience, and greater influence, even though she'd only been with the organization for a few short weeks. Her opinion carried weight, and her opinion of me and my work would have an impact on my day-to-day, either directly or indirectly.

I stumbled a bit over my report, now holding off an internal tidal wave of panic.

I looked at Adam, and while I got my words back under my feet, he gave me an almost imperceptible nod, which I took as a sign of encouragement and confidence.

As I continued my report, hating but trying not to think about the sound of my own voice, hoping I didn't sound too nervous, Louise increased her nonverbal communication campaign. She started making the tiniest sighs and huffing noises every time I paused or drew breath.

I plowed on, looking almost unconsciously at Adam again. This time he was looking at Louise, now mirroring her look of disdain back at her, with a touch of impatience in the way he had twisted his body weight toward her.

I was able to finish the report, but not before my heart had crawled all the way up my chest and come to rest somewhere in my throat, making it difficult to form words around the lump that had congealed there. Adam then provided his own succinct executive summary of our plan, perhaps spending a few more words than he normally would have done detailing why he thought (though he actually said "we think," everyone in the room knew he really meant "I think"—a common hidden meaning in an organizational context) it was the best plan to accomplish our goals.

Later, about an hour or so after the meeting, Adam came by my office.

"I'm hoping you can help me with something," he said, hands casually in his pockets.

"Of course," I replied, beckoning him to come in. "What is it?"

"In that meeting this morning. I'm wondering if I was the only one who noticed. Did Louise seem, I don't know, a little put off, when we were talking about our strategy?" (Again there was that high-context use of "we" when he really meant "you," but wanted to ask the question more delicately and promote a sense of inclusion and teamwork.)

Adam's tone was exceedingly relaxed and light, careful not to put me on my guard, not to influence my response one way or the other.

"Yes," I said emphatically, nodding with probably too much vigor, elated and a little frightened. Internally I was having another minor panic moment about where he might go next. Was our carefully crafted plan being scrapped? Were we going back to the drawing board?

"Okay, so I wasn't the only one who saw it, then."

"No, I saw it too," I affirmed. But I didn't dare ask him anything else, not sure whether he expected me to agree with Louise or to combat her. On the one hand, she had more experience than I did, and so her opinions clearly held value. On the other hand, we had spent months building out a comprehensive plan that we believed made the most sense for where we wanted to go and how we wanted to get there.

Adam proceeded to let me know that Louise was leaving the organization for a position somewhere else, which was a little shocking to me since she had only just started. Our conversation shifted to other topics more directly related to our current work, and Adam said nothing more about our plan, about Louise, or about any of it.

It wasn't until a day or so later, replaying that interaction in my head, that I realized a couple of key, high-context, hidden meanings took place in that short exchange:

- When Adam came in and began the interaction by asking for my help, he subtly shifted the power dynamic between us, to temporarily raise my perceived power and lower his own. As boss and direct report, our natural power balance was usually the opposite. If instead he had come in and said something like, "Are you okay?"—he would still have been in the position of power, and I would have felt weak, somehow, that he had felt like he needed to come "check on me." In reality, that is *exactly* what he *was* doing—making sure I was okay—but he did it in such a way that made me feel stronger, rather than weaker. The hidden meaning in that message was something akin to: "Look, I want to make sure you didn't take that experience too

personally and you're still 100 percent committed to
your work and our plan, but I know you can take care
of yourself, because you are just as capable a professional as I am."

- By bringing up the negative nonverbal cues we both
  saw from Louise, but not then succumbing to any
  negative conversation about her or what she did in
  the meeting, and instead sticking to the fact that she
  was leaving, Adam subtly reinforced his confidence
  in our plan. He didn't have to say outright, "Despite
  what Louise might advocate, we're sticking with our
  plan." All he had to do was tell me she was on her way
  out, and that was that. The subsequent implication—
  hidden meaning—was that we were continuing down
  the path we had set for ourselves, as there was no further reason to think otherwise.

If Adam had come in and just said these two things directly to me—"Are
you okay? Regardless of what Louise thinks, we're sticking to our plan." It
would have accomplished getting that basic message across. But it would
not have accomplished the infinitely more important messages for the long-
term: "I have confidence in you. You should have confidence in yourself. We
are confident in our plan."

AN IMPORTANT NOTE:
YOU WON'T CATCH EVERY HIDDEN MEANING

You might catch some much later, many days after an interaction. It's not the end of the world. But it's better to miss a few than to spend too much time looking for shadows that aren't really there. Don't go down a rabbit hole of assuming hidden agendas that likely don't exist. When in doubt, you can always ask the other person if they really meant "X," and chances are, when faced with an honest question, they will give you an honest answer.

When Someone Says One Thing but Means Something Else

Sometimes, a person will—either accidentally or on purpose—say one thing when they really mean the exact opposite, or something else entirely. It might be intentional sarcasm; it might be a "Freudian slip"; it might just be someone getting tongue-tied or having too many thoughts in their head, so they come out a bit jumbled.

In all these cases, prioritizing your contextual knowledge, rather than relying on the low context of the exact words that the person says, can be beneficial.

This one is super difficult for me, because not only am I naturally low context, I'm also very literal, so if you tell me A when you really meant B, I'm going to have a very hard time.

For example:

"Pasta for dinner?" I posit to my husband, my head in the fridge.

"Sure. But we've had a lot of red sauce this week—it's starting to give me heartburn. So see if you can make it with red sauce."

"Okay." I fish the leftover noodles out of the fridge, and head to the cupboard to get down a jar of sauce. I open the cupboard, and my hand is on the jar of red sauce before I have repeated to myself in my head the words my husband just said.

"Wait," I say, confused. "Why would I make it with red sauce if it's giving you heartburn?"

He looks up at me, eyebrows knit in puzzlement. "That's why I asked you to make it with white sauce."

"No you didn't."

I can see from his eyebrows raising that he is getting annoyed. "Yes, I did. I said: 'We've had a lot of red sauce this week and it's giving me heartburn, so see if you can make the pasta with white sauce.'"

I'm getting annoyed now too. "No, you said red sauce."

And now we are in a silly and unnecessary (though potentially explosive if we let it get there) argument over whether or not my husband said red or white sauce—rather than sharing a positive moment about how I am making dinner for a change, when he's usually the one in the kitchen.

It might have been true that my husband said "red sauce" when he meant "white sauce," and that is confusing, but it is also true that he had just finished setting the context of too much red sauce giving him heartburn, and so the fault was equally mine that I did not weigh that contextual knowledge into the equation to balance out my overly literal dependence on his actual words. The higher context of my husband's impending heartburn from too much red sauce should have trumped the lower context of him using the wrong word and saying "red" when he actually wanted to say "white" (probably because he was thinking so much about red sauce, and it just came out unconsciously—which happens a *lot* to a lot of people).

It's a good idea to practice putting your contextual knowledge of a person or situation first to get better at realizing when someone says one thing but actually means something else. In the above example, when I finally reheard everything my husband had said, instead of letting myself just get confused and then accuse him of saying something odd, I could have recognized the confusion as a sign that a higher-context view might help. Then I could have taken myself up out of literal interpretation, taken in the larger context, and realized that he probably had meant to say "white sauce."

If I was still unsure, or wanted to clarify, I then could have said something much less likely to raise his defenses, like, "I know you just said to see if I could make the pasta with red sauce, but I think you might have meant to say white sauce, since the red sauce is giving you heartburn. Right?" And that would probably have stopped any potential argument before it started.

Tactfulness and White Lies

I mentioned tact above. Being tactful is a high-context skill because it requires someone to say or communicate things in a very indirect or subtle way, using surrounding context to convey meaning, rather than saying something directly. It is also a very useful skill for when something might be potentially embarrassing to you or another person (see the earlier example of someone offering a breath mint), or when the subject matter might be particularly emotional or difficult to deliver.

Tact is also a great skill to have for mediating disputes—helping each side of a potential conflict feel validated and heard at the same time, and not appearing to personally take sides or endorse a particular perspective. This way, the parties can continue to work together through you, using you as a kind of safe middle ground.

But wait! Isn't honesty always best? You've probably heard that it's okay in some cases to "tell a white lie" or to tell "a little lie," as opposed to "a big lie." Lying for the purposes of harm is never a good thing. But by a "white lie," people mean lying for the purposes of good, primarily to avoid hurting someone's feelings or causing them unnecessary distress.

Honesty is a thick concept—much like the big-T "Truth" and little-t "truth" I explored in the previous chapter, I find it helpful to think of big-H "Honesty" and little-h "honesty." Context matters here. Let me illustrate:

Say I am visiting my mother-in-law's home for the first time, and she baked an apple pie from scratch. She is eager for me to try it and tell her what I think. I taste it and it's okay, but I've had better. Do I proceed to shrug and say, "Eh, I've had better"? Not if I want to stay on my mother-in-law's good side!

In this context, the taste of the pie and how it factually compares to other pies I've eaten is not what's important. The pie could taste like petrol and that would not matter. What's important is building a positive long-term relationship with my mother-in-law, who is probably nervous about serving her pie to a new addition to her family, wanting to impress and welcome me, wanting to showcase her baking skills, whatever the case may be.

Even if the pie is not that great, I'm not going to tell her that. Instead, I'm going to tell a "white lie." Someone who is better at white lying than I am might come out with something spectacular and say, "Wow, Mom, this is the best pie I've ever had!" All that I would probably be able to manage in that situation is a warm smile and an "Oh yeah, it's great! Yum."

I am not good at white lies. They make my brain hurt and my mouth feel dirty, and I try to avoid them whenever I possibly can. But in some cases, the higher context of what is most important in the moment justifies the use.

Now, in this example, there's no reason that later on, after I have established a good relationship with my mother-in-law, I couldn't "come clean" and tell her the truth about her pie—especially if it was awful and she really wants to learn how to make a good pie. But that would come later, after we had built a mutual relationship of trust (I know, ironic, right? That a white lie can build trust?) and shared experiences.

The white lie example above fits under the big-H Honesty category, because that type of honesty is not about telling the exact true <u>words</u> in that exact moment (low context). It's about being honest in one's <u>intentions</u> and <u>actions</u> (high context). In that moment, my *intention* is to make my mother-in-law feel good and cared for. My words are not the exact truth in their *literal* meaning, but they *are* the exact truth in my overall intention.

AN IMPORTANT NOTE: WHITE LIES

There will be people in your life who do not need, want, or even appreciate white lies. Some people despise them. This type of person is like a breath of fresh air for me—this is the person who says "give it to me straight" and "I will never lie to you." This person is solid enough in their own perception of themselves and their reality that they may not need the "lubricant" of tact in order to hear and receive a blunt message without judging or taking offense. If there is someone like this in your life, it will be important to learn how to turn your "white lie" subprocess off when you interact with them, as the higher context priority with this type of person is not to care about their feelings (which belong to them, and no one else), but to care about their values, and reciprocate with your own.

High Context versus Low Context in Emails

One quick note on high context versus low context communication in written and in-person interaction: Emails are almost always best kept low context. With most written communication, the high-context cues of body language, nonverbal communication, intonation, and shared contextual space are absent. If someone is reading an email, the most important thing is likely the information contained in the email, not necessarily the context in which it was sent.

Knowing this, I have found that it is usually better to be direct in email text—not to "bury the lede" with a lot of exposition or providing surrounding contextual information—and get to the point in your email as quickly as possible. After the customary email "window dressing" of "Hi [name]," put the most important thing that you want the other person to retain FIRST in your written message. If it's something that does require more context in order for the other person to get the full picture, you can always fill that in farther down in the email or with a follow-up in-person conversation.

Especially since a lot of people don't read through every word of every email, get your main point right out there in the first full sentence of content, even if it seems a little blunt.

LARRY'S TWO CENTS

One of the most important components of good communication is establishing and maintaining trust. There are many ways to do this. In fact, we subconsciously start to assess trust levels from the moment we're introduced to another person. If communication is coming from a company, say in the form of marketing or a press release, we subconsciously think about what we know of the company, and that helps inform how we receive the message.

In all cases, for good communication to happen, we need to feel that the information being offered is reliable. Depending on the importance of the information, the amount of trust does and should vary. When ordering a cup of coffee from your local coffee shop, you trust that if there is an item listed on a menu, like a cappuccino, that the establishment and the barista know how to make a quality product for the advertised price. Now if you are ordering a half-caff, no-foam, upside-down latte, you are trusting that the barista has some experience, but you might be more tolerant if the first effort was not of good quality, as long as the barista apologizes for being new and offers another cup, this time made by a veteran barista. On the other side of the spectrum, you'll need a lot more trust in your tax preparer, realtor, or (ideally!) boss. This is especially true if what is being communicated could affect you negatively.

To illustrate this, I have a story about when Sarah and our friends lovingly gave me the nickname of "LarLar." During the brief period after MapQuest and before Google Maps, the best piece of technology to have in one's car was a portable GPS. One brand was called a TomTom, and my favorite feature was that you could pick the narrator's voice.

Fairly early on in our relationship, Sarah had the opportunity to come down to New York for the weekend. Before leaving, she printed out the directions, filled up the car, and packed some snacks in case of traffic. Fortunately, she also had a fully charged cell phone, for what was about to become a significant exercise in trust—and unintentional declaration of commitment. With less than an hour left in the journey, Sarah called to update me that all was well and she was getting close. A fair bit into the last hour, however, I received another call that things didn't look right and Sarah was no longer on a road that matched MapQuest's directions. My first suggestion was to read off some street signs and let me know what road she was on, so I could pull up a map and gauge where she was. A few minutes later it was determined that rather than crossing a bridge into Queens, she had made an inadvertent right and now was heading back north, away from me. Quickly, what would have been a fifteen-minute mistake turned into a minor calamity, as Sarah was not prepared for driving on an unknown freeway without any help. At this moment, it would have been less stressful (though sad) for her to just drive back home, because her mind so hates stress and the unknown. To avert this outcome, I asked her if she would stay on speakerphone so I could help her finish the drive.

Thus we embarked on a forty-five-minute shared journey, with her reading off signs and following my directions. In a stroke of luck, I promised her she would reach me in forty-five minutes, which was fifteen minutes longer then the web was telling me. As she rolled up to the parking space, I gleefully commented that she was right on time. Sarah responded by parking the car and throwing me her keys. To this day, whenever possible, I do the driving.

At this moment where I became "LarLar," much more happened. I earned so much trust from Sarah, and she earned so much appreciation from me for persevering through what was a highly stressful situation. Knowing now how stressed she must have been only amplifies how much I appreciate those forty-five minutes. Through good times and bad, we've shown that we can utilize the parts of our collective selves to succeed, and Sarah specifically learned that she had someone in her life who she could talk to when needing to figure out a problem, rather than staying quiet and missing out on an experience she wanted to have.

Though we tell this story to most new friends, as it is a great bit of not-that-small talk, it wasn't until we began to write this book that I realized what a turning point it was. I mentioned it to Sarah, and she laughed and confessed that if I had just told her the directions and then hung up, she would have driven home. That doesn't surprise me now, but at the time, it probably would have been the end for us. Never underestimate how important it is to feel heard, to feel safe.

Rapport and trust are earned, over time and through circumstance. Don't attempt to manufacture moments or contrive tests for the other person. What you can do is learn to allow them to happen, to not give in to your fears and avoid making the phone call in the first place. This is how you establish trust in yourself, the most important kind.

CHAPTER THREE

Workplace Communication

"The world needs many different kinds of minds
to work together."

—TEMPLE GRANDIN

There are many reasons why effective communication in the workplace is important. Not the least of which is that, if you are working full-time, you are spending most of your waking hours at work and interacting with people fairly regularly. No matter what you do for a living, if you can't communicate effectively in your vocational setting, your overall happiness will likely diminish.

Minimizing Stress

Lack of effective communication in the workplace can mean you carry that stress home with you, and it can negatively impact your relationships with your friends and family. Workplace stress should be about the work, right? Not about the people! I would much rather be stressing about making sure I can meet my next deadline than about what Bill said to me in the office pantry and why I didn't know what to say back. We all have enough life on our plate without having to worry about why we can't seem to build friendly rapport with our colleagues or get what we need from our bosses.

I didn't realize how much work-related communication stress was affecting my home life until my husband helped me see it more clearly. I figured everyone had misunderstandings at work, and that everyone worked through it and went home and tried to leave their work stressors "at the door," and that was that. But if you have ASD, missteps in social interaction and communication can have a greater impact on your overall demeanor than you may realize.

One of the things I tend to do, and that I know a lot of people with ASD do, is repeat negative things people have said to me (about my actions or my work), or awkward social interactions that could have gone much better, over and over again in my head. Long after the other person has forgotten the interaction, I will be able to recall the entire experience, moment by moment, and how it made me feel. This creates a lot of unnecessary internal stress. I would go home, and that thing someone said to me or that awkward misstep would still be running through my mind while I was trying to spend quality time with my son and my husband. I was preoccupied, instead of engaged. I was melancholy, instead of nurturing. Larry would ask me if anything was wrong, and all I knew to say was that I was tired. It wasn't a lie, but I didn't realize that more was going on below the surface. I didn't think burdening him with work-related stress that had nothing to do with work, and everything to do with silly interactions with colleagues, was appropriate.

Finally one night, Larry pulled it out of me, and I reluctantly shared that a colleague and I had a less-than-ideal interaction that day when I followed up on something I had asked for the previous week. She'd snapped at me and said she hadn't forgotten but had run into other priorities and would get it to me as soon as she could. He pressed for more information about why something that seemed so small would bother me so much that it was still visibly affecting me when I got home. I couldn't really answer him then, though I know now how an ASD brain will play and replay these kinds of negative experiences over and over again, almost like a subtle form of slow torture, looking for what exactly went wrong in the interaction (Had she snapped because I'd asked her via email rather than in person? Should I have worded or framed it differently? Did I miss some larger context that I should have spotted? Should I have waited an extra day before following up?) and how to avoid it happening again in the future.

At the time, Larry told me to write it down, which was excellent advice, even without knowing exactly what was going on inside my head. This is a form of cognitive behavioral therapy, and it works very well to combat the internalization spiral that can be common in ASD experience—writing it down so it gets out of your head and lives somewhere else.

Getting Ahead

Another good reason for learning how to communicate effectively in the workplace is that it can help tremendously to advance your career. Technical expertise and being good at what you do are also important, of course, but increasingly, as you move to higher-paying positions, your day-to-day work will be less about the technical skills and more about managing the people around you who are doing the work.

And managing other people well—not to mention working well with other managers—takes a *lot* of communication.

With effective workplace communication, you can also demonstrate that you have the capacity to communicate *up* the hierarchy, not just down. Reporting to decision-makers and executives grows more complicated the higher up in the chain you go, as different leaders have different perspectives and priorities. You can show that you understand this by adjusting your own communication to accommodate the bigger picture.

Managing Expectations and Capitalizing on Strengths

It is also important in the workplace to be able to effectively advocate for yourself and your staff, and to set boundaries around your work. Active communication helps you manage the expectations of the people you are reporting to and the people who report to you, as well as your peers across the organization. There have been many times when I have needed to use some highly complicated communication strategies in order to protect my time or the time of someone on my team from something that another person or department should be taking care of.

Being able to communicate your strengths is a hugely essential skill in the workplace, especially for someone with ASD. You need to seek out opportunities to do the work that you are best at, in the way that makes you most successful, which may be different from how a lot of other people work. You also need to actively get help on things that you might struggle with, like generating new ideas or thinking strategically about the big picture. One way to do this is to find a workplace mentor who can help you learn different approaches or tools for success. I include a separate section just on finding a mentor in this chapter.

EXECUTIVE FUNCTIONING IN THE WORKPLACE

The Merriam-Webster dictionary defines "executive functioning" as: "a set of cognitive skills used to control one's thoughts and behavior, especially the skills needed to focus on and organize tasks."

A whole host of tasks and functions exist under this umbrella, and difficulties in executive functioning should not be categorized as simply being "disorganized." There are plenty of people, myself included, with difficulties in executive functioning who are also extremely organized. The difficulties are much more nuanced than that and will differ greatly from person to person.

Prioritizing

For me, the most pressing challenge I face under this umbrella, among others, is prioritization. While I am more adept than most of my peers at staying organized, staying on task, organizing others, and project management, it can be very hard for me to recognize that certain needs or tasks are more urgent than others, why that is, how to tell the difference, and how to execute on the decision. My default is simply to set out with the intention of accomplishing everything. Everything is important, so why not just do it all? Well, because there are only twenty-four hours in a day. Time is finite, and the number of things that we each need and want to do in our lives—and for the purposes of this chapter, in our work—is infinite.

What is most important in the workplace? That is up to each individual person to define according to their own work and circumstances, but here are some of the steps I have found most useful in determining the relative urgency of tasks in my work life.

Level of Collaboration Needed

This one is so hugely important, and yet so easy for a single-minded individual focus, like that of an ASD brain, to miss. I listed this one before "deadline" on purpose, even though most people will cite the date or time something is due as the most important factor in determining priority. The reality is that even if something is "due" weeks from now, if it will require significant collaboration with others in order to complete, it needs to be a higher priority now than something you can finish completely by yourself in a few hours by tomorrow. Gears need to start turning as soon as possible when it comes to highly collaborative projects or you will find yourself in the home stretch of a deadline, having completed all your own individual tasks, but having nothing that you need from anyone else because they all have their own priorities they are dealing with on top of the one you just handed them with only a few days' notice.

I learned this the hard way early on in my professional career, with one of the first grants I ever wrote for a nonprofit organization.

I was excited. This was the first time I was going to be 100 percent responsible for the entire life cycle of a grant proposal—the initial prospect research, the program needs-matching, the program budget, the narrative proposal, the supplementary documentation, the approval process, the submission on a deadline, and the follow-up. I'd worked on a few grant projects as part of a larger team, but this was the first one I had spearheaded myself.

It was a request for more than ten thousand dollars, and as such, it required a program budget beyond the typical organizational budget and audited financials that accompany most grant requests.

In the case of the organizational budget and audited financials, these were the type of informational documents that the nonprofit organization simply had on hand as part of their annual process. So in my mind, a program budget would be a similar type of document—something that the organization's Accounting department or Program department would have in their files as part of their regular documentation—and I could request the document the day before the deadline and receive it via email attachment within a few hours. I had no idea the amount of collaboration and program development that was going to have to go into creating, apparently from nothing, a budget for the program. Because the current program budget was formulated to match current funding, and this was going to be extra funding, it required extra consideration.

You can imagine the Accounting department's reaction when I asked for a program budget and told them it was due the next day.

I had sent my request via email, but the CFO himself came upstairs from the floor below to talk to me in person in response.

"When is this grant proposal due?" he asked me. I assumed he was asking just to confirm, since I had diligently included that important piece of information in the email. I was not yet adept enough at reading nonverbal and vocal inflection cues to know that his tone of voice was bordering on annoyed (a slightly higher pitch than his normal speaking voice, and coming out more forcefully than normal due to the increased velocity of the air coming from his lungs), and his body language was a little aggressive (he was leaning forward, almost on the balls of his feet).

"Tomorrow," I affirmed for him, "by five p.m."

He employed more body language, all lost on me at the time, that this was not an acceptable situation, crossing his arms over his chest and sighing deeply. "When did you find out about this grant? Have you finished writing the narrative?"

Now I was getting a little confused, not sure why he was asking these questions. Not sure why, in fact, he had come all the way up here to talk to me about this in person, when he could have confirmed the deadline via email. Was he afraid that I wouldn't finish in time? As a new junior employee on my first big project, I hurried to assuage his fears. "Oh, the narrative is finished. I've been working on it for two weeks. I just need to write the budget narrative once I get the numbers from you."

"You've known about this grant for two weeks!?" he exclaimed, and now I could definitely tell that he was upset for some reason, as he raised his voice and threw one hand up in the air. In childhood, I'd successfully interpreted similar cues from my mother as "getting angry." But I still had no idea why, which made it hard for my brain to accept the fact of his feelings. If I don't know <u>why</u> an emotion exists, I'm fairly blind to the fact that it exists at all—a common occurrence, I have since learned, in the ASD brain.

All I knew to do was simply to answer his question. "Yes," I said.

"Why didn't you tell us sooner?" he asked. "We can't just crank out a new budget overnight. We needed to know about this two weeks ago." His tone was calming down again, and I saw that he was consciously employing professional restraint. Perhaps it was becoming clear to him, from my quiet, surprised acquiescence, that this was not a case of malicious intent, but simply misunderstanding, stemming from lack of professional experience. This was, after all, my first full-time job out of grad school.

"I'm sorry," I said. "I didn't realize. You have to make a new budget?"

He proceeded to explain how a new funding source would fundamentally change the nature of the program budget enough that yes, they would need to create something that did not already exist. I explained how I had thought it would be something that already existed, and therefore need no time to provide. We came to an understanding that Accounting should know as soon as I did about a new grant opportunity, in order to give them enough time to create the materials that I would need.

In the end, we worked together on this particular project to create the budget and were able to submit the grant proposal on time. Good thing, too, because we got the grant!

In the above example, I learned about a lot of things—in particular, the existence of "little-i" information, which doesn't just exist on its own but needs to be formed (see chapter 1), and the importance of prioritizing collaborative projects over individual projects. I also learned, though I didn't internalize it at that particular time, that some conversations—like the relatively heated one that the CFO anticipated we were going to have—are best conducted in person, rather than via email. That was why he took the time to come up and talk to me in my office, rather than send back an emotional email response. He was able to tailor his own emotional response in real time based on the cues I gave him while he spoke—a two-way interaction, rather than the one-way exchange that an email would have forced him into (see the "Written Communication versus In-Person Communication" section of chapter 1).

Deadline—Including Interim and Final

This one may seem simple, but in fact there are a number of things to consider when taking into account the deadline (by when something needs to be done) of a need, task, or project, and how that affects its place in your ultimate lineup of priorities.

First, there are such things as "hard" and "soft" deadlines—a submission deadline for a government grant, for example, is as hard as a deadline can get. But there are also "soft" deadlines—dates by which something is <u>ideally</u> due, but which are flexible enough to allow for some wiggle room, especially if advance notice is given. Reports are often a good example of something that typically has a softer deadline, as long as you are not submitting something for publication. A deadline on a report can often move back a few days or even weeks, if the person or team working on the report deems more time necessary in order to increase the quality of the reporting.

Second, there are often "interim" deadlines to consider, on top of the "final" deadline. Interim deadlines can be set by an external party or by you. I have found that giving myself interim deadlines, especially inside of a long runway, is an excellent time management tool to make sure I stay on top of a long-term project. (More on this in "Benchmarking Progress" on page 120.) Externally set interim deadlines are just as important to meet as the externally set final deadline, as they engender confidence and trust in the external party, and may even help buy you credit to spend if you end up needing some leniency when the final deadline comes (no guarantees, of course).

Audience and Impact

Internal versus external audiences. Another important thing to consider when you are prioritizing certain work projects over others is who the audience, or end consumer, of your project is going to be. Usually external audiences (outside of your organization) require higher priority, greater collaboration, and have harder deadlines than internal audiences. A grant proposal, for example, is going to an external audience, while a cost-benefit analysis of a new initiative is going to an internal audience.

This was another one that I learned the hard way in real time when preparing a presentation for our organization's Board of Directors, considered an "external" audience due to their distance from the day-to-day operations of the organization, and also one of our most important external audiences, as they exercised such influence over the success and health of the organization.

As I walked into Deborah's office, already a little nervous at the prospect of presenting my work to my boss's boss, she peaked my anxiety even more with a declarative—and surprising—statement: "This is the most important meeting of my day."

At first I wondered whether she might be joking, as a meeting with me couldn't possibly be her "most important" meeting, when she had so many other much more important things to be deciding on and worrying about besides anything that I might be working on.

But one look at her told me she wasn't joking. There was no trace of a smile on her face or in her eyes, and she was crossing her arms over her chest as she sat down next to me.

I found the fact that she wasn't joking very confusing. In fact, she looked worried—with eyebrows raised and mouth tight—and that worried me.

Worried in the most important meeting of your day? Not a good combination. I started into my presentation, adrenaline building up in my bloodstream and propelling me forward, but I didn't get very far.

"Wait, tell me what this slide is again?" she interrupted. "And why are we leading with this?"

Deborah proceeded to dismantle my entire presentation before my eyes, reordering content, changing core messages, pulling out extraneous information, identifying key missing pieces, etc. She was visibly stressed at finding that so much work still needed to be done on my presentation before it would be ready for the upcoming Board meeting.

"Sarah," she chastised with barely concealed exasperation, "why didn't you bring this to me earlier? This is for the *Board*. You did all this work, but it wasn't the *right* work—you needed to come to me much earlier in the process to get direction and make sure you were going down the *right path*. Now you've wasted all this time and we won't be able to send this to the Board in advance of the meeting with the rest of their materials. They need to see these things *weeks* in advance, you know. We're already way past that."

I waffled a bit about not wanting to take up more of her very coveted time, still not fully understanding, without my own time to process, why this presentation was so much more high stakes than other presentations I had successfully given in the past.

"This is for the *Board*," she reiterated. "I will spend the extra time on the Board. It's my job. And it's your job to set yourself up for success by coming to me earlier."

I agreed, realizing that—very similar to the grant proposal example under "Level of Collaboration Needed" on page 108—even if I was working on a project by myself, if it was going to an external audience as important as the Board, it was going to require more collaboration during the final review stage, and therefore higher timeline priority than a purely internal project.

Impact related to the audience, and the breadth and depth of the *impact* your project will have (who or what your work is going to directly affect), is also important in determining your deadline's level of priority. If your project, for example, will only have a direct impact on your own department, it might take a lower priority than a project that will have an impact on multiple departments (a wider breadth of impact). By the same token, if you have two projects that will only directly impact your own department, but one of them will impact many more aspects of your work than the other (its impact goes deeper), the one with greater depth may need to take priority, depending on other factors involved.

Influence and "Rank"

There are many other minor factors that may impact the priority level you place on a project, but the last major factor that I have found useful to include in this decision-making process is the level of influence, or professional power, of the people who will either be involved in the project or impacted by it.

It is a truth that in the workplace, people with higher-ranking titles, or more perceived power, usually take higher priority than people with less perceived power. Sometimes, this can be merely because of the title, but I have found that someone with a higher title usually has more responsibility—more people reporting to them, more initiatives under their direction, more strategic input to the overall organization, more pressing deadlines or external reporting needs—and therefore, just by nature, work that involves them (and therefore has more breadth and depth of impact, more external audiences, and more collaboration) takes higher priority than work that might only directly impact or involve people with less power in the organization.

In the introduction of this book, there is an example from my work life of a moment when my priorities had to change because a higher-ranking person requested a report that would delay my ability to finish a different report for my boss on time. In that instance, I let my boss know about the change, and prioritized the higher-ranked need, which also had a quicker deadline.

Time Management

Another area of executive functioning that has wide-reaching impact on many different aspects of work is time management.

If I can't manage my time effectively, I can't get things done when they need to be.

Time management is difficult for a lot of people, ASD or no. Add in the neurological traits that make this area of executive functioning harder to access, and it can be nearly impossible to do without concerted effort and concrete tools.

There are many resources available for improving time management skills, providing tips and tricks to make it easier. Here I want to focus on several specific tools I have found most useful in redirecting the ASD parts of my brain toward success.

Special Interests

The first and biggest hurdle a lot of people with ASD face when trying to manage time is dealing with a special interest.

Let me delve into "special interests" for a minute, which is a uniquely autistic concept, to illustrate the point:

My brain does not reward me in the same way a neurotypical brain does for normal, everyday occurrences, like seeing a friend on the street, sharing a light moment or joke with a coworker, and so forth. A neurotypical brain lets off a shot of feel-good chemicals, like serotonin, when these things happen, like a momentary buoy to help sustain energy and focus throughout the day. My brain, on the other hand, lets off a shot of cortisol, the fear and anxiety chemical. All day I am getting little doses of anxiety chemicals as I move through the world interacting with family and coworkers, hearing every tiny sound and seeing way too many details, replaying each moment over and over again in my head, and trying to hold on to the threads of many different contemporaneous responsibilities. Rather than buoys to keep me afloat, each tiny chemical output from my brain is like a pebble dropped in my pocket, weighing me down.

So at some point—more often than with a neurotypical brain—my body chemistry goes looking for some serotonin to balance out the anxiety, drop some of the pebbles, and keep swimming. That's where special interests come in.

For me, it's the magical world of Harry Potter. (Go ahead and laugh. Yes, I'm thirty-two, I never went to Hogwarts, and yet I am a Ravenclaw, and my Patronus is a squirrel.) For my son, who is four years old at the time I am writing this, it's cars. Any type of toy vehicle with wheels—even if he's just looking at it through a glass case—will give him a small modicum of calm.

Some special interests are in fact highly useful or productive and can be turned into vocations—like coding or painting. I believe one of the best things a young person with ASD can do, for long-term success in life, is explore how their special interests might translate into vocational interests in adulthood—the same way that any person who loves what they do will do it better, for longer, and reap more rewards from it. For an ASD brain, finding work that directly relates to a special interest can instantly make time management much simpler, as productivity delivers those crucial serotonin rewards.

Of course, other special interests—like mine—are purely for entertainment and can easily suck time away from more pressing needs if not managed properly. If you have one (or several) special interests that are not necessarily productive, like a fantasy reality or video games, the best way I have found to manage time around it is to use it as a reward system, or as a temporary break. It should be consciously used in order to spur forward momentum with other life tasks. Don't want to do the dishes? Give yourself fifteen minutes of your special interest after they are done as a reward. Too overwhelmed to focus on a major project for work? Take a ten-minute break with your special interest to recharge. As a preventative measure, maybe set aside one day every month or every two weeks when you have no limit on the amount of time you can spend with your special interest—that's your major boost of serotonin to keep you moving forward through the rest of the month, tuning up now and then with shorter indulgences.

The trick with a nonproductive special interest is not to overindulge, or to engage with it mindlessly. Given no other responsibilities or cares in life, I could easily spend every waking minute immersed in the world of Harry Potter (and in fact, as a teenager, I spent many blissful days that way). But what kind of life would that really be? I would imagine it's almost like the temporary high of a narcotic—it might feel incredible in the moment, but it's not worth sacrificing the rest of your life if you overdose.

Prioritizing Time

Another reason that time management can be tricky is because it directly relates to prioritization. The reason we manage our time is so that we can put the most important things first, to ensure they get done in the finite amount of time we have to spend on this planet. If I'm already having trouble deciding what is most important, how can I be sure I am allotting my time correctly?

Using the above tools for prioritization has greatly helped me to maximize my effectiveness at work. But in some cases, I need to remember to think about the priorities involved above and beyond just the work itself—like the priority of me being able to focus, or me being able to do the work in the first place:

"What's up?" Larry asked me one morning as we got the coffee going before our son woke up. I supposed he had noticed that I was quieter than usual, or slower to respond to stimuli.

I pulled myself out of the deep recesses of my brain in order to register that he had just asked me a question, and that his question was communicating concern.

"Oh, it's nothing," I replied. "I'm just thinking about work."

"What about it? Maybe I can help." He was reaching for the cereal boxes while I got a bowl from the cupboard. Then I realized that he was also going to eat cereal and it would be more prudent for me to get two bowls down. The texture of the bowls on my fingers made my teeth hurt, and I let go of them as soon as possible.

"Uh, well," I said, trying to marshal my thoughts into speech. "I'm just thinking about how I have to go into the city today for a meeting, and whether I'm really going to have time to finish this thing I have due tomorrow because it's hard to work on the commute, and I'm losing an hour into the city and an hour or more back, and—"

Larry cut me off, as he is wont to do. "Why are you coming back?"

"What?" I was in the middle of getting the milk out and wondering why I hadn't put a sweater on before subjecting myself to the coldness of the fridge. I couldn't understand his question. What did he mean, why was I coming back? Because I loved him and our son, and wanted to eat dinner as a family together like always, and sleep in our bed? Why was he even asking me this question? Why was it relevant to my current dilemma? "What do you mean?" I asked.

"I mean, why are you coming back?" he repeated, a bit impatient, perhaps thinking that I hadn't been listening. "Do you have another meeting in the office this afternoon?"

"No." I was still confused, standing frozen, quite literally, in front of the open refrigerator. But now that he had asked a deepener about meetings, my brain was catching up to the fact that he was speaking purely within a work context. I realized that I should have automatically assumed he was asking about work, given the content of our conversation, though of course for me, things that should be automatic are usually not. Especially before coffee 😉

"Then," Larry continued, "why waste work time commuting back to the office when you could work remotely from the city after your meeting?"

This idea was so novel that it took a few minutes to sink in. "You mean, I don't need to go back to the office after I'm done with my meeting in the city?" I had simply always assumed that unless one was sick, on vacation, expressly "working remotely," or required at a meeting off-site, one worked in one's office.

Larry looked at me over his cereal bowl as I unfroze and brought the milk over. "Not if you're working. As long as you are working and meeting your deliverables, and your office policy allows working remotely, it doesn't matter *where* you're working. You should prioritize your own productivity over normal routine if your timeline is this tight. Would having that hour-plus of commute time back in your workable hours make a difference for your deadline?"

"Yes."

"Then find a cafe or somewhere in the city and work there for the rest of the afternoon, and don't come back until after five p.m. That way you spend all your work hours on work, rather than wasting time on an unnecessary commute in the middle of the day."

In this case, in addition to prioritizing whatever work I needed to finish on a deadline, I also needed to prioritize how and where I was spending my time—was it more important to get back to the office, or was it more important to get the work done? If I'd had another meeting back at the office to get to that afternoon, or if my office policy was less flexible about remote work time, this time management solution might not have worked. But in this case, it allowed me to both meet my deadline and attend my meeting off-site, because I did not blindly prioritize being physically in the office when, after critically thinking it through, there was little reason to do so.

Benchmarking Progress

A great strategy for executive functioning in the workplace—in both time management and prioritization—is not only setting end goals but also setting benchmarks along the way, and tracking progress along those benchmarks. The goal becomes your <u>priority</u>, and the benchmarks become your <u>time management</u> strategy leading up to your priority.

Benchmarks make the concept of reaching a big goal much more concrete. Say your end goal is to have a big report written by the end of the week. In order to finish the report, you need to do some research, meet with two different people who have information that you will need to incorporate into the report, and set aside time to do the actual writing. You could set the following benchmarks:

- Monday—Outreach done to Benia and Madhu to schedule meetings
- Tuesday—Research complete
- Wednesday—Both meetings complete
- Thursday—First draft of the report complete
- Friday—Final review complete and entire report ready to submit by five p.m.

Being able to track progress along the way allows you to shift your strategy as needed and still reach your goal. So in the above example, say that on Tuesday, in the middle of your research, you hear back from Madhu that he's on vacation until Thursday. You'll need to shift your strategy, because you had benchmarked to have both of your meetings completed by Wednesday. So now perhaps you'll take the time on Wednesday that you had planned to use for meeting Madhu and instead use it to write as much of your first draft before Thursday as possible, so that once you meet with Madhu later in the week you can slot in his information and make only minimal changes before your final review on Friday.

If you hadn't laid out benchmarks in the beginning, you might have gotten all the way until Wednesday before realizing that you still needed information from Benia and Madhu, and only at that point reached out to get their input. Maybe by then Benia's whole week would have been booked up, and your end goal would have been delayed.

Typically, I find benchmarking most useful with more long-term projects, which will take at least several months, if not a year, to complete (as opposed to the one-week example mentioned earlier). It can be easy to put off or even forget a long-term goal in the bustle of everyday life. But if you are tracking benchmarks every week, you'll be able to course-correct very quickly.

Driving Team Performance

All of the above tools can be applied in a team context, or if you are in a situation where you are responsible for team success, either in whole (as the team leader) or in part (as a team member).

One of the specific ways that my brain gives me trouble when I am responsible for driving and guiding the work of other people—either vertically with direct reports or laterally with peers—is knowing when to step back and when to get more involved.

It is infinitely easier, not just for someone with ASD but really for anyone, to do the work yourself. You know that phrase "If you want something done right, do it yourself"? This is not a realistic approach. There is simply too much work to be done. No one person can accomplish everything. Eventually you have to trust other people.

There are many resources available on how to be a manager, how to be a team player, or how to drive team performance. For the purposes of this book, I want to focus solely on this issue of handing work that you know how to do well over to someone else, when the other person may or may not know how to do it the same way as you. Just reading that sentence may be sending some ASD-minded readers into a minor panic. But trust me, it will be okay. You know logically that you are not the only capable person in the world; you know that others have skills and methods and ideas to contribute.

By working as part of a team of people who are all committed to success, you will find that there is actually incredible benefit to people doing things in their own way, which will likely be different from yours. Different perspectives working together on a common goal or team project is what will ultimately make success possible—especially if the goal is a big one.

And yet it can be hard, as a leader, when you know that in the end, you are the one who will be judged by the quality of work that other people put out. Your instinct is to keep it as close as possible.

There is a way to keep it close, without keeping it yours.

One of the best tools I have found for maintaining overall control of the end product of a project is the "Slice of Cake" method.

Take a Slice of Cake

The essential idea is this: Think of the entire project as a multilayer cake. It's got icing on the top and icing in between the layers. It's big and round and, while one person might be able to bake it on their own, nobody would ever want to consume the entire thing by themselves.

The project you are handing over to someone else is the cake. They are going to bake it. You will have very little hand in the overall baking process. The end users—your executive team, your customers, whoever your "audience" is for this specific project—will be the ones who eat the cake, and who judge its quality.

First, you will metaphorically sit with the person who is baking the cake that you will ultimately be judged on, and you will lay out your strategy together: Will the person baking the cake follow the recipe and use four eggs, or do you think it's important to incorporate one of your grandmother's secrets and use three full eggs and two egg whites? What is the best oven to bake the cake in for maximum moisture-retention and time effectiveness? The person you are working with may have their own experiences, which add something to the work that you never would have thought of yourself—maybe their brother is a baker and adds a pinch of cinnamon to get just a little extra zest in the final taste, etc. In reality, for a work project, this strategy-building may take the form of several meetings with various stakeholders, conducting a needs assessment, pulling together knowledge from various sources, building the foundation of what will become an eventual solution, etc. And then, at the moment of handing over the project, a summary meeting with the person who will be driving the project, to codify your final strategy.

In that meeting, you will work together to set the end goal, determine the appropriate benchmarks, and set priorities within the larger context. You will let the person you are working with know a date by which you will be taking the first "slice" of the "cake"—familiarizing yourself with the progress of their work up to that point—and what layers you expect to see in the cake at that time (i.e. what work you expect will be done by then).

When the time comes for you to take that slice of cake, you won't ask to see how far the person has gotten in the entire project—you won't taste the entire cake. You will ask only for your slice. This one piece gives you the power to extrapolate how the whole rest of the cake is going, without having to see it firsthand.

You are able to "taste" the work and provide strategic direction as necessary—maybe the icing on the second layer is a little too thin, which is allowing it to slide a little too much—or, in a work context, perhaps the second phase of solution implementation is lacking an oversight mechanism that would allow for feedback from the consumer of the solution to be incorporated back into the development and implementation of the third and final phase of the project. This "slice" of the other person's work gives you the opportunity to strategically share your knowledge and expertise and make sure that the quality of the overall work is at a level you would be comfortable presenting to your end audience, even though you aren't doing it yourself.

Depending on how long a project is going to take or how big the end goal is, you may structure in several of these "slices" so that you can track progress at the beginning, middle, and near the end of a project, without eating the whole cake every time.

THINKING STRAIGHT

In addition to executive function issues, I want to explore some of the other key ways that my brain, and many (though not all) ASD brains, differ from neurotypical brains in our perception of the world as they relate to the workplace. I hope some of these will ring a bell and help you build your own unique solutions or work-arounds.

Struggling with Central Coherence

An ASD brain can be more prone than a neurotypical brain to have what is known as "weak central coherence." The simplest form of central coherence is finding the "main idea" or "theme" of something, like a paragraph or story. Extrapolating the unspoken moral from a fable or pulling out the key argument being made in a debate. But these things are not a problem for me, nor are they a problem for a lot of people with ASD, or those who have central coherence issues. Where weak central coherence becomes an issue for me is in the much more convoluted and abstract areas of life where certain skills related to central coherence are necessary, such as:

- **Big-Picture Thinking.** I have a much harder time "seeing the forest through the trees."
- **Black-and-White Thinking.** To me, everything is default "black or white," and I have a very hard time recognizing or functioning in "gray" areas.
- **Generalization.** I struggle with appropriately generalizing skills or ideas from one context to another, usually ending up overgeneralizing or under-generalizing.

Big-Picture Thinking

Due to an acute focus on small details, a lot of ASD brains can struggle with big-picture thinking. Why does an ASD brain tend to hyper-focus on details? Most literally, it has to do with how my senses take in the world. Most neurotypical brains will look at a person's face, and the first thing they will think is "face." They see the full context, filling in the details later. My brain processes in the opposite direction. When I see a person's face, the first thing I think is not "face," it's "brown eyes flecked with green, flat nose, high cheekbones, thinly shaped eyebrows." It's incredible the number of details you can notice about a person's face. This is true for everything. A table is not a table at first glance, it is a black, round, wooden slab about two inches thick with three legs and a varnish finish, leaning slightly to the left. After many years of operating this way, I am usually able to process the overload of information in a nanosecond and recognize a face or a table, quickly enough to pass for neurotypical. But imagine this same issue applied to larger concepts—the strategic vision and purpose behind a work initiative, for example, or the fundamental reasons for a significant life decision. The challenge of not being able to see the forest for the trees becomes much more problematic.

This issue is very much related to the "high context" versus "low context" exploration from the previous chapter. The details of any particular situation are low context—the solid facts, the smaller pieces that make up the whole. The bigger picture of a situation is high context—how all the pieces come together to make a whole that is greater than the sum of its parts. When you can see the larger context of a situation, you can decipher more clearly what is really important in that moment (a.k.a. my mother-in-law's feelings about her pie, rather than the factual taste of the pie itself), and prioritize those things.

The inability to see the bigger picture can significantly impact certain types of work and working environments. Here is an example from my work life of struggling with big-picture thinking:

"I have made this type of correction before in our messaging. I need you to be more proactive about learning from and incorporating these edits into future work before you submit it to me for review."

Jodi's critique stung less only due to the fact that it was delivered over email, rather than in person, so I was afforded the time to digest it without emotions running high, and before having to formulate any kind of real-time response.

She had been making edits to a grant proposal that was going out later in the week. When I looked at the section she was referencing in her comment, I saw that her edits were to include more specifics about the program's history, including an award it had won the previous year, the year that the program started, and the evolution of the program's name over the years as the services were more narrowly defined and deeply qualified.

Her edits, on their face value, made sense. All these pieces would serve to show a more complete picture of the program and build a stronger case for funding. However, her comment indicating that she did not appreciate having to make the edits in the first place, and implying that I should have done these things already by learning from previous edits she had made to other projects, confused me deeply.

Logically, it made sense. I would be annoyed, too, if I was in a position to have to keep correcting what I perceived to be the same behavior over and over, especially if the person I was correcting seemed perfectly capable of learning from the experience and doing better the next time.

But just the previous day, Jodi had edited OUT similar program specifics from the narrative of an email that was going out today to our donor base. And that wasn't the first time her edits had included taking out the program name entirely and using more wide-reaching statistics rather than focusing too narrowly on the specific benefits or history of a particular program.

At face value, her edits to one narrative seemed completely contradictory to her edits on the other narrative, and the fact that she expected me to know in advance which way she was going to go with her edits this time, frankly, rankled. How was I supposed to know if she wanted it black on Tuesday and then white on Wednesday?

All three of the above-mentioned ASD-linked traits were at play here—black-or-white thinking, over/under-generalization, and lack of big-picture thinking.

In the past, I might have internalized the whole thing and spiraled into confusion, feeling lost and incompetent and unsure of how to fix the problem. Since I had learned to take a step back and not internalize as much, I was able to bypass unproductive feelings of incompetence and take an even further step back to look at the bigger picture.

When I looked at both interactions at the same time—the edits to the grant proposal and the contradictory edits to the donor email—and then combined those two with other edits Jodi had provided to other projects, I was able to discern the larger thought patterns.

From a bigger picture lens, Jodi's edits were in fact consistent over time, when I also took into account the type of narrative and the audience for the messaging.

On previous grant proposals or other long-form narratives going to more well-informed audiences such as funding institutions or nonprofit partners, she had made the same type of edits for depth of program description and history. At the same time, on previous emails or other messages going to individual donors, she had made the opposite edits on breadth of data and fewer specifics on one program.

So what to me initially looked like contradictory directions—randomly black on one day and white on another day—because I was too focused on the smaller details, was in fact two different patterns of direction related to two separate types of work, once I looked at it as a much bigger picture.

Black-and-White Thinking

Another common ASD trait that is directly related to "weak central coherence" is inflexible thinking, or seeing everything as "black and white."

It is very difficult for me to recognize or operate in what people call "gray areas." But most of life is in fact lived in the gray areas, because we are all human, and nothing is ever really absolute or always one way.

I don't know why it's so hard for me to conceive of, and function in, gray areas. I just know that whenever I am navigating a gray area, it feels like trying to walk through a room full of furniture in pitch blackness. I logically know that I'm in a room with a floor and that I will encounter obstacles, but I can't see them to prepare for them, nor can I avoid them. I also have no idea how big the room is or which direction I need to go to get to the light switch, or wherever it is that I want to go.

A gray area is anything that does not have clear parameters and which might be evaluated subjectively. I thrive on precise expectations. If you tell me you need something back from me "any time next week," it feels like you just threw a helium-filled balloon into the air and told me to chase it. Do you really mean "any time," as in, I can get it to you by 5:30 p.m. on Friday? Or do you really need it by Wednesday, but you feel like it would be too rude to say that outright and so you'd rather I intuit that you actually need it by Wednesday without you having to tell me? *Why are you making me chase after your balloon?*

And yet, people do this all the time. This is how people normally interact. Life is too big and full and complicated for all of us to be precise all the time. There are so many people and the human existence is so varied and wonderful that most of our lives must exist in gray areas.

One of the best concepts I have come across in my work for combatting the perfectionism that can be a result of black-or-white thinking is the phrase "Don't let the perfect be the enemy of the good." Basically it means that, sometimes, it just has to be good enough in order to move forward and exist at all.

For me and my default of black-or-white thinking, if something is not 100 percent right, then it's 100 percent wrong. But that is an impossible standard to live by, especially after leaving the world of academia and entering careers and marriage and parenthood. I used to spend hours, for example, fixing the formatting of a particular report or presentation, when the content was what really mattered and the formatting could have been handled adequately in less than thirty minutes. It might not have looked perfect, but how it looked didn't really matter compared to what was in it. At some point, 85 percent or even 70 percent "right" just has to be *good enough*, because there are only so many hours in a day.

If perfectionism is keeping something from ever happening, then it's actually a bad thing—a barrier standing in the way of success. Good is still good, even if it's not perfect.

Generalization

Another issue I experience related to "weak central coherence" is difficulty in generalizing. Often I will either overgeneralize (apply one thing to too many or to inappropriate contexts), or under-generalize (not be able to take a skill or concept learned in one setting and apply it to a similar setting where the skill/concept would also be appropriate).

An example of overgeneralization could be my coworker not saying good morning to me like they usually do. I might think to myself, *Oh, we're not saying good morning anymore. Okay.* And then never say good morning to them again. But in reality, my coworker was probably just having a particularly busy morning that day or came into the office more preoccupied than usual. Not following their usual routine in this one case does not mean that the routine has changed forever. They will probably go back to saying good morning when they come in the next day, and not even remember that they broke their pattern the day before.

An example of under-generalization could involve my boss sending me an agenda template in advance of my weekly one-on-one meeting with her, asking me to fill it out for our meeting this week. I might do it and send it back to her before our meeting, and we might then have a great meeting. The next week, we might get to our meeting again, and my boss might ask me, "Where's the agenda?" In her mind, when she asked me to do the agenda for that one meeting, it implied that I was to be doing the agendas in advance of all our one-on-one meetings moving forward. Whereas in my mind, she had only asked me to do it for that one week, perhaps because she didn't have time that week or any number of other obscure, yet still entirely possible, reasons. Due to under-generalization and lack of natural ability to apply one learning to future contexts without explicit thought and energy, I might not have realized that this was the new process by which we were to formulate the agenda for every meeting, as opposed to just a one-time request.

Struggles with generalization are related to the concept of black-and-white thinking—if you tell me something is "never" a certain way, I am apt to believe you literally (black-or-white thinking), when in fact no one who says "never" really means "never." They just mean "rarely," or "never in this context" (gray areas).

One of the reasons I find it hard to generalize is—again—the sheer number of details that I take in. If I see one table that is bar height, made of metal, with four legs and painted white, and next to it I see another table that is much lower, made of wood, with three legs and painted red, my brain does not automatically generalize the larger category of "table" to both. I have to manually tell myself that both of these items are tables, and that comprehending their existence at this generalized level is good enough to be getting on with.

This trait can be advantageous in many situations. For example, it is very hard for me to make assumptions about people based on commonly perpetuated stereotypes, such as "all women are emotional" or "all millennials are entitled." These kinds of stereotypes are usually not only untrue, they are also damaging, and therefore it's a good thing that my brain rarely accepts them.

On the other hand, there are far too many trillions of people and places and things in the world—too many data points—to have to understand each one of them in individualized, unique detail. Some level of categorization— or generalization—is necessary to be able to make sense of all the data and go about everyday life.

This is where I falter. It is hard for me to find my footing in the "gray area" of generalizing enough for comprehension and action, but not too much—well, how much is too much? How much is enough? Does it differ in different circumstances?

The answer, of course, is yes.

The key for me has been to take all these traits in tandem—my struggles with big-picture thinking, black-or-white thinking, and generalization— as all facets of one larger struggle with central coherence. To make better decisions and perform better in various capacities, I have learned to take that extra step back. Take a step back and observe your work from the outside looking in, or from a "bird's-eye view"—whatever metaphor works for you. That way, you give your brain the space it needs to recognize where there might in fact be patterns of behavior when you were just seeing contradictions, or where you might be under- or overgeneralizing someone's expectations, or where you might be spending too much time on making something perfect when it's already good enough.

LARRY'S TWO CENTS

One of only a few truly universal truths is there are twenty-four hours in a day, or at least close enough, when rounding and taking into account a leap year day once every four years. With this truth, we as a society have developed what the consensus considers to be "normal life." Exceptions notwithstanding, we plan our day from roughly when the sun comes up until sometime after the sun goes down. Even those who work night shifts or variable schedules still follow some sense of a regular time table.

From that twenty-four-hour time slot, we lose 25 to 33 percent on average to sleep. This leaves us with sixteen to eighteen hours of awake life time, which we split between work, family, and fun. You can further subtract from the remaining time things like eating, commuting, and any number of other items that are unique to you. All of this is to say ultimately that time is precious, and this is especially true in the workplace. Depending on your job, you may have a specific shift to work within or you may be (un)luckily salaried, where you have a minimum amount of hours you have to work, but it's okay with the company if you go over those hours. Regardless of where you end up in this equation, what is true is that the more time you spend on a given task, the less time you have for other work.

Learning to be efficient is thus a key component of being successful. At times, however, being efficient can mean not being absolutely perfect, and to a perfectionist, that can be more than just maddening, it can be a significant problem. One of Sarah's traits has been well cultivated from early in her schooling, when she impressively was valedictorian of her high school. It is quite impressive that someone who can be a bit of a procrastinator, though nowhere nearly as skilled as me, was able to achieve the academic heights she was able to. In talking about this with her, one thing I learned was how she considered time to not be as important as I did. Where I would gladly turn in something that might warrant a B+, she would forgo entertainment and sleep until it was worthy of being turned in. Of course, in school this is well rewarded and rightfully so, at least to a point. The one significant drawback of this academic system is it doesn't always prepare you for how the workplace has evolved, where things need to be well done, but they don't always, every time have to be perfect.

This balance—of being very good at times but not perfect—is not easy to identify, let alone be good at it. Learning to estimate the volume of a canister is easy enough in math, but learning to estimate how long a task will take, can be impossible in certain conditions. Now, for a scientist, a philosopher, and others in such jobs where time is not the most important aspect of the equation, this is all perfectly acceptable. In the corporate world, deadlines are real, and delivery is an absolute necessity. If one does not do their part of the bargain, say for example, when Sarah was learning to finish a presentation that was due to be given to an executive. If the presentation isn't done, the consequences are much more significant and cascading. Also, unlike the school years, there is only so much one can do after hours. You can't always stay at work all night, and people may want something finished the night before so they can review it prior to a big meeting the next day.

Over time and with enough close calls or minor glitches, mistakes and missed deadlines, Sarah has developed her estimating skills and prioritization skills, though they are under constant tweaking as new priorities emerge that change a previously known calculus.

Another learned skill that has helped with Sarah's time equation, particularly in the interpersonal communication category, is having premade decisions that include planning what to wear the night before, to having a few go-to choices when it comes to food and drinks. There is a lot of time one can spend thinking about how to look or what to eat, but there is a big difference if you stay up a bit late the night before versus missing your train because you didn't give yourself enough time in the morning to dress. The same principle applies when it comes to making a drink or entrée choice while out at a business meeting. With Sarah's rapid ascension in the professional world, so too came the need to have various out-of-office meetings, usually at restaurants for lunch, dinner, or during an event.

Being able to draw on the experiences in taking Sarah to a diner for breakfast and witnessing fifteen minutes of careful consideration of each item on the menu, I took the initiative and began the conversation about how being out with a person is often more important than the food or drink choices. Unless you are going to a four-star amazing restaurant, it is much more likely that the most important part of any get-together is about the people, not the food. After a bit of cajoling, with examples, Sarah came around to my counsel and began to taste wines, beers, and liquors, so if someone offered to get her a drink, she could bypass the menu process and just pick, for instance, a vodka seltzer. This investment and now, ability, removed a significant amount of strain and tension Sarah would have otherwise experienced at the beginning of a conversation, which of course presented its own stressors. Equally, with the food options, learning various enjoyable enough food choices for a given cuisine, or pre-checking a restaurant's website to review a menu, allowed Sarah to reallocate that time, energy, and intention to the person or event.

All of this culminated in one last major milestone, interacting with a member on the Board of Directors. By its own titling, for a young professional, this is intended to be met with an air of cautious foreboding. Board members are perceived to be well-off, accomplished professionals who are giving a small amount of their precious time to one, if not several organizations. With this limited time comes enormous pressure to make the most of it, and to get out as much support, often in terms of dollar contributions, as possible. This responsibility now sat with Sarah and her peers on the executive team. It was one thing to prepare the quarterly meetings for the overall Board, which is plenty overwhelming, but another thing entirely to set up and conduct one-on-one meetings with an individual member.

Wesley. Wesley to this day is a name Sarah or I invoke when thinking about these times, usually in comparison or contrast to a current Board member Sarah happens to be dealing with. In working with Wesley, Sarah found a great, early success, and learned so much in preparing for said success.

What started with a high stress IM that a one-on-one meeting with Wesley was now on her task list, lasted for two weeks where much of Sarah's professional and personal time went into preparing for the meeting. Like a midterm, it had to go well. This was the time when faking it could not be invoked; it had to be a make-it moment. As the time passed, Sarah became sort of relaxed, in a still-stressed sort of manner, as she overprepared and had a huge amount of data at her disposal, both memorized and in printed form.

Not more than a day before the meeting, during a discussion confirming times to meet, Wesley sent over the location of the meeting, which happened to be an Indian restaurant. Up until now, not only had Sarah not thought about not meeting in an office, she had never had Indian food before, as it's not the most common cuisine in the Midwest. This led, as you can guess, to a flurry of stress-filled IMs, which I responded to, after having Sarah take a nice calming walk and coffee break. Sometimes I insisted on this strategy of taking a few calming moments, and this was a time when I would not budge. After returning, I asked the name of the restaurant and did a quick look, to see what was going on. With the meeting happening during the day, they had some nice package options and were well prepared for quick lunches as well as more extravagant menu choices. Finishing my quick review, my simple response was "Not spicy, Chicken Tikka Masala," a very lovely dish which can be found on most menus and is fairly consistent between various restaurants regardless of what region from India the restaurant's cuisine is modeled after. Had it been a vegetarian restaurant, I would have amended their variant of tikka masala with equal confidence.

Though I know Sarah spent several minutes herself looking online at the menu and pictures of the restaurant, having a food choice in mind calmed her nerves and she was able to focus on final preparations. Literally a day later, not only did she report that the meeting was a success, she also enjoyed the meal and we had a new cuisine we could add to our takeout menu collection. A double win, for sure, and one I have continued to celebrate.

Sarah has since internalized this learning of scoping out the restaurant and menu beforehand when possible, in order to allow her—during the meeting itself—to focus more entirely on the *person* involved in the meeting, rather than on the food.

Ultimately, through these first few years, having preached and witnessed the success of individualized support mixed in with a good work ethic, Sarah succeeded and was able to accelerate her professional learnings as she continued to climb the corporate ladder. It is not a timeline we would recommend, but maybe it isn't all that bad to have both high expectations and strong support to achieve them. We are all capable of great things, but how we go about them varies greatly. Once we get past our early math lessons where we are told to constantly show our work and are often penalized for not following the right steps as we get the right answer, we begin to learn that we are judged on our outcomes, and if the job is done right, very few people take umbrage with how we got there.

CHAPTER FOUR

Navigating Professional Relationships

"Walk with the dreamers, the believers, the courageous, the cheerful, the planners, the doers, the successful people with their heads in the clouds and their feet on the ground."

—WILFERD PETERSON

MEETINGS

The form and flow of meetings will vary greatly depending on the field or industry where you work, and the type of environment you work in. For the purposes of this book, I stick pretty closely to office working environments in Western culture. I also endeavor to keep these references as broadly applicable as possible, while acknowledging they cannot possibly encompass all work experiences. Feel free to skip sections that don't seem to pertain to your own environment, or take the pieces that do and tweak as needed.

Purpose, Roles, and Structure

When preparing for interpersonal communication in a work meeting, it's important to set the scene: the overall purpose of the meeting, the roles you and others are playing, and the structure the meeting will take. The way you prepare for an information-gathering meeting, for example, will be different from the way you prepare for a collaborative information-creating meeting. Just as the way you prepare to lead a meeting will be different from the way you prepare when you are just a participant.

First, consider the overall **purpose** of the meeting:

- Is it simple <u>information exchange</u> (which can sometimes turn out to be not-so-simple)? An example of this type of meeting could be that you are writing a report or a proposal and you need various pieces of information from different departments, which will be easier to gather with everyone in the room together for thirty minutes. You or another party could also have information to share—an example of this could be a strategic positioning meeting, where senior leadership lays out the overall organizational goals for the year, or it could be a meeting you have initiated in order to provide your team or another team with some new information that will affect their work.

- Is it more about <u>information-creation</u> or coming together to collaboratively brainstorm, discuss and solve a problem, or begin/continue a project? An example of this type of meeting could be a new initiative launch. You have an opportunity to partner with another organization in a new way or to launch a new project or product within your own organization, and you need several different types of expertise and experience at the table. Another example of an information-creation meeting is idea gathering. Perhaps your team or several teams are facing a larger challenge that no one person can solve on their own, and you would benefit from the input of different stakeholders within the organization, in order to formulate a plan with multiple strands of ownership.

- Is it a <u>regular weekly or monthly check-in</u> meeting, where you meet together as a team to track progress against goals and hold each other accountable to ongoing tasks? These types of meetings might be with the same few people each time, and therefore require less preparation in terms of communication strategies, but more preparation of information or reporting.

Next, consider the **roles** that you and others will play in the meeting. These roles can be fluid, of course, or they could be static. Specific roles will depend somewhat on the purpose and/or structure of the meeting, and vice versa.

Who is leading the meeting, if anyone? If there is no clear leader, are there several people who will be responsible for moving the meeting along and making sure the participants of the meeting stay on task and on topic? I have found that when there is no clear leader, one of two things will likely happen:

1. The person who called the meeting may be looked to as a de facto leader. This doesn't necessarily mean they need to lead the entire discussion, but they may be expected to set the frame at the beginning ("Why are we meeting?"), raise the appropriate questions related to the purpose of the meeting throughout, and keep track of timing. This means that if you are the one who sent out the calendar invite, even if you are not the most senior person in the room or even particularly knowledgeable about the subject, you should be prepared to be the "structure-keeper" of the meeting, and to take an administrative role if needed.

2. The most senior person in the room may be looked to as a de facto leader. This happens more often when very senior managers are present, like vice presidents or C-suite executives.

    -   If you are leading the meeting, you will need to consider not only your role, but also the role that you would like others to play. Do you want a co-leader? Do you want someone to provide a case study or a specific example from their own work to illustrate your point? Do you want someone to make sure to raise a specific topic or ask a specific question in order to lead the conversation in a certain direction? How much talking will you do, versus how much the group will amongst themselves? Will you need to take into account different communication styles? The roles and structure you create for your meeting will depend largely on what you hope to get out of it.

- If you are a participant in the meeting, and not leading, consider the role you will play with respect to the leader and the other people in the room. Is the leader your boss? If so, be prepared to be called upon in a potential impromptu support role. Are you his/her boss? If so, again, be prepared to play a support role, but be careful about how you do this, and ensure that any support you provide uplifts your supervisee, rather than strengthening the power imbalance or invalidating your supervisee's role as the leader.

Here is a concrete example of how I did this for one of my direct reports, modeling my own behavior after one of my bosses who had done the same for me:

Corinne was starting to go offtrack. I knew it, and I could tell by one highly subtle sideways look between the two executives in the room, and one furrowed brow, that they were preparing to redirect, as their time was precious and they wanted to make sure it was used productively. I also knew, as Corinne's direct supervisor, and as the direct report of one of the executives present, that it was my responsibility to attempt the redirect first.

I was careful to let Corinne finish her current sentence and start to take a breath before I indicated strongly, via body language first, that I wanted to interrupt. I leaned forward quickly in my chair, opened my mouth, and held up one relatively loose hand with a kind of slight bouncing motion, as if I were formulating my thoughts right then and there. Too solid of a hand gesture, like a stiff hand with one finger pointing up, without the pensive bounce, would have indicated too strong of an interruption and served to underline the fact that I ranked above Corinne. This empowered Corinne to recognize that I was going to step in, and to reciprocate with either "yes" or "no" body language—she could have refused my attempt to intervene, which I wanted to make sure she knew was completely within her rights. She chose to accept my interjection, probably sensing she was getting offtrack and not sure how to get back on. She closed her own mouth and leaned slightly back, nodding to me and gesturing toward me with an open, up-turned hand as an invitation to speak.

"I just want to add," I began, careful to keep my eyes on Corinne at first, as if we were having a collaborative discussion, just the two of us, rather than me stepping in to bat for her in her interaction with my boss and his colleague. The use of the verb "to add" was also important here because it served to validate everything that Corinne had said up to that point, and indicate forward motion, rather than negate or counteract any-thing she had brought to the table, which would have happened if I had instead said something like "What I think is missing here . . . " or "What we mean to say is . . ."

"I just want to add that, in addition to all the research Corinne has done into the best practices at other organizations"—and now I shifted my gaze toward the executives, having established that Corinne and I were on equal footing on the same team, and that this was still her meeting, and that I was going to hand her back the reins in a minute—"we've also done a great deal of thinking and information-gathering about the best ways to implement this in our organization, given our unique market." It was my turn to lean back, open my upturned hand and nod toward Corinne, to indicate that my point was done and she could step in. I knew, from having prepped for this meeting with her beforehand, that she had the information ready and would know where to take the conversation from here.

- As a participant in the meeting, will you be expected to provide specific information during the meeting, or to have prepared certain material in advance for reference? What roles are the other people in the room likely to play, and what do you know about their communication styles? For example, if I know I'm going into a meeting with someone who I know tends to take the conversation further "into the weeds" than is necessary, I prepare to redirect any points I need to make back to the bigger picture.

Finally, consider the **structure** of the meeting:

- How many people will be in the room? Is it a small meeting, like three people, a medium meeting—maybe five to ten people, or a large meeting, with ten or more people? The number of people in the room will affect how you engage.

  - A good standard I have found for being able to measure whether I am engaging effectively in a meeting is the "5-Minute Rule": If I am in a collaborative meeting with five people or less, and I have not spoken in the last five minutes, too much time has passed without my voice in the room. I know that I need to find a constructive way to add my voice to the conversation, whether this is a relevant question, an additional point that no one has brought up yet, or an observation that might shift the conversation to another level (noticing themes or patterns). This 5-Minute Rule extends to ten minutes in collaborative meetings with more than five, but fewer than ten people. If there are more than ten people in the meeting, then hopefully the meeting is not about collaboration, but more of a presentation or workshop, with designated times when specific people are supposed to talk.

- Who will be doing most of the talking? Will it be one person who is presenting or leading, several people who are presenting, or is the whole group expected to participate relatively equally?

- What are the agenda items that will need to be addressed by the end of the meeting? It is almost always very helpful to have these items, even roughly sketched out, on physical pieces of paper or an easily referenced PowerPoint slide or even a whiteboard/ easel pad, for people in the room to refer to at any point throughout the meeting, in order to reorient themselves to the task at hand. Meetings tend to run more smoothly when everyone in the room can keep track of where the group is in the intended agenda, and what is left to accomplish.

Planned versus Impromptu

There is a big difference between meetings that are planned—with a time, place, and subject matter that has been mutually agreed-upon in advance by the various parties involved—and meetings that are unplanned, or "impromptu," where two or more parties come together by chance in passing and end up having a mini "meeting" about substantive material. There is also such a thing as a planned "impromptu" meeting, explored a little later in this section, where one party seeks the other party out without previously informing the other party of the intention to meet.

In general, I find planned meetings, like those described in the above section, to be much less stress-inducing than unplanned meetings, due in large part to my ASD. With planned meetings, I know the main subject matter in advance, and can prepare what I will say about it, and what I will have prepared as reference material to answer relevant questions about it or to engage in productive discussion about it. Because I know when and where the meeting will take place, I am able to engineer time beforehand to make sure I am in the right mental state (two minutes of meditative breathing, or eating a piece of chocolate to stimulate the production of some oxytocin, or two minutes of "power-posing" for high-stakes meetings).[1] Because I know in advance who will be in the meeting, I have time to prepare myself for various communication styles that will complement the personalities in the room (if I know someone in the meeting tends to dominate the conversation, or tends to ask a lot of probing questions, etc.).

But, if you are like me and thrive with time to prepare, there are ways that you can prepare yourself for potential *unplanned* meetings, as well, without going overboard and swamping yourself in planning upon planning.

Quick-Reference Mental "Files" for Important Topics and People in the Workplace

One of the most time-effective ways I have found to help prepare myself for unplanned interactions in the office is, much like the quick-reference mental files mentioned in chapter 1 for initiating relevant small talk with acquaintances, is to take a few minutes—like no more than three minutes—to mentally prep the top one or two things that are most time-relevant for the few people who I might run into during my upcoming venture outside my own office. This is a very helpful strategy in general, not just to be prepared for unplanned interactions, but to be prepared to get what you need in terms of work follow-ups, especially with people who you might not meet on a frequent basis.

Here is an example of how this strategy was helpful for me recently in the workplace:

I needed to warm up my lunch in the shared office pantry microwave. I knew that several executives were in the office today, having seen them come in or in passing earlier in the day. It was prime lunch time, right around 12:30 p.m., when it was likely that others would be preparing their own lunches in the pantry as well. And knowing that my lunch would take four to five minutes to heat up, I was going to be in the pantry for longer than usual, thus increasing the chances that I would run into one of the executives making their own food.

So I took a few minutes and ran through in my head the number one thing that I needed from, or that I would like to bring up to, each of the executives in turn, in case one or more of them came in while I waited for my food to cook. From the chief financial officer, I needed his feedback on the cost-benefit analysis I had submitted last week. From the chief operating officer, I needed his approval to approach one of our new vendors with a sponsorship opportunity. I knew that if I brought this up to him, he might ask how much we wanted to ask them for, so I put that number in my head, too, along with the high-level justification for it. For the chief executive officer, I knew she might ask about the performance of our recent mailing, so I quickly reminded myself of our response rate and net revenue numbers.

Armed with my hit list, I walked into the pantry and was gratified, and slightly intimidated, to see the CEO already there taking her own food out of the microwave. Good thing I had taken the time to prep.

Indeed, after the obligatory pleasantries, she turned around on her way out and inquired, as an afterthought, about how our mailing had done. Ready with the numbers fresh in my head, I gave her the highlights, and some preliminary thoughts about what we might do differently next time to increase effectiveness. She nodded appreciatively and seemed satisfied that I was thinking proactively about my work, and offered some encourage-ment that the numbers sounded good before she left.

As the microwave hummed around my food, in walked the COO, to get his own lunch out of the refrigerator.

Again, the exchange of pleasantries, but this time it was my turn to proactively engage him, since he didn't have any direct follow-ups that he needed from me. "Atlas, did you see my email last week, about asking Mil-lennium to sponsor our event in the fall?"

I could see him mentally pulling up the email in his mind's eye as he dug his food out of the fridge. "Uhh, yeah, yes, I remember seeing that. Um, yeah, we should definitely ask them to sponsor. How much were you thinking?"

"Well, our contract with them is for over two hundred thousand in the next year, right?" I answered, setting up my response as my food finished cooking.

"Yes, I believe so," Atlas replied, putting his Tupperware in the micro-wave now and setting the timer.

I rummaged in the drawer for a fork as I said, "Then I think we should ask for at least five thousand, don't you think? Maybe more?" I wanted to set the bar but feel out how good of a relationship he thought he had built with this new vendor, and whether he thought we could raise it.

Atlas seemed to sense my prodding and responded positively. "Go for ten," he said, definitively. "Yeah, ten thousand. They can always say no and go for five thousand instead."

"Perfect," I responded, indicating with a satisfied, peremptory tone of voice that he had said exactly what I wanted him to say.

With my food done, it was acceptable at that point for me to leave the pantry and head back to my desk. "Thanks, Atlas!" I said as I left. "Enjoy your lunch."

"No problem. You too."

The Importance of the Engineered "Impromptu" Meeting

Sometimes, it can be very useful to proactively engineer what would otherwise appear to be an "impromptu" meeting. This requires knowing the schedule of the person you are trying to catch in passing, or having access to some form of shared calendar that gives you an idea of when they would be free. I generally use this type of engineered impromptu meeting in order to do something similar to what I did with the COO in the previous example, except instead of it happening by chance, I make sure I am in a place where I know he might likely be at that time so that it can happen on purpose. I might look at his calendar and see that he has a thirty-minute break in between meetings, and I will make sure I walk by his office during that break period so that I can see if he is indeed available (i.e. sitting in his office, but not on the phone or meeting with anyone else). Or if I am going to a meeting or other type of office gathering that I know he will be in, I will prepare and make sure to catch him as the meeting is wrapping up, before he leaves.

Another type of engineered impromptu meeting can be something that you cultivate on a more regular basis with a particular person in order to establish better rapport with particularly difficult, distant, or otherwise problematic coworkers. Sometimes a person is harder to work with simply due to the fact that the two of you don't interact enough in a casual context. Proactively creating that space can save a lot of time and miscommunication that might otherwise happen if each of you don't understand the basic motivations and baseline demeanor of the other.

Here is an example from early in my professional career of how I came to understand the existence, importance, and execution of regularly engineered "impromptu" meetings with a specific coworker:

Into my well-worn instant messenger app on my desktop, I typed:

> Need your help with a work thing . . .

Larry answered within a few minutes.

> Go ahead.

> I just got this really long email from Gavina. She seems really upset. I don't understand what happened.

I explained in text, feeling the despair starting to well up again as I mentally recalled some of the harsh words Gavina had used in her two-page email.

> Forward me the email.

While I waited for Larry to read the long email exchange, I mulled over what could possibly have gone wrong to prompt my colleague, Gavina, to send me such a diatribe. I had already learned—via an email etiquette crash course from my husband—that an email with that much vitriol, and that long, was not the most appropriate response to a workplace interaction. In my mind, the fact that Gavina had gone "off the norm" and sent me a two-page written attack, rather than coming to talk to me in person, indicated that I must have done something highly inappropriate in order to prompt her similarly inappropriate response. What had I done? Was it something I'd said? Was it a personal problem, or was it about a work-related issue?

"Firstly," Larry started typing back, and I refocused on his response, amazed as always at how quickly he could read and consume material and context. "She should not have sent that in an email. She needed to come talk to you."

I nodded absently at my computer. This I knew already. And yet she had sent it, and she had at least fifteen more years of experience in the workforce than I had. I must have done something awful.

"That said," Larry continued, "it is not your place to tell her that. That conversation would need to come from her boss or a trusted mentor. Instead, you, as her peer (see the note on peers on page 157), have an opportunity to make small changes in the way you interact with her on a regular basis in order to prevent this kind of outburst in the future. There are several factors you can control that may have been at play, which prompted her to send a long one-sided email rather than come to you. How often do you interact with Gavina in the office, as in face-to-face?"

"Really just in meetings," I answered.

"As in, with a bunch of other people in the room? Do you ever meet with her one-on-one?"

"No, always with other people."

"OK, that's the first problem. She's your director of Human Resources. Don't you need information from her on a fairly regular basis for grants and such?" he asked.

"Kind of, but nothing that can't be sent via email . . ." I typed back.

"Where is her office?"

"Around the corner from mine."

In my mind, I could see him rolling his eyes while he sat typing on his own computer. "OK. Not now, but for the future, after you get over this email spat, you need to stop into her office from time to time to ask in-person for the information you need, rather than relying only on email. The face-to-face time will help. You'll understand why in a minute."

"OK," I acquiesced, consciously suspending my disbelief until the promise of later understanding. Occasionally popping unannounced into a colleague's private office space in order to badger them for information sounded annoying to me, not helpful.

"For now, three things need to happen. One, DO NOT respond via email to Gavina's email. You'll address her in person, the way she should have done for you. You can write out some of your thoughts beforehand, but try not to focus on the details of her email—keep it high-level, and about repairing your working relationship. Fixing the details she brings up in the email can come later."

As I read his words, I could tell this was going to be tough for me. I had the data right in front of me—Gavina's email—just begging to be addressed. I had already started formulating specific, targeted responses to each of the points Gavina had brought up in her email, and here was Larry telling me that was precisely what I was not to do. I knew it was because he was directing me toward the bigger picture—the reason that each of the details in Gavina's email had become a problem in the first place, which was a larger breakdown of communication between the two of us. I knew logically that the bigger picture was the more important thing to fix right now, because if I didn't fix the bigger picture and instead tried to fix the details first, nothing would really change. Gavina wouldn't be in a state of mind to be able to hear and act on my detailed responses, and we would just end up bickering in email rather than addressing the root of the issue. But knowing that didn't make it any easier to push aside the details written out in front of me. I was going to have to allow myself to write out each of my point-by-point responses to Gavina's words first (a.k.a. "You said in your email that I should know and respect the volunteer background check policy, but in fact the policy changed just last month and there was no notice that went out to anyone in the agency of the change and how it would affect our use of volunteers. Of course I would respect the policy if I knew it had changed, but am I supposed to go myself and look in our policy records every week to cull through any changes that might have occurred?"), and then go through the exercise of coalescing and smoothing out my responses into bigger themes (a.k.a. changing the above to: "I didn't know the volunteer policy had changed, and I wasn't the only one who didn't know. It seems like there are areas where a lack of communication, on all fronts, is causing misunderstanding, and it can feel like disrespect, rather than simply not having all of the information."), and then pull the themes up into even higher-level big-picture context (a.k.a. refining the above change to: "I'm sorry that I was not aware of the volunteer policy change. What are some ways that we could improve overall communication, to avoid misunderstandings like this in the future?") before I could get to the actual words that I would say to Gavina in person.

"Two," Larry continued. "You need to engage JoAnne."

I shuddered, unwilling to let this one slide in suspended disbelief. "Why??" I typed back before Larry could finish.

JoAnne was my boss and also Gavina's boss. She was the executive director. Engaging her on any level in this peer-level "spat" felt to me like running to the teacher to tattle on someone. Something that, as a rule-stickler all through elementary and middle school, I had learned the hard way was not acceptable behavior. I was also nervous about appearing incompetent to my ED—this was my first full-time work experience out of college, and I was miles younger than any of the other directors in the agency. Running to my boss—let alone to the ED herself—whenever I had a disagreement with a coworker was hardly the precedent I wanted to set.

"Not to complain about Gavina," Larry explained. "But it is important for JoAnne to know that two of her direct reports are actively working out some interpersonal conflict. You don't need to tell her the details—that you got a two-page email and it felt like an attack. You just need to give her an FYI that you've had some less-than-ideal interaction with Gavina, and that you are taking steps to address it. This way she knows you are on top of it. And if Gavina comes to her complaining about you, she will know that you are aware of it, and already being proactive."

Now, that felt like a perfectly reasonable strategy to me. It didn't feel like tattling at all. Just an FYI. "But what if JoAnne asks for details?" was my worry.

"She won't," Larry responded. "She's the ED. She has way too many other bigger things to worry about than squeezing details out of an inter-office conflict that you present you are handling on your own."

"She has worked with Gavina for years," I typed, spotting another potential problem. It seemed to me that there might be some background of understanding in the prior relationship between Gavina and JoAnne that I would be treading on if I told JoAnne that I was having any kind of issues with Gavina.

But Larry cut off my train of thought. "Good. Then perhaps she has run into issues like this with Gavina before, and she will appreciate you taking the initiative to address it directly. She won't begrudge you doing what you need to do in order to advocate for yourself and get your work done, despite whatever prior relationship she might have with Gavina. She hired you, just like she hired Gavina."

"OK." That seemed reasonable to me, but I knew I would have some higher-level details ready to share just in case she asked, and that I would be careful to keep them respectful and solution-oriented, nothing that sounded like a complaint.

"What's the third thing?"

"Third, after you have addressed Gavina in person about the higher-level context behind the email, you need to start engineering regular five-minute weekly check-ins with her. Like, coffee in the pantry on Tuesday mornings."

"???" I typed back, lost for words. This one confused me greatly. Social coffee every week with a colleague who, in my mind, clearly didn't like me? What would that accomplish?

"Yes," Larry affirmed. "This way, you can structure idle time when each of you can keep the other informed about anything big that is happening with your work. So for example, you would have known in advance that Gavina was planning to put through a volunteer policy change, and she would have known in advance that you were going to need volunteers for MLK Day."

"OK . . ." I responded, using an ellipse to indicate that I was still unsure and would appreciate further reasoning to justify this strategy, and instruction on how exactly to do it.

"Trust me," Larry answered. "It will also help the two of you get to know one another in a more low-pressure setting. It's harder to send a two-page tirade to someone who you just swapped a good story with the other day."

"OK, that makes sense." Though now my heart was pounding at the thought of coming up with a "good story" to "swap" with Gavina, but that was a whole other ball of wax to deal with at a later point. "So how do I ask Gavina out for coffee in the pantry on Tuesdays?"

"Just tell her, at the end of the in-person meeting you are now going to set up with her to address the bigger-picture around the email, that you think it would be a good idea for the two of you to start catching up for a few minutes every week. Ask if there's a time when she generally likes to take a coffee break, and if you could join her once a week. It doesn't have to be a permanent thing—it's just to give you and her a chance to interact more casually and set a baseline of positive emotion."

I followed my husband's advice, but in the end the Tuesday coffee chats never worked out with Gavina. We did have a good "debrief" meeting to unpack the big-picture communication problems around her email, which she apologized for sending, knowing that it had been an inappropriate way to communicate her frustration. And JoAnne did appreciate the respectful

FYI of interpersonal conflict that was being actively addressed and did not press for details. But Gavina cancelled our first engineered casual coffee interaction last-minute, and we never tried to schedule another one. I really got the impression that Gavina just did not care to get to know me better in a casual context, and honestly, that was fine with me. Because of the professional way that I handled her unprofessional email, and because she knew that I had alerted (though not tattled to) JoAnne, she never sent me another email tirade, and our overall communication in the workplace did improve.

I have taken this model of engineered "coffee chats," however, and applied it in other situations where I felt the need to establish a better casual baseline with colleagues. This has even extended to engineering an in-person, low-pressure interaction with a colleague who is, consciously or not, blocking something that I need done, either something that I am trying to do or something that one of my direct reports is trying to do. The problem might in fact be that they don't actually want whatever it is done, or the problem might just be that they don't understand what I or my team are trying to do. By putting myself in a situation where I will run into the person outside their office, or even by going to see them in their office and having an in-person conversation about what might be concerning them, I can usually overcome it. I will often make a point of following up these interactions with another positive casual interaction a week or so later, with an update on how whatever I had been working on has since progressed thanks to their help. This helps to establish, as my husband explained, a baseline of trust and positive emotion that will make future work-related needs flow more smoothly.

OFFICE POLITICS

When someone refers to "office politics," they are not talking about an intersection of peoples' political leanings and work. Office politics has nothing to do with the politics we hear about in the news—candidates vying for reelection to a government office, presidential campaigns, house bills and lobbying Congress, etc.

Office politics refers to the way that people interact with each other within and around the implicit and explicit power structures that exist in a work environment. How your boss interacts with their boss on your behalf, or how you interact with a peer versus a direct report versus a direct report of your peer's. As much as it makes my brain hurt—and many other non-ASD brains hurt—all of these workplace relationships usually require a different type of interaction, a different approach, and different considerations for what and how much information to share, how to frame that information, and when to share it.

If you are in a position where you need something from someone who reports to someone else, for example, you will go about getting what you need from that person differently than you would go about getting it from a person who reports directly to you. You might go to the person they report to first, or you might use less direct and more deferential language ("It would be great if we could have a first draft of the design to review by— what do you think? Maybe Wednesday? Would that work?" as opposed to "I'd like to see a first draft by Wednesday.")

Managing Up and Across

Managing the work of people who report to you is one thing. Managing "up" to your own boss or "across" to your peers in other departments requires a completely different skill set. When you manage someone who reports to you, you are using direct authority to help shape and guide their work.

When you are "managing across" to your peers, you are using indirect authority to engender teamwork and progress toward common goals. You don't have control over your peers' work—they don't report to you—but you need their cooperation in order to do your job. The best way to empower your peers to help you is to provide a clear vision (the big picture, why should they give their time to this), clear parameters (what exactly do you need from them), and a clear timeline (when exactly do you need it), so that they can slot your needs into their other work priorities. Then it's your job to follow up with your peers at least one more time before the end deadline, because your project will not be as important to them as their own projects, and you are the one responsible for your overall work product, not them.

AN IMPORTANT NOTE:
PEERS

I used to think that peers were people who were relatively the same age. And this might be true, up to a certain point. Once I entered the workforce, however, the concept of who was a "peer" and who wasn't became much murkier. In the workplace, your peers are not necessarily your age-mates. Your relative responsibility, authority, influence, and scope of work is much more important than age in determining who your peers are in the workplace. So if you are a director and ten years younger or older than another director in a different department, they are still your peer.

Managing Across—Creating a Culture
of "Buy-In" and "Ownership"

It can be difficult to get other people to do work for a project that is not directly their own. If you or your team need time and energy from other departments in order to successfully complete your own work, your best bet is always going to be to create a culture of mutual ownership, and gain the buy-in of your and your teams' colleagues.

You can do this by:

- Showing your colleagues what they stand to gain from the successful completion of your project (i.e. a grant proposal which, if funded, would bring in revenue for the organization and therefore benefit their bottom line).
- Eliciting input from your colleagues on the timeline or content of your project (i.e. their opinion on what kind of funding opportunities to pursue, when certain things can be done based on their own competing priorities, etc.).
- Sharing progress updates so that they know their work is appreciated and making a difference, rather than just going into a mysterious black hole.

When you are "managing up"—to your boss or higher up—you are empowering that person to do what they need to do in order to help you with your job. It might be putting a reminder on their calendar for something you need them to do. It might be setting up a meeting to discuss something specific that only they can provide. It's also making sure they know enough about your work to be able to support you the way you need, and to articulate your work up the chain to their boss. Managing up is very often about creating the right frame for the message that you want to convey.

Managing Up—Framing Your Message

Because time is precious in the workplace, and becomes ever more in demand the more responsibility a person has, the frame that you put around the message you are trying to communicate—when either managing up or across—can make or break your interaction.

Imagine the vastness of your own work—everything you do in a day, everything you are working toward over the course of a year—it's enormous. Only you can hold all of that in your head, because you are the one doing it. But you need help from other people along the way, including your superiors, or your work will not be successful. So you have to share pieces of your work with others in a way that empowers them to help you. You have to take a small portion of your work and put it inside of a frame—think of a picture frame—and hand it to the other person (talk them through it). They will look at the picture in the frame (hear how you frame your work), and either understand what they need to do to help because the frame you used and the work you shared with them is clear, or they will be confused and need to ask for other details or more information because the frame you used was too small and cut out too much surrounding context, or too big and gave them way too many details so that they don't know where to focus their energy.

It takes time to learn how to frame your message the right way with different people. You might find that certain people like more detail than others, or certain people like to know the end product first (what you need from them) before you even get into the explanation of why or when you need it.

Learn how the people you are reporting to respond best to what type of frame, so that you can use their time—and yours—most efficiently.

Social Status and How It Affects Workplace Functions

As much as someone with autism may want to turn a blind eye to it, the fact is that the workplace is full of people, and people are social beings. Social underpinnings such as status (where you are in a social hierarchy), cache (breadth—how much influence you have socially), and rapport (depth—a shared social history) are prevalent, and essential, in workplace settings.

Understanding that these things exist at work, and how to recognize and use them to your advantage, is incredibly helpful in navigating office politics.

Bending the Rules

You will find that one of the greatest benefits reaped by someone who has built rapport with their colleagues is a certain amount of leniency with less important workplace "rules."

For example, Lane might get a pass after submitting a report three days late because she has built a personal relationship of positivity and trust with her boss. Whereas Tony, who keeps mostly to himself and has not built up any social cache with his superiors, might be criticized for submitting a report one day late.

It's not fair. But that's life.

As human beings, we are much more likely to give each other a break when we have a personal relationship or a shared history.

This doesn't mean that you have to go around trying to be friends with every person at your work (please, no). It does mean that you can aim to build a comfortable rapport with key people from whom you might need support in the future, or a favor.

Having at least a minimum of social workplace interaction with your boss, like a few minutes of small talk at the start of your regular meetings, or a few minutes of social interaction in the shared pantry or when passing in the hall, will give you a tiny window into their life beyond work, and them a tiny window into yours. This way if you run into an issue, such as submitting something late that is mid- or low-priority or making a minor mistake, you can spend some of the social capital you have built up to ease the tension.

Technical versus Social Skills

To a certain degree, high technical skill can do a lot to make up for low social skill.

If you are really good at your job, it might matter much less to your peers or superiors that you don't put time or effort toward building up social capital. You offer contextual value in other ways, via your specialized skills and depth of knowledge.

But technical knowledge and skill will only get you so far.

Technical skills are most efficient when directly applied to the work, rather than managing someone else who is doing the work. So if you are relying on your technical prowess as opposed to social status, you may be perceived as someone who does not have the aptitude or desire to advance up a career ladder into management positions. If this is in fact the case, then no problem. If you *do* want to advance, you will need to balance out your technical knowledge with more focus on building social awareness and aptitude.

Kindness Goes a Long Way

It's not a bad thing to be considered "nice." It might not hold as much social cache as being considered "funny" or "gregarious" or "powerful," but it's still a positive impression to leave.

Especially if you are just beginning to delve into the world of building your social capital at work, just practicing kindness in your interactions with other people can get you a long way toward laying that foundation of social cache.

Navigating Office Hierarchy (Explicit and Implicit)

A big part of office politics is knowing and navigating appropriately within the hierarchical structure of the workplace.

For example, say one of the people who directly reports to me, Priyush, is having an issue with one of his peers, Jared. Jared directly reports to one of my peers, Molly.

I wouldn't go directly to Jared and ask him to cooperate with Priyush. Instead, I would exercise the following steps:

First, I would guide Priyush, my direct report, to hopefully solve the issue on his own. Has he tried approaching Jared from X angle? Has he tried framing the work in X way?

If, after attempting to work it out himself with my guidance, Priyush is still having an issue, then I might go to my own peer, Molly, to whom Jared directly reports. But even then, I wouldn't go to Molly and outright complain about Jared. I might try to catch her in between meetings and casually bring up that Priyush is working with Jared on X project, which I'm excited about. I might share with her a few details about the project, why it's exciting, and some high-level points about what kind of help Priyush and I need from Molly and her department to be successful.

Molly will likely instinctually want to help, and may even outright ask me to let her know what she can do. If so, that opens up a window for me to say something like, "Well, actually, Priyush has been running into some pushback with Jared. Maybe you could speak with Jared to see where the issue is and how we can work together to solve it?"

If Molly doesn't explicitly offer help yet, then I would leave it at the high-level overview for now until after Priyush has tried again with Jared. If the problem still persists, then I would follow up with a more direct appeal to Molly.

Workplace hierarchy is more than just explicit work titles and who reports to whom. It is also implicit social status which may or may not follow along the explicit hierarchy. For example, in the above scenario, say that Molly is notoriously unhelpful when it comes to guiding her staff to work collaboratively with other departments. I might still try the above method with Molly, because it's always better to offer the chance, rather than assume the person won't take it. But if that doesn't work, I might go sideways to one of her other peers—perhaps someone she is closer to socially, a friend—and engage them in advocating to Molly on my behalf. Even if that other person doesn't touch my or Priyush's work directly, they might have more social cache with Molly than I do, and might be able to affect more change.

Avoid "Stepping on Peoples' Toes"

One common danger in office politics is either accidentally or more pur-posely "stepping on someone's toes" by doing work they should have been doing, overstepping work boundaries, or trying to use social status or power that you don't have.

In the above example, if I had gone straight to Jared rather than going to Molly, I would have been stepping on Molly's toes. It's her responsibility to guide the work of her direct reports, not mine.

Similarly, if Priyush had bypassed me and instead gone straight up to Jared's boss, Molly, he would have been stepping on my toes. He would have needed to at least ask me first whether it would be appropriate for him to go straight to Molly rather than me engaging her as a peer—which in the end may have been fine, but still needed my input in order to avoid over-stepping into territory that I would consider my, as opposed to Priyush's, responsibility.

Avoid Using or Creating "Work-Arounds"

You want to be very judicious about how and when you create or make use of a work-around, meaning getting to an end product in a way that you are not really supposed to, given your specific workplace structure.

If, for example, my organization has a stand-alone Marketing depart-ment, and I need to make a flyer to advertise a particular program, the proper channel would be to submit the request for the flyer to Marketing, and work directly with them to design the final product. A work-around, say if I'm get-ting a lot of pushback from the Marketing department for whatever reason, or their docket is so full that they won't have time to get to my project until next month, would be for me to create the flyer on my own. But then it might not have the right branding, it might not use the right colors or fonts, or it might not be cohesive with the rest of my organization's marketing materials.

Wherever possible, for key functions of your work, try to structure your department and your tools so that you automatically assume control over those areas, and don't have to depend on another department in order to get them done. For example, if you regularly send emails out to your constituents, you will want to have an email content management system that you or your staff know how to use and have access to, rather than relying on, say, a Communications department to actually send out your email every week.

And, whenever possible, follow the established protocols when it comes to which department does which work, even if it's something that you think you could solve yourself in less time than it would take for help to come.

Part of building social cache and trust is showing that you trust your colleagues to take care of you and your work, rather than going around or behind them to do something half as well as they would have done it in half the time. But don't just lay down and not advocate for getting what you need if another department holds the keys and isn't delivering. Be honest about your timelines and deliverables, and your colleagues will usually do everything they can to accommodate.

Setting Clear Boundaries for You and Your Team

I struggle with this one, as I am wont to say yes to everything, and that extends to saying yes on behalf of my department and my staff, even if it is not the most efficient use of their time or the most beneficial to our specific work goals. I have learned to be much more discerning about what I say yes to, especially if it's something that will require work from my team in addition to myself.

Others will appreciate your need to set boundaries for your team. They want you to be successful at what you and your team are best at, and the clearer you are about those delineations, the higher the quality of work you will be able to produce, which benefits everyone.

Finding a Mentor

One of the best things you can do for yourself and your sanity as you learn how to navigate professional relationships is to find a mentor at your work. Your mentor needs to be somebody who understands the social underpinnings and office culture, and therefore can help you troubleshoot and help explain or identify issues. They also need to be someone with whom you are able to connect to some degree on a personal level, and who can understand or empathize with some of the reasons why you might struggle with various socio-emotional context in the workplace.

Mentors can be highly advantageous for a number of different workplace-related reasons—advice on career advancement, moral support, and help with leveraging social or hierarchical status to get the results that you need.

Specifically with navigating professional relationships, a workplace mentor can help you dissect particularly confusing or otherwise emotionally charged interactions—perhaps when a colleague got upset about something you did (maybe you stepped on their toes and didn't realize) or when you got upset about something a colleague did (maybe they worked around you when they shouldn't have). Try to reserve these requests of your mentor to only very key relationships that you need to repair and keep on good footing in order to advance your work, rather than bring every little interpersonal issue to their attention.

A mentor can also help you tailor your communication style for various people, offering advice from their own personal experience of how particular people like to receive information (i.e. "Kavanah is a visual thinker, give her a chart or a graph to look at in order to illustrate your point" or "Jeffrey likes to chat for a bit before you ask him for something").

One of my mentors, who also happened to be my boss at the time, helped me through a particularly sticky situation in which I inadvertently stepped on the toes of none other than a Board member, and ran into a bunch of my own ASD-related roadblocks in both lack of tact and black-and-white thinking:

"But it *was* my job," I countered, confused. Adam had just finished telling me that it wasn't my job to be recruiting Board members to chair the Board committee related to my department. "Deborah asked me to see if John would be interested in taking on the role of committee chair."

Deborah was Adam's boss, but would often come straight to me with ideas or directives rather than going through him, which of course threw me off, but which I tried to accommodate as best I could.

"She might have," Adam said, "but once John declined, I don't think she intended for you to then take on the recruitment of a committee chair as part of your purview."

John, it transpired, had refused the role, but suggested another Board member, Alfie, instead. I happened to have a meeting with Alfie scheduled for later that same week, so I had approached him about being the chair, and he had also hesitated to accept the responsibility. After both John and Alfie passed on the role, I took it upon myself to ask the next Board member I had in mind who might make a good Chair, Myles, during my call with him the next day.

And so I ended up asking several Board members whether they would be interested in chairing the committee.

At some point after I had spoken to all three, I had the occasion to send an email to the Board chair, Bert, with an overall update on some of my department's work. I mentioned in my email that I had asked John, Alfie, and Myles to chair the committee, and that John and Alfie had both declined, but Myles was still considering.

Bert had responded almost immediately with an email that sounded, when I read it to myself in my head, peeved.

"I think we have too many cooks in the kitchen," he wrote, and proceeded to lay out that the appointment of Board members to chair committees was a responsibility that fell to him, the Board chair, not to staff, and that he would appreciate me ceasing to approach any other Board members about filling this role.

Yikes! I could tell that I had stepped on Bert's toes, so to speak, but I still didn't understand how or why. I was doing what my boss's boss had asked me to do. I was doing my job. I was taking initiative, following through—all good things, I thought.

Adam could probably see the consternation on my face.

"I can see," he continued, "how you would come to that conclusion, and I appreciate you diving in and taking initiative to get it done, based on your perception. However, it was the wrong perception, and now we have a mess to clean up."

"I'm sorry," I said. "I'm still having trouble understanding, though. Will you help me? If Deborah asked me to ask John if he would be the chair, but she knows that Bert is the one who assigns chairs—"

"She likely just wanted you to feel John out," Adam explained. "Not officially recruit him."

"Ahh," I said, comprehension starting to dawn on my horizon. Feeling out someone's interest level and leaving the actual commitment ambiguous was different from confirming roles and responsibilities.

"So in your email to Bert," Adam continued. "If you had said something more deferential, like 'During my meetings with Board members this week, I felt out John's, Alfie's, and Myles's potential interest in chairing the committee, and it seemed like Myles might have been the most interested,' that would not have set him off the same way. It would have just let him know that you had started laying some groundwork, to make his job easier, rather than trying to do his job for him."

"When it comes to Board members," Adam said, as I digested his words, "always err on the side of using *deferential language*. Defer to their authority, and you'll usually land on the safer side of things."

I was starting to see where I had made the mistake—with lack of clarity about what was expected of me and with lack of deferential tact when communicating my work to the Board chair, I'd inadvertently overstepped my bounds.

But then my heart started to sink.

If this had happened this time, when I had felt so confident that I was doing my job, that I was forging ahead and taking care of high-level things my department needed, then what was to say it wouldn't happen again? Where *were* the lines between my role and that of the Board chair or other stakeholders? What if the lines weren't always clear, or even moved depending on various circumstances? Should I even interact directly with Board members again?

This was my classic overanalysis, black-or-white thinking spiral ramping up into high gear. I voiced a small piece of this impending spiral to Adam, whom I had learned to trust.

"I see what happened," I said. "Thank you for helping me understand. But now I'm worried, because I had been so convinced that it was my job; I was so confident. What if something like this happens again? What if I overstep on something that I think I'm supposed to do, but in fact is not my job? Should I go through Bert now for everything related to the Board?"

And then Adam gave me one of the best pieces of advice I've ever heard, and which I will carry with me like a gift for the rest of my life.

He said, "Sometimes, there will be landmines. They exist, and we can't see them, and we don't know where they are, and we *will* step on them, and we will deal with it when we do. You can't avoid or precisely predict the landmines. You can only be prepared that one might go off at any moment, and be ready to minimize the damage and pick yourself up afterward as quickly as possible."

"Better to be confident and wrong and then have to defer," he continued, "than to be timid and not move ahead. We have to be strong enough to take the hit, learn from it, and not shy away from the next one."

This blatant, honest advice of "there will be landmines, and we will step on them" made it clear that (a) nobody can know or predict everything in advance, and (b) it's okay to make mistakes.

Two life lessons that not only helped me in that moment by giving me the confidence to move ahead because he would have my back if another landmine went off, but also that helped me with life in general. Directly addressing my deep-seated nature of overpreparing for every situation, and my strong bent toward perfectionism, both of which can cause significant paralysis if I let them get out of control.

COMMON OFFICE FAUX PAS

When it comes to work culture, I have to speak very much from my own experience, which is certainly not going to be the same as everyone else's experience. Different working environments, types of work, types of organizations, geographic locations, and overall cultural factors will be at play, and just like no person is the same as another person, no workplace is going to be the same as another workplace.

There are, however, some fairly common work circumstances—even if you don't experience them the same way in your own workplace—from which you might be able to extrapolate some learning and apply to your unique situation.

Office-Based Social Events

One of the most common work-related scenarios that can cause an ASD-type meltdown is when social life overlaps with work life, such as in office-based social events like holiday parties or after-work happy hours.

These situations can be particularly confusing for someone who already has difficulty with face-to-face communication, because now, the social "rules" bend a little bit. Suddenly, your "work life," which has a very different set of social rules, is mixing with your "social life," and it can be hard to suss out exactly how (and how much) to bend the work life rules to make room for the social interaction. A lot of people find this type of overlap awkward, not just people with autism. But imagine someone who just finds the everyday "good morning" in the office awkward—how much more thought process is going to have to go into the office holiday party for that person?

In an effort to ease some of that thought process, these are some of the areas I have found helpful to focus on when dealing with work-related social events, and ways you can prepare for them:

Attendance and Timing

Whether or not you choose to attend a work-related social event is completely up to you. Never let anyone pressure you into going if you really don't want to or feel that you would not be successful.

At times, attending social gatherings with colleagues can be a career booster. It can also be fun, and help you build more long-lasting relationships with coworkers who you might consider keeping in touch with beyond the job. On the other hand, they can also be stressful, take you away from your home life or your own social life, or not really be that useful to engendering good relationships or positive office culture.

As with anything, there is a balance. If you can make a point of strategically attending at least some work-related social gatherings, you will find some benefits in your every day and overall work life.

When I am deciding whether to attend a work-related social function, I weigh many factors. Aside from home-life priorities (is my husband able to take care of the kids that night, is one of them sick, is there any pressing reason for me to be home, etc.), I also take into account why the party is taking place, who else will be there, and what is expected to happen at the party.

Why is it happening?

- Obviously, if the party is happening because of me or a close coworker of mine (birthday, promotion, etc.), I will probably go. 😌
- If it's the annual holiday party, which many workplaces in the U.S. host during the winter season, I will also probably go, as this is the party that most people will likely go to, and attending is part of the "holiday spirit" of the season.
- If it's a regularly occurring after-work happy hour kind of party, I probably won't go. I might consider attending on one particular occasion if a close coworker specifically asks me to come, or there is some other extenuating circumstance which makes that occasion special.

Who is going to be there?

- If my boss or my boss's boss is going to be there (and I along with others at my level are invited), I might consider going as it is often beneficial to gain extra face-to-face time with the people I am reporting to and the people they report to. Even just the visibility helps keep you and your work active in the back of their minds.
- If a few of my peers are going, but no one who I really work closely with or want to stay top-of-mind with, then I likely won't attend.

What will happen?

- Some work-related social gatherings include annual, biannual, or other regularly distributed awards, like

"employee of the month" or "leader of the year," etc.
I still might not go if awards are being handed out, but
which awards and who might be in consideration for
them might influence my decision of whether or not
to attend.

- Some office social functions include "team building"
exercises and are part of a larger culture of building
teams. If this is the case, then likely the overall work
culture is that people attend. I might decide which
ones to attend based on who else I know is going to
which ones, who might be leading the "team building" portion, and other factors.

The other thing to consider, aside from whether to attend at all, is—if
you do decide to attend—when to show up and how long to stay.

Unless you are volunteering to help with something like setup, or if you
work in HR and it's part of your job to be early, I find that it is usually better
to be "fashionably late." I try not to arrive right on time to an office-related
social event, unless it has been made clear to everyone that an on-time ar-
rival is expected. I aim for a ten- to fifteen-minute window after the official
"start" time of the gathering. That way I'm not overly late, but I'm also not
one of the first people in the room when there are still very few people there
and social interaction is at its most strained and awkward.

How long I decide to stay at a work-social very much depends on the
situation. In general, I try never to be the first or the last person to leave.

If I have a pressing reason to head out, like if I'm trying to make it home
in time to say good night to my kids, or if I'm getting a headache, then one
tactic I will sometimes use to gauge a socially acceptable time to leave is to
aim for 15 percent. If there are about 100 people in the room, I might feel
comfortable leaving "early" after at least ten other people have already left,

placing me around the fifteenth percentile of folks leaving (and if there are a total of twenty people in the room, I would try to wait until two or three others have left already before I leave—again, 15 percent).

If I don't have a pressing reason to leave, then I might aim for closer to 40 to 50 percent (in a room of one hundred people, staying until at least thirty have left, or in a room of twenty people, staying until at least eight are gone).

Personal Appearance

What you choose to wear to an office social setting can be a nightmarish decision for anyone, but especially those with ASD.

In general, the way I get around this potential rabbit hole of unending debate is to simply wear something a little bit nicer, or a little bit more casual, than what I would wear to work on a normal day. Whether I trend in the "nicer" direction or the "more casual" direction depends on the type of event—for a holiday party, nicer. For after-work drinks, more casual.

The trick for me is that whatever I am wearing during the social event, I would be comfortable wearing all day at work. Because at the end of the day, even though I might not be working at the social gathering, I am still with my coworkers, as opposed to my friends or family.

Drinking

Many office-related social events will make alcohol available to attendees. Whether or not you choose to drink at a work gathering, again, is entirely up to you.

Personally, I will usually have one drink, and stop there. I might not even finish the whole thing—part of the point of having a drink at a social occasion is simply to be seen drinking it (sending the nonverbal message that "I'm here, I'm part of this party, I'm participating, I'm enjoying myself."). So if all I do is hold a single glass of wine all night and slowly sip from it throughout the evening, that's fine with me.

If alcoholism is not a problem for you, it's a good idea to explore various alcoholic beverages widely enough beforehand in order to cultivate your own repertoire of go-to drinks (not all in one night, please!). This way, whatever function you might be attending, or wherever you might be indulging in an adult beverage with friends or colleagues, you already know what you like and you don't appear overly naive, or have to rely on just ordering whatever the person next to you ordered because you know nothing about alcohol. Cultivate enough of your own preferences to know if you generally prefer white wine over red, for example, or if you prefer a heavier beer like a Guinness over a lighter one like an IPA. For mixed drinks, maybe you prefer something light like a vodka cranberry, or something with more oomph like a rum and coke. Try enough varieties so that when your turn comes to order something, you have a couple go-to options already in mind and aren't caught like a deer in the headlights trying to figure out what to drink.

What I will never do at a work-related social event is drink more than one alcoholic beverage, no matter how long the event is or how much food is available to soak up the effects of the alcohol. This is in part because I don't often drink anyway, so it doesn't take a lot of alcohol before I start feeling the effects. But more important, it's because—as above with what I choose to wear—I am not with my friends, who know me well and who perhaps have helped me through some emotional times or seen other sides of me that I would never take to work—I'm with my coworkers. And I don't need my coworkers to know any side of me that I don't have 100 percent control over, even if the context is a social one.

Know that even if you are in a social setting, if colleagues or bosses or executives are in the room, you will still be judged the next day at work (even unconsciously) by how you conducted yourself outside the workplace—because we are all human beings and that's just how we operate. If you got drunk and asked a colleague to go on a date with you at the office happy hour, they likely won't forget it the next day.

While it is important to have fun and enjoy a work-related social gathering, be conscious of the fact that you will have to go back to work with these same people, and don't put yourself in a situation where you might do something you would regret later.

Contributing and Volunteering

Often for work-related social events, a person will take up a collection around the office for folks to pitch in cash contributions toward a common purchase—like getting a cake for someone's birthday, or bringing in donuts on Valentine's Day, or whatever the case may be.

Another ask that might go around the office in advance of a social gathering could be a plea for volunteers, to help with setting up the event, or cleaning up after, or to take on some other volunteer role during the event, like ticket-taking, handing out raffle tickets, or greeting people.

Whether or not you decide to pitch in, with either your time or your money, is entirely up to you, and you should never feel pressured to do so. Just because someone asks you does not mean that you automatically need to say yes.

Generally, if someone asks me in person to contribute my time or money to an office function, to give myself time to digest the request and answer honestly, I will respond with an overall positive but noncommittal, "Oh"— smile and nod—"Let me see what I can do," or similar. This gives an impression of wanting to contribute in some way, but also doesn't commit me to follow through with anything yet until I have had a chance to think about how I want to be involved. Otherwise, I would just automatically say yes to everything, and while that might make people happy, it's not necessarily going to make me happy, and wouldn't necessarily be the best thing for my time, or my financial obligations.

If the ask comes through via email, it's obviously much easier for me to handle because then I have enough time to think about it and respond in my own time with a well thought-out answer.

It's a good idea to set some general parameters in advance for you to easily fall back on when deciding how to give your time or money to office-related functions, such as: giving five dollars to office collections, but no more than ten, or volunteering your time to pre-event preparations and setup, but never volunteering for duties in the latter half of a function. These parameters can be based on your personal situation, preferences, and needs, and can be flexible, of course, depending on various circumstances. They are more like principles you can use as a guide for deciding when and where to contribute, rather than spending too many brain cycles trying to start from scratch every time.

Trust Culture

Another workplace area where it is easy to make many common social mistakes is around the broader concept of "trust."

Trust in the workplace is a thick concept, because while we are all humans and we care for and trust each other, we are working for an organization and, ultimately, our employment is incumbent upon the organization's well-being over that of each other.

This can lead to a lot of confusing and hard-to-navigate situations.

A clear-cut example of when trust in the workplace gets tricky is, for instance, if you witness your colleague—especially one who has become your friend—stealing from the organization. Do you report your friend? This would destroy their trust in you, but ultimately it's your responsibility to report them if you want to keep your job, and if you want your organization to succeed. If your relationship with that particular friend is more important to you than your job, or if you don't like or agree with that particular organization, then perhaps you make a different choice, but just assuming that you like your job, you would find yourself in a situation where you would need to put the organization's well-being over that of the individual.

This is not always the case in situations where trust is involved. Short of finding a colleague stealing or otherwise putting the success of the organization in jeopardy, there are many different situations in which you might put individual trust before organizational trust, or vice versa, depending on various factors.

Respecting Privacy and Agency

One of the most common areas where trust comes into play in the workplace is in issues of privacy. If a colleague confides something to me that does not in any way put the organization at risk—perhaps it's a personal thing, like they are having marital issues, or their dog just died—it is not my business to be spreading that information around, regardless of whether or not they asked me to keep it private. It's my colleague's life, not mine, and it's up to my colleague to decide who and when they may or may not give that information.

This becomes especially true when you start dealing with various hierarchical levels in the organization, because often someone who reports to someone else will not want that person hearing something about them from a secondhand source.

For example, say Japir reports to Beth, and Shana reports to Micah. Beth and Micah are peers and often work together, while Japir and Shana are peers, but also have become good friends.

Japir has accepted a new position at a different organization and is about to give his two weeks' notice. He tells Shana first, because he works with her most closely and he wants his friend to know that he's leaving. He shares his personal contact information with her so that they can stay in touch after they no longer work at the same organization.

Shana takes the news well, but later that day, she tells her boss, Micah, that Japir is leaving, and that she is nervous about how one of the projects they had been working on together will pan out without Japir's continued input.

The next morning, while Beth and Micah both make their coffee in the break room, Micah—not realizing that the information got to him before it got to Beth—mentions Japir's impending departure. But Japir has not had a chance to tell Beth yet.

If Japir reports to Beth, and Beth hears from her peer, Micah, that Japir got a new job and is planning to give notice soon, Beth will wonder why Japir didn't share the news with her first. Japir will also probably not thank Shana for spreading his news without his permission, even though she only told her own boss. It's Japir's news to share, not anyone else's, and respecting Japir's agency to be the one to let his boss know directly would have been more tactful on Shana's part. It would have only meant waiting another day or two before raising her concerns to Micah, or checking in with Japir first as to whether he had yet told Beth.

By the same token, Japir would also have done better to tell his boss he had accepted another job offer before he told too many other people, so that Japir could control the narrative and Beth would hear it from him first.

The Gossip Trap

When people share information with each other, whether it's private information or not, it can be hard to pinpoint the source of the information and whether it's credible. A peer-reviewed research article is likely a reliable source for information that has been vetted to be true. A rumor from a colleague who heard their coworker who overheard their boss say something, is *not* a very reliable source.

When it comes to office gossip, if I worked in my ideal world, I would avoid it unilaterally.

I have better and more important things to spend my thoughts and energy on at work than who said what about whom, or who heard what about something that not many people are supposed to know about yet, or whatnot.

With that said, I have learned that some larger context and otherwise "hidden" meanings can be present between the lines of certain types of gossip, and therefore, rather than avoiding it like the plague, I exercise cautious, limited tolerance. If someone starts sharing gossip with me, I usually catalog what they say with a grain of salt (not believing every word), redirect the conversation away from the gossip if I can, and then refuse point-blank to spread the gossip to anyone else.

Later, I might spend some thought cycles dissecting what someone said to me that fell under the category of "gossip" to see what higher context might be hidden underneath. For example, if someone says, "It looks like they might be interviewing for a new facilities manager already," it might imply—if true—that the organization is serious about getting facilities under control, or that the previous facilities manager either gave advance notice of departure or was already on thin ice if the organization is prepared to look for their replacement so quickly. Or, "Trent told me that Julie left because she asked for a raise and they didn't give it to her," might imply—if it's true and I report to the same hierarchical chain as Julie—that now might not be the best time to be advocating for a raise.

You can discern a fair amount of underlying context from the type of gossip that you might hear. But a word of caution—don't go looking for meaning that isn't there, and don't put too much faith in what you might extrapolate. Like a children's game of "telephone," where one word or phrase repeated from person to person morphs into something else entirely, gossip is not a reliable source of detailed, factual information. It's a gray area. It can help you "feel" your way through a larger contextual landscape. But it can also often be harmful to the people being talked about and the organizational culture of trust.

Refrain from gossiping as much as possible—either starting it yourself or spreading something you heard from someone else. And if you come across it, log it away for analysis, but don't feed the fire by asking your colleague for more. Instead, discourage it by politely moving the conversation onto something else.

LARRY'S TWO CENTS

What we want out of life, personally and professionally, is very unique to each person. From our early years, we have people in our lives wishing the best for us, sometimes accounting for who we are and sometimes not. Include our personal interests and traits along with life experiences, and you are left with what can be a very challenging, seemingly never-ending series of choices about what we want to do professionally, let alone the personal ambitions.

For those who are autistic, like Sarah, everything can feel truly overwhelming, especially when going through the early years of all of this while being undiagnosed. There is this expectation that one can be successful in a given vocation just by performing a specific task with the appropriate training. Unfortunately, this expectation is not always fair for a multitude of reasons, including, for many on the spectrum, the reality that their personal traits are not similar to others, and thus, the training is not always suited. When that is the case, failing to perform the task can lead to failing in the vocation, and even the most ambitious person willing to give it their all may succumb to a horrible, negative feeling of unworthiness, and the sense that they themselves are a failure.

To counteract this negative spiral, a different form of training and assistance is necessary. What these different approaches are can vary greatly, but with at least one similarity: the more individualized the support is, the better the chance for success.

When I met Sarah, she was a grad student looking to begin her professional career in the Peace Corps, which would have been an absolutely amazing next step for her. There is detailed, low-level training and very managed expectations spread among a group. Had this worked out, I am confident her early efforts in the professional world would have been successful without additional supports. However, things did not go as planned, as they oftentimes don't. Just a few weeks before her service was to begin, the Peace Corps delayed due to an overstaffing problem. Simply put, there were more volunteers for the Corps than there were positions. Now, it is true that without this delay, our lives would be vastly different and quite possibly our relationship and this book might never have come to be. Using the lesson of turning lemons into lemonade, Sarah and I came together after a few brief months of dating and here we are, sharing the last several years of our lives publicly.

Digression over. What I really want to talk about is what came next for Sarah, especially those initial three years when Sarah went from part-time bookseller to intern and then, in almost a blink of an eye, a director and part of the executive team for a non-profit here in NYC. It was a crazy time, and admittedly there were multiple occasions where it all could have turned out much differently had the invention of instant message (IM) not occurred and had Sarah not been able to ask me for quick, on-the-fly translations to what in the heck to do with a given challenge. All that was transpiring for Sarah professionally was just as important to the efforts we were putting into our relationship, which was still building its foundation, and which I mention now to illustrate that she never really had much of a mental break from the constant change and churn during these years.

Early on, our IM conversations were scattershot in subject, ranging from how to ask to go to lunch once she had her first desk job with a not super defined schedule, to questions about why meetings were so painfully disorganized, not to mention unclear or incomplete task assignments. It was during the first year of professional life, as Sarah transitioned from intern to coordinator that we, and she, worked out how to create a sense of daily expectations that allowed for a bit better handling of the daily disruptions of changed priorities and endless emergency, must-do-now tasks. With each passing IM conversation, a routine between us developed which I continued to tinker with, usually along the lines of me pointing out how a given question was similar to something that transpired recently. Her response was to define why it was different, and then we would adapt the conversation to help with the understanding.

One thing I continued to be adamant about was the need for her to learn how to take a moment to take a step back and critically think about a question before asking. Not just because my time was somewhat limited, but really to help her develop her approach to learning to answer the questions herself, and thus learn and grow in her own confidence and capabilities. We had understood, if not ever talked about, the fact that she could not go through her entire professional career relying on our IMs, and for sure her ambition was to be successful without relying on her interpreter, as I had begun to call myself.

Toward the end of Sarah's time as a coordinator, she began to define what we termed micro-processes. This language helped us talk agnostically about not only a specific question, but to include the order of operations Sarah went through in approaching the problem. With each successive similar question being handled, these micro-processes were augmented with more details and clarity until she became self-sufficient at solving the problem. This, in turn, built up her confidence and slowly reduced her stress level as the work became easier to handle daily. Well, that is until her non-profit reorganized and she was promoted to a director position, reporting now to the executive director (ED) and the Board.

This was an abrupt promotion, one that was necessary in a struggling organization, as Sarah was more cost-effective then others would have been. Equally, though, it was a promotion based on her now new boss's observation that Sarah was capable of the work and would figure it out soon enough. The new phrase Sarah was told routinely, "Fake it until you make it," became often repeated by the ED, and one that sent chills up Sarah's spine, as she would IM me the first chance she could get.

In all the classes taken from elementary through college, along with her previous responsibilities until just a week prior, nothing had taught Sarah how to fake performing her job. Never had she been asked to really develop, define, and execute work without a supervisor's help, without a team to consult with. To make matters more stressful, the people who were left in her department had just weeks prior been her peers, in age and experience. Now she was expected to come up with the work for her staff, review it, correct it, and make sure it was complete in an appropriate time. This did not sit well with Sarah; she did not understand it was really what one's own abilities are that matter in the workplace, not the age of the person performing the task at hand.

The best I could do was to remind Sarah of her experience in managing volunteers, and help her learn to evaluate how people approach a job and how to evaluate a work product before it was complete. Normally in the professional world, this takes years of experience and a slow attrition, but for Sarah, it was a big part of the "fake it" aspect of her job. Fortunately, in this case, it was evident very quickly that there were distinct differences in how her former peers approached and conducted their jobs, and with that, a clear understanding that she would be successful. Now I was able to share a new phrase, "See, your ED was right," whenever Sarah had a positive work milestone. As much as I'm sure she rolled her eyes upon reading this in my IM, it served to give her a positive affirmation, which there can never be enough of.

Through this fake it to make it phase, Sarah learned just how valuable self-confidence is, and that it cannot always come from a book. Rather, to reach the goals she wanted, to inform groups of people and to lead change, more than just a modicum of belief in oneself is necessary, and trusting instincts is part of what leaders have learned to embrace. It doesn't have to come naturally, but it has to come. With this understanding, Sarah learned where she fit in when it comes to the business world. Never would she want to be a CEO or even a vice president within a company, but rather, to support a good leader's vision and be a strong director or senior manager who appreciated there was a bigger picture while being able to focus on the more detailed components of such a vision.

Coming to a point in one's life, professionally or personally, where you have a true sense of who you are and who you want to be is very rewarding. It doesn't mean things won't evolve and change, because they will. The good news is, once you have found yourself once, it is so much easier to do so again because you realize that you can. You are no longer just faking it. You made it, and that confidence should never leave you.

CHAPTER FIVE

Long-Term Neurodiverse Relationships

"If soul mates do exist, they're not found.
They're made."

—*THE GOOD PLACE*

Not everyone will want to engage in romantic endeavors, or seek out long-term relationships. For those who do, the importance of such interactions will be highly individualistic. You will have your own reasons why a romantic connection will be important to you.

Personally, I knew from a young age that I wanted to have a partner in life. My mother courageously raised my sister and me alone, and I saw the toll it took on her—mentally, emotionally, and physically. I knew that I wanted to be a mother, and that I did not want to do it alone. I also knew that I wanted my children to benefit from the presence of two separate adult perspectives in their home, and to experience first-hand the type of mutually uplifting relationship that a good marriage can provide.

But, of course, it had to be the right person—someone who could know and love me unconditionally, and for whom I could do the same.

When pursuing romantic connection, it's worth taking a moment to fully define your motivations. It will be important, at various times throughout the process of finding, building, and sustaining long-term relationships, for you to step back and see the bigger picture—why you are putting yourself through this, and what is most important to you in the result.

Because love is not easy. We all know this, whether we have lots of relationship experience or none. It takes hard work, patience, and understanding—even in the best circumstances.

And for someone with ASD, or for a long-term partner of someone with ASD, there can be unique challenges that are harder to troubleshoot.

One of the best resources I have found specifically for identifying and navigating the unique obstacles that can come from an NT–ASD romantic relationship is Ashley Stanford's book, *Asperger Syndrome (Autism Spectrum Disorder) and Long-Term Relationships, 2nd Edition*. Throughout this chapter, I will refer to things that I learned and applied from her book. I would encourage you, if you are serious about creating or sustaining a neurodiverse long-term relationship, to read it and build your own toolbox from the experiences, insights, and strategies she shares.

A note about this chapter: In this chapter about communication, I will be focusing on the "building" and "sustaining" stages of a long-term NT–ASD relationship. There are many other resources available for the "seeking" stage of romantic connection (a.k.a. dating). In my own experience, I never really "dated," and my own path to finding love was so unique that not many people would benefit from hearing my advice. But I have since learned two important things related to dating that would have been helpful for me had I known them earlier:

- Remember that, as someone with ASD, it can be easier for others with less scruples to take advantage of you, due to your tendency to take people at their word, interpret communication and contexts literally, not see the subtext or the possible ulterior motives behind someone else's words or actions, and to assume sincerity and honesty from others (since that is how you are communicating, and you reasonably expect the same in return). You don't need to start believing the worst of everyone or go into every date looking for shadows, by any means—just be aware that you may be more vulnerable to manipulation than someone who is neurotypical.
- Take particular pains to actively and verbally advocate for yourself and for your needs/desires. A common ASD trait is to lack "theory of mind" abilities—simply

put, the ability to understand that others may have a different perspective than you do, or that others may not know what you know in a particular context. Just because you know that you don't like making out, doesn't mean your dating partner knows that you don't like it, or that they feel the same way. Speak up—it's okay to be direct and to repeat yourself when it comes to your needs.

OPPOSITES ATTRACT

There are so many clichés out there when it comes to love and romance. "Opposites attract," "like calls to like," etc. These exist because there's always a kernel of truth, but it's rarely the whole truth.

Studies do show that, when it comes to romance, humans are more commonly attracted to potential partners who possess a certain amount of "likeness," whether it's similar backgrounds, socioeconomic experiences, personalities, religious or spiritual beliefs, or vocational interests.[1] Not surprisingly, we also tend to geographically group ourselves according to similarities, so we're meeting people like ourselves on a daily basis. But there is also evidence to suggest that we seek equality and equity when pursuing long-term partnerships. We tend to strive, consciously or otherwise, to find our "equals."

Along with a certain amount of similarity, humans can look (again, whether consciously or not) for a certain amount of difference in potential long-term partners, as well. There are evolutionary reasons for this, since forming a partnership with someone who has strengths in areas where you have weaknesses can increase your own chances for survival. For instance, most of us know at least one couple wherein one partner likes "the quiet life," while the other is a social butterfly. The key is finding a balance that works for you and your partner—a balance which will rarely materialize on its own, but will need to be shaped, nurtured, and maintained constantly.

For my part, I knew that it could be nice to share my life with another quiet, introspective person, but that type of person would do nothing to help me grow, or to face challenges that require a different skill set. I needed to partner with someone who could do the things I couldn't do, who could see things I couldn't see, and who could teach our children things I couldn't teach them. In turn, I also needed to be able to do things my partner couldn't do, see things they couldn't see, and teach our children things they couldn't teach them. A healthy partnership is one between two whole, separate people, who bring different strengths and weaknesses together to complement, enhance, and support each other.

Here is an example from fairly early on in my relationship with my husband where we were able to "divide and conquer" in a way we likely would not have, if we did not see and interact with the world so differently:

This is it, I thought to myself excitedly. *Larry and I are finally at that point in our relationship where we are shopping for our first home together.*

In my naivete, growing up in a small town in the Midwest, I had always envisioned this step as shopping for an actual <u>house</u>, but my year-plus exposure to New York City had updated that perspective.

By this point in our apartment-hunting experience, we had seen at least eight places over several weekends, and I was starting to get a feel for the housing search—how quickly apartments got snapped up, how listers will have several places in mind to show you beyond what you originally reached out to see, how different apartments have different combinations of appealing and not-so-appealing traits (i.e. no washers/dryers in the basement, but a close walk to the subway; great view of the city from the windows, but crappy noise protection from the apartment above).

We had also learned a lot about each other from the experience: what each of us valued most in a living situation, how each of us was willing to compromise to accommodate the other, etc.

And we had *very* different strengths and weaknesses when it came to the logistics of the hunt itself. My husband is a big-picture people person. I am a detail-oriented data person.

So we soon found a rhythm that worked very well:

1. First, I culled through hundreds of apartment listings online to find the ones that seemed to meet most of our mutual requirements. This was highly detail-oriented, repetitive, and meticulous work, and would have driven Larry insane.

2. Then Larry took a pass through my curated list and cut it down by half, according to some bigger-picture, larger-context parameters that I didn't know to account for (i.e. this is a largely Hasidic neighborhood, and as we're not practicing Jews, we might want to avoid living in the heart of it; this apartment has been listed for more than a hundred days, there's probably something wrong with it that they're not telling us).

3. Once we narrowed down the list, I sent the initial emails letting listers know we wanted to see the apartments, giving them Larry's cell phone number to follow up, and keeping track of them and their apartments in an Excel document, so we knew which places we had already seen and which listers we had already contacted.

4. Larry took the callbacks from the listers and set up the dates and times to see the apartments, getting an initial feel for the people representing each apartment by how they interacted on the phone. Aside from being good at talking to and reading people, Larry was also much better than I was at scheduling activities—taking into account our prior

commitments, where each of us would be at any given time, where we might get lunch beforehand or dinner afterward, and how long it might take us to get to a certain neighborhood and back.

5. During an apartment viewing, Larry handled almost all of the direct interaction with the lister, talking about the place, hearing their perspective, building rapport and trust with them to encourage their sharing potential insider information that they might not otherwise freely offer up, learning about any history with the previous inhabitants or the relationship with building maintenance or the landlord, talking about the feel of the surrounding community, etc.

6. While Larry engaged the lister, I went around the apartment, making note (literally, taking notes on a pad of paper) of details in the layout, where each room was located (is the bedroom <u>right next to</u> the front door or situated back a little ways in the apartment?), roughly how big each room was, what kitchen appliances were included (dishwasher? gas or electric stove?), how the windows did or did not do a good job of letting in natural light, the state and size of the bathroom, and so on. Nuanced details that one would not necessarily be able to glean easily from the online description or photos.

This way, when we finished seeing each place, we could compare notes and combine different sets of knowledge into one overall picture of each apartment. I might have seen something in the details of the apartment, like a drop-ceiling in the bedroom rather than insulated plaster (ZERO noise protection), or he might have picked up something in his interaction with the lister, like the people living in the next apartment over had a bedbug infestation last year, that would strike a place off our list.

Working together, recognizing where each of us was strong and weak and making sure that each of us could play to those strengths and support the other's weaknesses, made for a well-rounded apartment search in the pitiless jungle that is the New York City housing market.

EQUALITY VERSUS EQUITY

Over the years we have been together, the most difficult concept for me to comprehend is the difference between "equality" and "equity"—owing to my own (perceived and real) deficiencies when it comes to interpersonal communication, executive functioning, flexible thinking, and emotional intelligence, related to my ASD. I had been taught, as many of us are, to think of romantic partnership as fifty-fifty—that is, each partner contributes exactly half of all things the relationship requires.

This is simply not the case—not in neurotypical relationships, nor, perhaps even more acutely, in neurodiverse relationships.

To lay the foundation for this distinction, let me turn to my favorite referential duo, Merriam-Webster. The dictionary defines "equality" as: "the state or quality of being equal, in quantity, value, degree, rank, or ability." Conversely, the definition of "equity" reads: "the state or quality of being fair and just." The difference is clear. Two things do not necessarily need to be "equal" in quantity or ability in order to be "equitable," or fair.

But alas, life is messier than Merriam-Webster. There are times when the partnership will feel more like 70/30, or 40/60, or even 90/10. There are different contexts in which one partner will excel and the other will flounder, and vice versa. These may be fluid contexts, or static—it might <u>always</u> be that one partner is better than the other at X, or that dynamic might shift over time. The key is not to strive for equality, but to find <u>equity</u>. To continually seek a balance that is fair and just for the strengths, weaknesses, needs, and desires of both partners.

As I mentioned, this has been particularly challenging for me, due to my ASD. I find so many things about daily life and emotional connection difficult. My husband has to pick up the slack in those areas, and at times it can feel lopsided. Yet trying to keep track, though so innately part of human nature, is not helpful, nor productive. I have learned this the hard way. What is helpful is continually referring back to the equity question: Do we each feel fairly treated and cared for, even if we are not necessarily "equal" in ability or outcome? Do we each feel that our strengths are being utilized, and our weaknesses supported? If not, something somewhere needs to shift.

I used an example in the previous section, illustrating how opposites can work together, of how Larry and I consciously played to each of our different strengths and weaknesses during our first apartment search together. This time, to illustrate specifically the concept of "equity" versus "equality," I want to use the example of our next apartment search, when we were ready to move from a one-bedroom to a larger space, as we began to think about growing our family, and as our commute and community needs evolved.

This time around, I knew what to expect. I knew, having lost one of the apartments we had been seriously considering last time, that if we saw a place we really liked, we would have to grab it right away. Waiting even twenty-four hours to decide might not be an option. This was tough for me to accept, as someone who (a) has trouble making decisions in the first place, and (b) thrives in being able to mull things over with time and think through all the possibilities. But it was a fact of life in New York.

Having lived together now for a few years, I also knew better what to expect out of a housing search with the man who was now my husband. We recalled and made use again of our "divide and conquer" strategy for tackling the apartment hunt, with me handling the data involved, and Larry handling the people involved.

I found one two-bedroom online that looked, from the photos, like the perfect place to live: high ceilings with exposed beams, an attic for storage, an outdoor front porch, huge windows with lots of natural light, and skylights in the ceiling. But I knew that pictures never told the whole story, of course, so I tried not to get my hopes up too much as I added it to our list of apartments to view.

Larry contacted the lister and set up a time to meet that coming weekend to see a few of his places.

That weekend, and during the week leading up to it, we had seen so many places together with different listers that the ideal photos of the high-ceilinged apartment drifted to the back of our minds. When the time came to meet with this particular lister, neither of us remembered specifically that it was the guy with the high ceilings and big windows.

He took us to another apartment first and listened to us as we walked through it together, talking about the sizes and placements of the bedrooms. Larry did his thing, chatting with the lister, while I did my thing, walking through and taking detailed notes.

In the car on our way to the next place, I sat in the back and listened to the two of them. The lister talking about the next place he was going to show us, and how he had one other place but he didn't think he would take us there because the second bedroom was pretty small, and he didn't think we would like it based on what we were looking for.

I started to run through in my mind all the places we had picked out to see this week and flashed on the place with the high ceilings. I couldn't remember precisely, but I had thought we were going to see that place this weekend, and this was the last lister we had booked. Was this the guy?

Wanting to cover all of our bases but feeling awkward and out-of-my-element, I tried piping up from the backseat of the car. "I think we would like to see that other place, too, if we have time . . ."

Larry, full into his trust-building mode, countered gently. "No, he knows what we're looking for now. I trust him; let's follow his lead."

That night when we got home, I looked again at my notes and the online listings I had bookmarked, and discovered that, indeed, the high-ceilinged place we had both loved the look of was one of this guy's listings. And was likely the place he had decided not to show us because he thought the second bedroom was too small.

I insisted, and Larry had to eat his words and call the guy back to ask to see the other place as soon as possible. He did it with a grace and humility that I would not have easily mustered if I had been in his position, and the very next day we were looking at the place, along with another couple whom the lister had booked at the same time.

It was gorgeous. It was exactly what we wanted. The only drawback was that it was a twenty-minute walk from the nearest subway, which only took us about ten minutes of thought and discussion to overcome. Walking was good for us. We should do more of it anyway.

As the lister showed both us and the other couple around the apartment, I noticed several times how he sidled up to Larry when the other couple was in a different room and whispered to him that the place was ours if we wanted it. The lister obviously felt bad that he hadn't shown us the place the previous day, and my husband had built up enough of a rapport with him that he felt compelled to give us a leg up.

We went straight from viewing the apartment to signing the lease. And not a moment too soon—the next day, the lister told us that the other couple had decided they wanted the apartment, too. I was validated in my insistence on following up with the detailed research I had done, and Larry was validated in building the positive relationship with the lister, who had made sure we got our chance at the lease first.

"We are better together," Larry said to me as we opened the door to our new apartment for the first time. This had become a refrain between us over the years, acknowledging how we accomplished so much more together, despite (or perhaps because of) our differences in thought and opinion and methodology.

As I write this book, we have been living happily in that apartment for nearly five years, and the location has worked out spectacularly, in ways neither of us could have predicted. Having a home we love has empowered us to stay in New York City much longer than either of us thought we would.

READING MINDS (OR NOT!)

Nobody can literally read another person's mind. That's the stuff of carnival psychics and romantic comedies.

I used to think that this was wholly and unequivocally true—that what we think of as mind-reading is really just coincidence, or knowing another person well enough to predict their feelings and actions with relative accuracy. But what I didn't realize was that neurotypical people really do read minds—at least a little. They intuit another person's thoughts and intentions from cues delivered in body language and vocal inflection. They can often recognize and understand perspectives other than their own—even those of people they've just met.

An ASD brain, on the other hand, may have difficulty recognizing and interpreting body language and vocal inflection, or realizing that another person may think differently about something. Suffice it to say, we're not mind readers.

This can become particularly problematic, you can imagine, in a long-term romantic relationship, where a neurotypical partner might reasonably expect their "other half" to anticipate and intuit their needs, wants, and feelings. Nobody expects perfect accuracy, of course, but in a neurotypical world, it's assumed that two people who have been together for years will be "in sync."

I find myself perpetually "out of sync." Not just with the world, as many people with ASD feel, but even with my husband of nearly ten years. It is not necessarily an uncomfortable experience for me, though of course it can become so when we really need to present a united front on something. More often, it's just a state of being.

While I am perfectly able to recognize patterns in my husband's behavior that allow me to anticipate many of his needs—he likes hot coffee black but iced coffee with cream and sugar, he needs time to unwind and not have to think in the evenings, he does not like surprises—I am also usually unable to read his emotional state unless he explains how he feels. And if his immediate need is something unpredictable or unprecedented, I am often unable to see or understand it, and therefore do anything to meet it, without explicit verbal information.

Here's an example of how this plays out in real time. We were in another city, on a road trip with our son. We were about to meet someone new—a friend of a friend—who lives in the area and suggested this coffee shop as a good place to meet up. I had been driving all morning.

1. I was anxious about meeting a new person, which is always difficult for me, as my brain simply feeds me "fear" chemicals during interactions with other people (even familiar ones) because it is wired differently than most brains, and a new person is by definition unpredictable.

2. I was already overloaded by having spent the last couple of days in a new city, with an entirely new routine, sleeping in a different bed in a different room with different sounds, accommodating my toddler through all of these changes, smelling different air, seeing different people, etc.

3. I was in that moment particularly full of brain activity, having just been driving, which takes a significant amount of

manual concentration for me, as I accommodate potentially
life-threatening factors and make in-the-moment decisions
about what to do, and I had not yet had the time to wind
down from this flurry of thought.

In the backseat, Larry was getting Sirus ready to leave the car and head
into the coffee shop. I was making sure I had the car in park, checking that
I was equally positioned within the parking lines on either side, unbuckling
my seat belt, and making sure I had everything I needed in my purse and
was leaving nothing important in the car.

"The sooner you can get out of the car the better," came Larry's voice
from the backseat. I could hear that he was stressed about something, but
I didn't know what.

Wanting to be as helpful as possible, I quickly sped up my leaving-the-
car-now process and opened my door as fast as I could. "Why?" I asked as I
got out of the car, looking around the immediate area to see if I could spot
why he wanted me out of the car so quickly. Was the person we were going
to meet approaching? Was there another car in the vicinity posing a potential danger? Why did I need to get out of the car?

"Just get out!" Larry repeated, frustration in every word.

I got all the way out and closed the door, panicky now about what was
wrong that I couldn't see.

"Come over here!" came Larry's voice, now shouting from the other
side of the car.

I hurried over, feeling useless and clueless. I didn't know what to do, so
I clung to the only thing I could understand—Larry's explicit instructions.

"Take Sirus," Larry nearly growled. He passed Sirus into my possession,
struggling to get him out of the car and into my arms. I saw that Sirus wasn't
happy, but I thought it was because he was picking up on whatever invisible
but highly palpable strife was going on between Larry and I.

I stood there, in the parking lot next to our rented car, holding onto a distressed Sirus and watching my husband try to extricate himself from the car, waiting for him to tell me what he needed me to do next. Why was he so agitated? Had something spilled in the backseat, maybe? Did he need me to run to get napkins to mop up? Had the friend-of-a-friend texted to say they weren't going to make it anymore, and Larry was frustrated that we had come to this particular coffee shop for no reason?

Larry turned and saw me standing there, doubtless with a blank and confused look on my face. "Go inside!" he said. "Why do I have to tell you to go inside? She's in there, probably waiting for us, and you're just standing here watching me!"

Hurt and confused, still not understanding what had happened, resenting the fact that Larry hadn't told me when I had asked why, I turned and took Sirus into the coffee shop, feeling my anxiety shoot through the roof as I realized that I, rather than Larry, was going to have to make the initial introductions to this stranger we were meeting. I could barely focus on getting Sirus safely across the parking lot and into the right restaurant, as I now started trying to run through what I was going to say to this person, how they might react when they saw us come in, how I was going to find her when I didn't know what she looked like, what kind of impression we were trying to make and what the right approach would be.

Later, after we had successfully met the new person and had our coffee and pastries, and were in a position to discuss what had happened with some emotional distance, I resurfaced the interaction and asked Larry what had happened. He had since forgotten about the whole thing. This shocked me, as it had been weighing heavily in my mind for hours and hours, as I replayed what had happened over and over again and tried to figure out what went wrong and where I could have done better.

He explained that it was simply that Sirus was acting up, not wanting to get out of the car for whatever reason, and Larry had been in the backseat with him all morning, and was tired and fed up and just needed my help handling Sirus, getting him out of the car and into the coffee shop successfully. He was flabbergasted that I apparently hadn't intuited—read his mind—that he needed help with Sirus. In his mind, all I had to do was glance at the situation in the backseat, and I should have realized what was wrong and how I could help.

Instead, wrapped up in my own eccentricities of manually going through each step in my routine because I was in a new place doing new things (driving a new car, so double-checking that I put it in park correctly, and that I had the keys in my purse, using a different purse than usual so double-checking that I also had my phone and my wallet), I hadn't had the room in my brain to see that Larry needed help.

In turn, wrapped up in Sirus (literally) and already worn out and frustrated, Larry hadn't been able to simply shout "Help!" to alert me to the fact that he needed me. He assumed I knew already that he needed me. So instead he got even more frustrated at my lack of action, and started issuing instructions, and when I asked why, it just added fire to the flames.

Neither of us could read the other's mind in that situation, as we were each thinking in such a contrary way to what the other person would have expected.

It is hard to pinpoint exactly what could have gone better in the above example. Sometimes, negative interactions will happen, and that is okay.

If you have ASD, know that you may feel the negative effects of an interaction like that for much longer, and much deeper, then your NT partner might. That is okay, too, but if you would rather not feel the negative effects for so long, there are things you can do to help cease the negative spiraling and consciously pull yourself out of that fugue state. I go through a few of them in chapter 7. One key thing that I have found helpful to remember is that the other person may have already forgotten about the thing that is weighing on my mind, and therefore it is okay for me to start forgetting about it too. I can always bring it up again later if I need to better understand what happened, but I don't need to let it permeate every minute of my thoughts until then.

I do want to note one strategy I have read about in Ashley Stanford's book on ASD and long-term relationships, which is for an NT partner to alert their ASD partner to the fact that something is wrong and the NT partner needs help, because the NT partner, knowing that their ASD partner needs the alarm bell, needs to say outright, "I need your help."

It seems so simple, and yet most neurotypical people would not think to do it. First, it is not always easy when you are in the throes of whatever problem you are having, to come out of it long enough to ask for help. Second, a person who is neurotypical may expect other people to easily see what they need and know how to deliver it. This, as illustrated above, can lead to big misunderstandings. Had I not enlightened Larry to the fact that I had no idea that he needed help, he might have simply assumed I was ignoring him. That is not who I am. That is not the impression I want my husband to have of me. That kind of assumption, over time, happening repeatedly, can lead to resentment and toxicity in any long-term relationship.

If you're NT, it might take some practice, but the simple act of providing that verbal alarm to a partner with ASD, who may not be able to see or interpret all the other nonverbal alarm bells going off, can save a lot of strife and misunderstanding.

Staying Attuned to Nonverbal Cues

That said, there are also things that the ASD partner can do to avoid misunderstandings and aid in the process of "mind-reading."

One big way is taking the time, explicitly and purposefully, to start to identify the nonverbal cues your significant other uses to communicate specific emotions, or at least broad emotional groups. You probably have a greater opportunity to do this with your life partner than you do with other people, due to the amount of time you likely spend together.

You can refer back to the section in chapter 2 about the most common forms of body language, and you can do your own research into different types of body language relative to what you notice about your partner, specifically. You can also engage in active research, telling your partner that you noticed they used a specific form of body language and asking them what they are usually feeling when they fold their arms across their chest, for example, or when they cover their face with their hands. It's best to do this at a time when you are both on emotionally stable ground, NOT in the middle of an interaction where they are employing the body language in question. If you find yourself noticing a particular nonverbal cue (or a few) from your partner during a fight or a heated discussion, make a note to ask them about it after you've both cooled down and are ready to have a reasonable conversation.

Mirroring Emotions (Avoiding Overanalysis)

When trying to read my husband's mind, I can easily fall into overanalysis, performing what feels like endless mental gymnastics to deduce what he is feeling or what he really means. This can be paralyzing and inhibit the in-the-moment emotional reciprocity that is so important for nurturing close interpersonal relationships.

One of the strategies I have found most helpful to stop the spinning and fast-forward to the "action" stage—where I am reacting to my husband's needs and emotions in real time, rather than just absorbing and analyzing—is mirroring. This is when you try to reflect the other person's emotional state and concerns back to them and try to internalize their emotions as if they were your own.

Mirroring is helpful on two distinct fronts:

1. It increases my ability to engage in "theory of mind," or to explicitly empathize with how another person is feeling by

way of making myself feel the same way even though I don't yet understand exactly why. Usually I need to know <u>why</u> an emotion is being felt, either by me or by another person, in order to recognize the emotion. Mirroring helps me skip the why and go right to the feeling itself.

2. It communicates to the other person that I am sensitive to their needs and feelings. As my body language starts to mirror their own, as they hear their own words repeated back to them, they feel understood and validated. It may still feel superficial to me, but to a neurotypical person, it implies that I understand and relate to what they are going through.

After all, every couple has areas where they'll probably never see eye to eye. But when it comes to strong emotions, simply feeling understood by your significant other can go a long way toward assuaging hurt and creating a more positive emotional state.

MAKING SPACE FOR MISTAKES

In any relationship, it's important to make space for mistakes. No one is perfect. Acknowledging this outright is especially important for someone with ASD, for whom expectations, and perfectionism, can be such intense drivers.

It's easier to make space for mistakes when you truly understand each other's weak areas, where mistakes are more likely to happen.

If I forget to pack my son's sheet and blanket for nap time on a Monday morning, thanks to our understanding of ASD, my husband and I both now know that it's not because I am being careless, but simply because my mechanics are different. We know that it takes my brain extra effort to adapt to a change in routine, and the fact that we only send his nap things once per week throws me off, because I don't do it regularly enough to remember consistently.

The mistake is okay, but letting it happen more than once becomes an issue.

In this case, I need to take particular care on Monday mornings, or perhaps in advance on Sunday nights, to account for extra variables. So perhaps we start a Sunday evening process of taking ten minutes to prep for the next morning, transitioning out of weekend mode and getting ready for the week ahead.

Understanding and Valuing Intentions over Outcomes

When dealing with mistakes, it's important to place greater value on a person's *intentions* rather than on the exact *outcomes* of those intentions. Knowing that I did not intend to hurt my husband's feelings, or forget my son's request, or whatever mistake I may have made, does not mean it hurts any less. But it does mean that any potentially longer-lasting damage—building resentment or a feeling of neglect or hostility—does not persist.

It's hard to stay mad at someone who only meant to help.

Here is an example of a time when I made a minor mistake in the moment, and took the opportunity to make space for it and move on quickly, valuing the intent behind the mistake as opposed to the outcome itself:

Because my commute to work is so much shorter than my husband's, I usually focus first each morning on helping him and our son get out the door, before then getting myself ready. I always run through a series of checks in my morning routine that take into account the needs of both my husband and son, which usually goes something like this:

- Does Larry have coffee?
- Does everyone have breakfast?

- Does Sirus have a lunch?
- Has everyone taken their morning vitamins?

Larry's breakfast needs are in fact less predictable than our son's, because Sirus will reliably eat only one of three possible choices in the morning: cereal, a waffle, or a banana. Larry, on the other hand, may never actually eat anything, may not eat whatever food I make for him, or may need to eat at a time when having his food ready is not convenient.

It bothers me immensely when my husband leaves the house without eating, so I usually try several different tacks to get him to eat something, the same way I do with our son.

"Will you eat a banana this morning, love? They'll go bad soon."

"Sure," he answered, one eye on the mirror and the other on his razor. "I'll split one with Sirus on our way out."

Well, that's better than nothing, I thought to myself. He'd already refused the idea of an English muffin.

I convinced Sirus to start working on a bowl of dry cereal as he played with train tracks on the living room floor, while I got out his clothes and finished making his lunch.

Larry finished shaving and got dressed while I dressed Sirus.

"Okay, let's get our shoes on," I said, directing Sirus toward the hallway. "Oh, and here, take this banana to Daddy. You're going to split it on your way to school."

"Mmm, banana," Sirus said, clutching it to his chest. "I want my own banana."

"Well, you and Daddy are going to split it," I answered. "Come on, shoes."

"But I want a whole banana!" Sirus protested, his voice skyrocketing.

"Sarah, let him have a whole banana," came Larry's voice from the hallway where he was getting on his coat. "Why are you arguing with him?"

"Well, I don't know, I thought the plan was for you to split—"

"Never mind the *plan*. If he wants a whole banana, that's great, he's al-lowed! We have plenty of bananas."

Larry's tone was sharp and impatient, and in addition to the confusion I was feeling—which was gradually morphing into embarrassment—I felt wounded that he was upset, when my intentions had only been to make sure that both my husband and child got something to eat before starting their day.

He saw me struggling, and his tone softened. "I know you just want to feed us. And I know we made a plan that now we're not following, and that's challenging for you. But you have to be quicker to recognize the need to change plans—especially when it has to do with something that Sirus is happy and willing to eat all on his own." A rare feat in our household, to be fair.

I had been so entrenched in our original plan—which, frustratingly enough, hadn't really even been a super thought-out plan to begin with, just a version of how things could go—that I didn't see the bigger picture staring me in the face. That if my son wanted a whole banana and we had enough, he shouldn't be forced to split it just because that was "the plan." But I wasn't intending to be rigid or to deprive my son of half his banana. My good intentions, despite lack of big-picture critical thought in application, won out, softening my husband's response to one of learning rather than purely exasperation or disagreement.

Repairing Strategies

When you are in the heat of the moment, it can be hard to see the source of the contention, identify what mistakes may have been made, and address the core issue. Instead, as the conflict begins to unfold, it can be very help-ful to cultivate some tools for real-time conflict management—"repairing strategies" for troubleshooting when something seems to be going wrong between you and your partner (or anyone, really) in the moment.

Without knowing about these tools, I have in the past found myself in many situations where an interaction starts heading down a path I did not intend, but having no way to stop it or redirect the conversation, I just ended up letting it crash and burn, or kept plugging away, trying to get back on the track we were on before, without success.

Emotional Reciprocity

The first repairing strategy is to match the emotional level or tone that the other person is giving off.

If you are having a conversation with your partner, for example, that's starting to go off the rails—maybe the other person seems to be getting upset, or they are upsetting you—try to take a step back and assess the emotional state of the other person. Do they seem agitated? You might not want to appear agitated in turn, as that might fuel the other person into further agitation, but it actually might help them calm down if you at least become a bit more animated, or communicate with your body language or tone in some way that the topic is just as important to you as it is to the other person. Showing that you are on the same emotional wavelength, even if you are naturally not as expressive, automatically helps their brain produce calming, "I feel safe" chemicals.

On the other hand, does your partner seem turned off or depressed by the conversation? This might not be the right time for them to discuss whatever the topic is, or they might have just realized something disappointing, or had a rough day. In a situation where the other person seems to be powering down, rather than powering up, you can always take a step back and literally ask them if they are all right. You can suggest that perhaps you talk about something else right now, or ask them if they need anything, or if you can help in any way. Showing that you are concerned for the other person's well-being has a similar "I feel safe" calming effect on their brain chemistry.

State the Obvious

Another repairing strategy is to state what you see, even if you don't know exactly what to do or say *about* what you see.

This one is very useful for me, because when conversations start to get emotional—as they often do with close family—my brain can overload quickly, and it becomes very hard for me to recognize appropriate next steps.

So if the person I'm interacting with, be it my husband or someone else, starts to get upset or angry about something, I have learned to take a step back and state exactly what I see and what is happening: "I see that this is important to you. It's important to me, too. But I don't know what to do about it." Or repeat back to them, respectfully, what you are hearing: "I hear you saying what I did was not okay. I hear you. I am trying to understand why, so that I don't do it again."

This way the other person knows that they are not alone, that you are there with them and agree on the importance of the topic at hand, but also that you are a little lost or unsure. Sometimes this can calm someone down right away—they see you are engaged, trying to help, but that you need help, too. Sometimes, they may still be angry or continue getting upset, but they will at least feel like you are both in this together and therefore other negative emotions like hopelessness or loneliness are less likely to seep in and complicate the momentary frustration with longer-term damage.

Take a Break

Sometimes, it is okay to give yourself, or you *and* the person you are interacting with, a "time out."

It might just be that one or the both of you are too agitated, too close to the emotion, too affected by what has just happened, to have a constructive interaction. To avoid getting angry or resorting to emotional outlets like yelling, you can say, "I need to talk about this later," or "I need a time out," or "Just give me a few minutes to cool down." You can even say this if it's not really you who needs to cool down.

Reminders of the Bigger Picture

One of the most effective ways I have found for accepting that mistakes will happen, and that they are okay in a long-term close relationship, is to use key phrases or visual reminders of the bigger picture.

In moments of strife, I will remind myself: What, ultimately, is the most important thing? Is it that I feel incompetent in this moment? No. Is it that we had a miscommunication that led to our day going completely sideways? No.

The most important thing is that I love my husband, and he loves me, and we'll get through this together.

In the first several years of our relationship, we cultivated this bigger-picture reminder—for both of us—in the phrase "we are better together." You glimpsed it earlier in this chapter, when I described how we each found ways to capitalize on each other's strengths in meeting the various needs of our everyday lives.

It became a kind of mantra that I would repeat to myself over and over, especially during the first few years, when I lived in constant fear that my husband would wake up one day and realize that I was not the person he thought I was, or that I had less to offer than I made it seem. (This was actually one of the biggest obstacles to getting my diagnosis later in our relationship, but I'm so glad I finally did.)

"We are better together" became the "why" that pulled us through to the other side of any conflicts that arose.

Later, as we began to grow our family, Larry brought home a piece of wall art for our new two-bedroom apartment. Without a word, he hung it up on our bedroom wall, right by the door, so that every time I woke up in the morning and came out of our bedroom to start the day, I couldn't help but see it.

The funny thing was, it wasn't exactly visual art, it was one set of words repeated over and over and over.

> hello darling,
> I adore you I adore you
> I adore you I adore you
> and tomorrow I plan to
> adore you even more.
>   xoxoxo

This is where I turn now when I need to remind myself that everything will be okay. When I need a reminder of the "why," to keep myself from plunging into the trap of black-or-white thinking that makes every mistake seem like the end of the world.

The words are there for us to see and remember, even when we might not be able to say them directly to each other right in that moment.

EXPRESSING LOVE

I want to take a moment to focus on this one particular, and very important, part of a romantic relationship, and that is expressing love. You might think this is a no-brainer, but don't ever take it for granted. You can never tell your partner that you love them too many times. You can never over-appreciate your partner.

Small reminders of love can go a long way in sustaining mutual positivity through the larger trials and tribulations of everyday life.

It doesn't have to always be saying "I love you," either. It can be a gentle, intentional hand brushing against your partner's shoulder as you move past them in the kitchen. It can be a text at lunchtime asking how their day is going.

These small moments are so important that I have specifically built them into my subconscious activity—which took, and still takes, a lot of conscious effort. Not because I want to show contrived love or put on airs—but because I know that if I don't intentionally set up the structures to facilitate this behavior from myself, I won't naturally perform it, even though I love my husband deeply. I have to compensate for my body and mind's lack of natural response, in order to send the message of love that I intend.

Mindfulness

One of the more subtle ways to express love is to practice *mindfulness* of your partner and their needs.

Mindfulness goes beyond just making a point of asking how their day is going. Mindfulness is making a point of being especially attuned to what they might be going through, what they might be thinking, what they might desire, what they might be dreaming of, what might make them smile.

This can be hard for me to achieve, as I can't "read minds" the same way other people might be able to, and it is nearly impossible for me to intuit what might be going on inside my husband's mind at any given moment. But the point of mindfulness is not necessarily that I always have to know; I just have to be curious.

Maybe Larry rolled his ankle yesterday.

This is new information that I will struggle to remember unless I specifically write it into my brain and create opportunities for myself to be mindful. I might take an extra moment that night to find his ankle brace and put it near his shoes. I might make a point of asking him how it's feeling the next morning.

My brain has so much trouble incorporating new information quickly that I have learned to simply give myself the space to practice mindfulness.

When I have a moment of calm, or when I am seeking one, I try to take a step back, and think to myself, *What new things have happened with Larry in the last day or so that I should incorporate into my active thought process?* This might be the moment when I remember that Larry rolled his ankle the previous day, and so I will make a note in the electronic calendar on my phone to look for his ankle brace that evening. Understand that if I don't put it in my calendar in that moment, I might forget to follow up.

Actions like this let your partner know (high context) that you are thinking of them even when they are not around. That you have their needs in mind, even when they are not explicitly asking you for help.

Being mindful of my own forgetfulness, and using tools to actively combat that tendency so that I remember things that are important to my husband, is an assertive expression of love.

TOOLS FOR SUCCESS

Executive functioning is a set of skills that is applicable to more than just the workplace. Being able to prioritize, manage time, set goals, track progress, and make adjustments to actions in real time—all toward advancing the bigger picture—are all essential skills for maintaining a household as well, where each family member has their own goals and priorities that fit into the overall tapestry of the family.

In this section are some of the most effective tools that Larry and I have found for maximizing household success with my ASD.

What's the Schedule?

My overall ability to keep track of everything going on has improved infinitely through the use of scheduling and calendar tools.

At work, if something is not on my calendar or written down on a to-do list somewhere, there is a good chance I will not remember to do it. The same is true for a lot of home needs.

Sharing a Family Calendar—Electronic and Analog

First, we maintain a shared family calendar. We have an electronic version that exists on both of our phones, which can be updated by either one of us in real time, and we have a dry-erase version of the current month that hangs in our living room.

This way, while I am sitting on the couch, I can passively remind myself what is happening in the next week. Will Larry be out one night this week? Does Sirus have a school event coming up? Having the visual advance warning is very helpful for my planning brain, as wheels start turning in my subconscious to be ready for the variables presented by off-routine events.

The digital version gives us the luxury of seeing right on our phone screens the next few upcoming items on the calendar, and also provides reminder notifications that pop up on our devices before a scheduled event.

Inevitably, whenever I forget to do something household-related, like refill a prescription, or stop by the store on the way home to pick up emergency diapers, the question will surface: "Did I put it on the calendar?" And the answer will undoubtedly be, "No . . ."

Setting Reminders

Any smartphone can do this for you. We also have the option of voice-activated reminders on our Amazon Echo device.

Reminders are *essential* for me, because if I don't do something right at the moment when I think about doing it, there is a good chance it will never get done—*unless* I set a reminder to do it at a later time. Before I discovered the power of reminders, I was forever at the whim of a brain that would randomly remember something important at the most inopportune times.

"Where are you going?" Larry would ask, peeved.

"I just remembered something," I would answer, my back turned.

"But I was in the middle of telling you—oh, *never mind.*"

Instead of completely derailing whatever I am doing in the moment (which could be any number of important things with a toddler and a baby and a husband and a job and a home), I can just pause for a second to set myself a reminder for later that night, or in one hour, or perhaps the next day, to take care of whatever had just popped into my head.

Framing Unstructured Time

One of the most helpful strategies we have found as a neurodiverse family is making sure to frame our unstructured time (weekends, vacations, and similar) together.

Weekdays have their own automatic cadence, with school and work. But weekends can quickly devolve into chaos unless we have specific plans.

It's not that every minute of every weekend needs to be planned out; it's just about having a frame within which to function, like a bucket holding sand. The framework of the bucket gives shape and purpose to the sand, when otherwise it would just be left to mix with the vast and untamed beach.

For an adult or child with ASD, lack of structure can introduce too many unknown variables and cause a lot of unnecessary stress.

Just knowing that our plan on a particular Saturday, for example, is to hang out in the morning, have lunch with a friend at one p.m., then do laundry in the afternoon, is enough. We sit as a family in the morning on each weekend day, and just spend five minutes laying out what our overall framework is for the day, so that everyone can set our larger expectations and start mentally preparing in advance for the major activities that will take place.

Household Management

When it comes to partnership in running a home, there are several areas where neurodiversity between partners can be both a help and a hindrance. Below are some of the key strategies we have used to maximize success.

Clear Delineation of Responsibilities

Sensing a theme? The ASD brain craves structure—clear expectations, consistency, transparency. You would, too, if you constantly saw eight different ways that any given situation could go and any number of extraneous and completely irrelevant details that may or may not be important.

So when it comes to household tasks, clearly defining responsibilities can go a long way in making sure the things that need to get done are taken care of—and by the person who is best at taking care of it.

In our house I handle bedtime routines, because I am good at them.

Larry handles social planning (lunch with a friend, inviting people over, etc.), because he is good at that. Larry cooks, and I do the dishes. I buy the kids' clothes; Larry buys the household supplies.

Things are not divided between us 100 percent one way or another (sometimes I might cook, sometimes Larry might do dishes) but for the most part, we have found what each of us is better at than the other, and we each take the lead in caring for certain aspects of our home life.

Be careful not to depend on these delineations too much, however. Keep the bigger picture in mind in order to avoid getting stuck in a "but I thought you did it" trap:

"Uh-oh!" Sirus exclaims, waving his tablet in the air. We'd just sat down at a restaurant for lunch after being out all morning and had been looking forward to some quiet time. While we are out, Sirus is only allowed his tablet when we are at restaurants and need to buy his willingness to sit still and let us eat.

"What happened?" Larry asks, taking the tablet.

"Looks like the battery died," I say, seeing the blank screen change hands.

"Yup," Larry affirms. "That's exactly what happened." He starts rummaging in the baby bag but comes up empty. "Where's the portable charger?"

My blank look is enough to tell Larry that he's on his own.

"Didn't *you* pack the baby bag this morning?" Larry asks, his voice tense. Baby bag packing was my wheelhouse, after all. I was always the one to prepare our bag before we left the house, making sure we had everything we'd need for both kids.

"Yes," I answer, confused. "But, well, don't you handle the technology?" I'm not trying to make excuses for not packing the portable charger, but I am genuinely confused as to why he is insinuating that it was my job to pack it.

"Yes, Sarah, but you are responsible for the *bag*! And the bag *includes* technology. You packed his tablet, yes?"

"Yes . . ."

"So whenever you pack his tablet, you have to make sure you also pack the portable charger for it! I should not have to tell you this! I didn't *touch* the bag—*you* did—how would I know it's not in here already?"

"I see your point." I had let my automatic assumption that Larry always handles whatever technological needs we may have, in or out of the house, trump my overall responsibility for the baby bag. And Larry, in turn, had assumed that I reigned supreme over the baby bag territory and would remember technology needs that he had recently introduced.

Explicit Teaching and Learning

I have read in other books about neurodiverse relationships that a lot of the interactions between partners can look like codependency, on the surface. The term codependency has a negative connotation, implying that one or both partners has gotten to the point of not being able to function as their own independent person, and instead depends on the other person for too much.

But when ASD is involved, I would argue that what looks like codependency may just be an example of explicit teaching and learning.

Sometimes, I just need my husband to spell something out for me:

"Your sister is getting married in a year—you need to be on the phone with her at least every other week, even if you end up talking about nothing to do with the wedding, just to be an active part of her support system."

I love my sister, and I want to support her, but never in a million years would I have thought on my own to set up bi-weekly calls with her in the year leading up to her wedding in order to provide that love and support. The fact that my husband had this idea and shared it with me, explaining why and how, is extremely helpful for me, because it helps me accomplish something that I want. It also teaches me, explicitly, skills that I can then use again in the future or, with effort, apply to other areas of my life.

Soon after setting up biweekly calls with my sister, I expanded this idea and did the same thing with my mom, on the off-week. So now, every Wednesday night is my night to be on the phone with either my mom or my sister after the kids are in bed.

Throughout the first few years of our relationship, Larry explicitly taught me a great many independent living skills that I had never learned on my own, such as more advanced methods of cooking, pairing wines with foods, caring for hardwood floors, building a credit score, and the fact that it was acceptable to have more than a single coat to wear year-round, whether in a cool spring breeze or bitter winter wind.

The teaching-and-learning dynamic might not be customary in most long-term relationships. But remember the "equality versus equity" conversation—do what feels right to you and your partnership. If the partner with ASD is open to learning, and the NT partner is willing to teach in a mutually empowering way, then why not? Just because it might not fit into the mold of what a traditional partnership should look like, doesn't mean it isn't the right fit for you. And remember, the partner with ASD has many things to teach the NT partner as well.

External Outlets

It is important, in any relationship—but perhaps especially in a neurodiverse one where each partner may have more unique mental, physical, and emotional needs—for both partners to find outlets outside of the relationship. Maybe it's friends, hobbies, therapy, going to see a movie on your own—whatever it may look like to you or your partner—having time away from each other is an important part of being together.

For Larry and I, this time is especially important because it gives Larry some of the emotional feedback he needs that I alone cannot provide, and because it gives me much-needed alone time.

We are very different people, and we glean energy and wind down in very different ways. Our custom since entering parenthood (likely the most physically and mentally draining era of what will be our lives together) has been for Larry to head out for a short walk after the kids are in bed, while I get comfortable on the couch and read a book. Larry might head to the local bar and chat with all the people he meets, or walk to the park listening to a podcast instead. I might dive into the latest novel I've been reading, turn on the audiobook of an old favorite, or crack open one of my illustrated versions of Harry Potter to get lost for a little while. This way we each get to wind down for an hour in our own way, and then come back to each other refreshed.

Whatever makes sense for you and your partner, find ways to give each other space. Space to be alone, space to hang out with your own friends, space to pursue separate interests, and, yes, even space to vent about each other to people you trust. It's important to exhale. And sometimes the best way to do that is to use an external outlet, rather than keep everything bottled up between the two of you.

LARRY'S TWO CENTS

Let's not compromise.

As we progress through life, our understanding of what it means to be in a relationship evolves. In the beginning there are our parents or caregivers, families and friends, who establish our ideas of how relationships work. As we progress into our adolescence and are attacked by hormones, we learn much more through the internet and media than we ever imagined, and we start to dabble in our own romantic attachments. Eventually, most of us settle into long-term relationships. We may marry; we may divorce. As Sarah mentioned at the beginning of this chapter, our advice is geared toward long-term relationships. What works for us, why it works, and how we continue to work together to keep it . . . working.

Compromise is a word which we absolutely try to avoid. If this surprises you, it did to me, too. Like everyone else, we were taught that compromise would be a key element in successfully joining our lives together. Very common questions like what to eat tonight for dinner, where we would live, and how we would decorate our new apartment were constant topics. What wasn't as common, at least for me, was the length of time each conversation would take, how much energy Sarah needed to expend just to choose pizza toppings—and forget it if we also had to pick a pizzeria to order from. Fairly quickly we both realized we needed to find a better way.

Rather than asking what Sarah would want for dinner, I would suggest we have Chinese takeout if we were tired and running late, or that I could make some pasta if we had some time and weren't starving. Equally, Sarah had lots of ideas about how to decorate our newfound first apartment, so I often said yes to the first choice. Let me emphasize, I was not avoiding look-ing at ten different bookshelves because I didn't care, but rather, because I did, and Sarah was so good at it.

Thus we began to organically eliminate the word "compromise" from our vocabulary, instead evolving toward a "we are better together" ap-proach—a sort of delegation that suited both of us.

When we do disagree, which is rare now, we choose to trust each other, and let the other person's happiness influence our own. This frees us up to reap the benefits of our labor and of each other's company.

In my world, I have the responsibility of leading teams and making final decisions, but I have always prided myself on listening and truly hear-ing those who I am working with. It's this honed skill that gives me the confidence to know, based on how Sarah is feeling, what she most likely would like to watch on TV, whether it be a twenty-minute improv comedy or a seventy-five-minute Netflix drama. So rather than asking the question, "What do you want to watch tonight?" I now ask, "Do you want to watch *Whose Line Is It Anyway*?" This frees Sarah up to answer a simple yes-or-no question, and it's fine if the answer is no. Maybe I misread the situation, or maybe it's just an *America's Funniest Home Videos* night. (I'm fine either way, and I have no fear we will ever forget to watch a new episode of *Whose Line*, as I simply wouldn't let that happen.)

For Sarah's part in this better-together approach, she does have an obligation to speak up and give an opinion when it is important to her. As most of the time the thought of having to make such decisions can over-whelm her, she is able to take comfort knowing dinner and entertainment are covered, so she can spend those minutes decompressing from her work-day rather than spinning unnecessary brain cycles. Sarah has shared with me the profound sense of relief she feels, knowing that I am comfortable making these decisions, and knowing that the door is always open for her to contribute to the decision-making process when she needs or wants to.

Ultimately for us, knowing that we are both taken care of and are doing our part to make the other person feel cared for is a wonderful feeling. In the end, it isn't the multitude of decisions or compromises that we make together, trying to win or get our personal preference picked most often, but rather that we lay down each night happy, knowing that we are loved.

There is nothing more grounding, nothing more supportive than having the love of another, and that is truly what drives us each day.

CHAPTER SIX

Communicating as a Parent

"There will come a time when—
after longing for the sleepless nights to end,
after counting down the days—
you will count the many ways
in which you yearn
to have them back again."

—ANONYMOUS

If you are a parent, you have probably already consulted multiple sources of information to try to learn better ways of doing things, of supporting your kid(s), of supporting yourself, of caring for your family. (Or maybe you are perfect and never read a parenting book in your life! 😉)

In this chapter, I want to focus on the specific intersection of ASD and parenthood, and the ways that being a parent is different for me. This dynamic is even more nuanced by the fact that my son is autistic as well. I also want to explore the partnership of parenthood between an ASD and a neurotypical parent, a unique pairing that presents its own challenges and advantages.

STRENGTHS AND WEAKNESSES

A key aspect of being any type of parent, but especially a parent with ASD, is understanding and accepting where you are strong, and where you are weak. This self-knowledge is important for any person, but as an ASD parent, it becomes even more essential to know where to put your limited energy, and how best to position yourself for success in guiding your growing children.

One of my greatest sources of my strength, as a parent of a child with ASD, is my insider's perspective on what it's like to have a brain that works differently. I understand intuitively what my son is going through. I think all parents or guardians feel a certain amount of this with their children. But my lived experience gives me a window into my son's head that most neurotypical people would not have.

To illustrate the power and uniqueness of this strength, I want to share a story of a time when my perspective into how our son's brain works facilitated immediate de-escalation of a potential conflict:

"Are you kidding me?!?" comes the exasperated cry of an overextended parent in the other room.

I know why he's exasperated. I am too. Still ringing in my head are the words I'd near-shouted a moment before: "He just woke up the baby!"

Our son, age four, is cringing from the tone of our voices, running to the couch for refuge.

"He didn't mean to," comes my less-exasperated resolution, as I lean over the crib in our bedroom to pick up a newly awakened—and unhappy—six-month-old.

"I know he didn't mean to!" answers my husband, still unable to move from the other room. He is lying prone on our son's bed, recuperating after a long morning out with Sirus. The morning has unexpectedly exaggerated the wound that is still healing from his recent minor surgery. "But why? How did that happen?!?"

Sirus has curled up in a protective ball on the couch underneath a blanket, waiting for the energy in the house to calm down. I carry the baby into the room where Larry is in pain and feeling helpless, to reduce our need to shout—an active attempt at quieting the household, to lower our son's anxiety.

"How does that happen!?" Larry repeats, both upset and wanting to understand.

I'm still frazzled, and trying to marshal my thoughts. "What do you mean?" I ask, unsure whether he blames me, or Sirus, or circumstance, or if he's asking me to recount everything that happened in exacting detail because he couldn't see it, or if he wants an executive summary, or if he's just exasperated and doesn't actually want me to explain anything. I recognize the warning signs of my brain going into hyper-analytical spiral mode, and instead of letting it continue to trundle away, I reel it back in, take a mental step back, and refocus on the most important thing. Love. Care. De-escalating negative emotions. I bypass my brain's need for further clarification, seeing already that my seemingly inane question only turned up the fire on Larry's emotional burner.

I skip to the essentials. "He thought you were in our bedroom, love," I say, trying very hard to make sure I don't come across as patronizing or upset in any way—I'm aiming for gentle and calm, not preaching from a high horse. I have to be very conscious of this balance because, in the past, my logical tone and lack of body language has been misinterpreted as condescension. "So when you called for him to come, he came to where he thought you were." *And unnecessarily banged open the door to our bedroom so loudly that it roused his sister from her nap,* I think to myself, but that much is already obvious.

"But he *knew* I was in here! How does that happen?" Larry persists.

"You being in Sirus's room to rest, rather than ours, is a new process for him," I explain simply, knowing that I need to consciously stop myself from saying any more and save further detail for later. I have neither the time nor the brain capacity to find all the right words to explain more fully in this moment. Even if I did, I have learned to recognize that Larry is not in a state to be able to hear a long, logical explanation right now anyway. Emotions are still running too high.

Seeing Larry visibly release some of the tension in his body—either because he is starting to understand, or simply because he is giving up for now—I assess that it is time to move on to the other member of our household who needs help.

I carry the baby, now calm, back into the living room, lay her on her play mat, and place some of her favorite toys within arm's reach.

I set my sights on the wriggling mass of blanket that is my son, likely feeling ashamed and embarrassed and confused and scared all at once. I sit down on the couch next to him and lean over close to his body so that he feels me, warm and gentle, not angry. "It's okay, Sirus," I say. "It was an accident."

He pokes his red face out of the blanket, tears in his eyes. He can't speak yet. I know that feeling—I've been in his position many times before.

"I know it was an accident," I say again. "So does Daddy. Your sister is fine. Look, there she is, playing. It's all okay."

It takes a few more times of me repeating gently that it was an accident before his throat unclenches and his brain gives him back the power of speech.

He nods at my words, still curled up under the blanket. "I forgot that Daddy was in my room," he croaks, his voice still tiny. And I know, viscerally, how painful it is for him to force the words out of his throat. "When Daddy lays down to rest, he's always in your room."

"I know," I say again.

"I don't like Daddy lying down in my room." On the surface, this might look like a moment of possessiveness or resentment, but I know—because my brain does the same thing to me—that it is simply a reaction to the change.

"I know it's a new thing," I say, "for Mommy or Daddy to rest in your room, instead of in our room. But none of us wants to wake up your sister, right? Your sister is here now. She's been with us for a few months, so we need to change and adapt how we do things to make room for her."

Sirus nods absentmindedly from under his blanket, glassy eyes on his sister, and I know that his brain is whirling through various accommodations we have made to our lives to account for the new baby.

"You need to add an extra step to your thinking now," I continue. "You need to take an extra second to think to yourself, *Where is my sister, and what am I doing?* Especially when the bedroom door is closed, and you know that your sister is sleeping."

"Okay," he agrees, blood visibly leaving his face so that it is not as red anymore.

I engage him in helping me to make lunch, so that he has forward motion and something productive on which to focus his energy. He immediately uncurls from the blanket and is eager to be helpful and positive.

Later that night, I'm able to offer my husband a deeper understanding of what had happened in our son's brain in that moment. I explain that, while Sirus might have logically known Larry was in the other bedroom, he has nevertheless amassed over three years of data telling him that when Mommy or Daddy is lying down to rest, they're in Mommy and Daddy's bedroom. The baby—who sleeps in a crib in our room—is a new variable in Sirus's data set, which has not been actively accounted for in all of his trillions of brain pathways. When he is in the middle of something and responding to a primal call from a parent to come, he—like anyone—will rely on the vast automatic unconscious of his brain to tell him where to go, rather than take an extra step to think critically about all the variables he must now take into account. A neurotypical brain—after six months of living with a baby—would perhaps have already built the new pathways of information for someone to automatically rely on when they don't have (or can create) a moment for critical thinking. Though, of course, most four-year-olds will still be developing this sense of external awareness, ASD or no, and Sirus's struggle at this age may not be that out of the ordinary for a new older sibling.

Like me, Sirus does not learn—at least not quickly—from passive exposure. He must be actively engaged in creating the learning, and even then, his brain will still try to automate processes for him with obsolete information that he must actively purge many times over before a new automatic pathway can be formed.

• • •

For me, the above example is the crux of the ASD brain's relationship with routines. My brain does not give me the same luxury of automatic information absorption, and so my routines become my safe, known automatic pathways—times when I can turn my brain off instead of thinking so hard about every variable.

The momentary conflict in this example occurred because Sirus's routine—his automatic knowledge that Mommy and Daddy rest in one room and he rests in the other room—was disrupted. It might not be the last time that this very same or similar thing happens, either. I know that in my bones, because I have been the victim of an obsolete brain pathway more than once. It happens to me in small ways multiple times a day, and I know how long it can take to actively rewrite new information on top of the old.

The important thing for both me and my son to remember is that it takes our brains longer to incorporate new information—but that is not an excuse. We must still strive to learn from our mistakes, to do better next time, and understanding how our learning is different from the norm is key. My greatest strengths in parenting our son lies in my lived experience of how he operates differently from other people, my ability to help him with tools and knowledge that have helped me, and my position as an advocate for his perspective toward a world that largely does not agree or understand.

Along with this and other strengths come some very specific weaknesses, that together my husband and I have learned to recognize and either mitigate, compensate for, or redirect toward greater success. I'll explore several of them, along with the specific tools that have helped, throughout this chapter.

PARTNERSHIP

In any relationship between two or more adults caring for a child, a sense of partnership is key.

You are in this together. You may not always be in it equally, as explored in the previous chapter, but you are always in it together.

Sure, we are all humans, and things may happen that leave you or your partner feeling alone. But if your bigger picture is always that you are a team, you can get through those inevitable lonely times more easily. It is also important for your children to see you in partnership. They will develop their baseline sense of love and teamwork from watching how you do it, deciding whether to emulate or diverge in their own lives.

One of the basic keys of partnership is to support and respect each other's unique perspectives, and to endeavor never to undermine each other.

This means that, if I say one thing, and my husband does not agree, he will consult with me first before he says something contradictory to our children, and vice versa. It means that neither of us speaks disparagingly about the other—ever, if we can help it, but especially in front of our children. It means that if we are not sure where we stand together on an issue, we check in—"What did Mommy say?" Larry might reply to a question that could have multiple answers, or "Let me check with Daddy," I might say if our position on something is unclear. It means honoring and respecting the other person's words and actions when they are not in the room, while still honoring and respecting your own point of view. For example, in response to something like "But Daddy always lets me jump off the couch," I might say, "All right, that's up to Daddy, but when Daddy is away and you are here with me and I am the one responsible for keeping you safe, I don't want you jumping off the couch," instead of something disrespectful and untrue (though likely easier in the moment and therefore tempting) like "Well, Daddy's wrong."

Another important aspect of partnership is working together to build on each other's strengths and compensate for each other's weaknesses.

When it comes to parenting, one of my greatest weaknesses, related directly to my ASD, is how slowly I adapt to change, and how rigid I can become in moments of stress or change or emotional tension.

Children grow at an alarming rate. They change every day: They learn new things and think new thoughts and become new people all the time.

This is especially true of young children, but teenagers go through their own period of rapid mental and physical growth as well. The truth of the matter is that I just can't keep up. I know this now. It is impossible. I have to let myself get lost and then find myself again, trying to make sense of a brand-new normal. I can't begin to try to follow and track and account for all the new variables in the data set that is a growing child.

When and how did he learn how to climb out of the crib??? Never mind, it doesn't matter, he's about to fall on his head. New normal: mountains of cushions lining the floor around the crib's edges while we frantically research toddler beds online. (To be fair, this one took *both* me and my neurotypical partner by surprise.)

How did he suddenly become aware that we are spelling words we don't want him to hear?? Whoops, no time to worry about it now, he is asking what C-A-K-E spells and he's already starting to sound it out and I don't have any cake to give him right now and I don't want to raise his expectations only to let him down and cause an unnecessary emotional spiral—quick! Distraction tactic . . . "Tag, you're it!" New normal: explicitly ask our son to let Mommy and Daddy talk for a minute when we need to discuss risky information, and DON'T spell any words we don't want him to hyper-focus on right away.

Larry understands that this is a particular weakness of mine, and helps me to recognize when I am reverting to old tactics (my brain not yet having finished rewriting the new learning on top of the old) or remaining stuck in an outdated frame of mind. But it can get frustrating for both of us, because Larry is not always around to help me, and because I need to be independently confident in my own role as the mother of my children.

Here is an example of a time when Larry was able to help me transcend a moment of rigidity, both in terms of being stuck in outdated knowledge/ methods, and being unable to originate another way of getting to success in the moment:

"Come on, Sirus. It's story time." I was getting our son ready for bed, a task that we entrusted to me specifically because a reliable bedtime routine is an important aspect of toddlerdom, and I am good at routines. But Sirus was giving me grief tonight.

"Find me, Mama!" he called from under the sheets on his bed.

"No, it's not playtime, hon. It's story time. Come on, pick out your two books."

"No! Playtime, playtime!"

"Sirus, we always do *stories* after pajamas. We're getting ready for bed now. What stories do you want to read?"

"You can't see me! I'm hiding, Mama, find me."

My voice was rising, and I was already losing my usually boundless patience. After a long workday, I wasn't prepared for my son to suddenly overturn his bedtime routine. Before our interaction could escalate into an unnecessary conflict, Larry appeared at the door.

"Sirus, can I talk to Mama for a minute?" he asked.

"You can't find me!" Sirus persisted, which we took to be as much of a yes as we were going to get.

I was grateful for the momentary break. Only now that I was stepping out of the spiral did I realize that my shoulders were tense, my head was starting to spin, my teeth were clenched, and I had been metaphorically digging my heels into the ground of Sirus's usual bedtime routine.

"He wants to spend some time playing with you," Larry reasoned, bringing my awareness up to the bigger picture. "He hasn't seen you much today."

Elevating my perspective above the consistency of our routine, I understood what Larry was saying, but I didn't know how to act on it. "Okay, but we can't go off and play now. If he doesn't get to sleep soon he'll be overtired, and he'll be up and down for another hour, and—"

Larry put a gentle hand on my arm to halt the negative spiral. "I know, but it doesn't have to be all or nothing like that. He's getting older now.

He has the right to some level of input in how he wants to spend his time. Maybe you can just give him the option of five minutes of playtime instead of one of his stories?"

"You think five minutes would be enough? And then we'd still read one story after, to wind down?" I asked, trying to buy into this new strategy.

"Sure. Let's try it, anyway," Larry said, shrugging in a "What do we have to lose?" kind of way.

I have learned to trust my husband's instincts when it comes to evolving perspectives and taking into account the bigger picture. It's hard because my brain perceives trying anything new as being fraught with risks—risks which I want to identify and catalog and develop contingencies for—but I have Larry's partnership to depend on if things go sideways.

"Okay," I agreed. "Should I set a timer?"

"Absolutely."

"Come find me!" called Sirus again, for the fifth or sixth time.

"Okay, Sirus," I answered. "We're going to try something. You want to have some playtime, yes?"

"Yes! Playtime!"

"Okay. So, we normally read two stories before bed. But if you want playtime, we can do five minutes of play instead of one story, and then only read one story before bed. How's that?"

"Play, play!"

"Okay." I used the Amazon Echo device on his bookshelf to verbally set a five-minute timer so that he heard it, and set about playing hide-and-seek with my son giggling under his sheets, rather than spiraling into a battle of wills with me on one side of the routine and Sirus on the other.

Ever since then, the option for five minutes of play in the place of one story has become a regular part of our bedtime routine, so that Sirus has the opportunity to choose and has some level of control over his time.

As he continues to grow, our bedtime routine will of course continue to evolve, with ever more complicated elements that, over time, transition the power over to him and, little by little, get him ready to take the lead in his own process for winding down at night.

When I don't have Larry around to pull me out of a moment of teeth-grinding rigidity, his partnership has helped me learn to be conscious of taking a step back and recognizing when the status quo has changed. And when a novel solution is available.

SETTING EXPECTATIONS

One of the most helpful sets of tools for a parent with ASD, or the parent of a child with ASD, is setting expectations.

Not just your child's expectations, but your own as well.

These tools are helpful for any parent, but especially parents of toddlers. From an autism lens, setting the right expectations can mean the difference between a perfectly easy and well-ordered type of day, and a chaotic, meltdown-ridden, emotional-roller-coaster type of day.

With so much of our brainpower focused on the details, and diverted from the bigger picture, it can be hard for me (and my son) to find the "why" that sustains us through any number of seemingly small hardships along the way. Life can often feel like it is spinning out of control. There are too many details that we can't control, and yet we see them all individually, usually without being able to perceive of them all as part of one big picture.

It's hard to describe what this is like to someone who has not experienced it. It's like trying to hold on to sand. There are so many tiny little grains—each one seems equally important, and yet it is impossible to hold on to all of them.

Setting expectations mitigates some of this lack of control. Simply knowing the structure in which my life is being held—even if just for the day or for the next few hours—can offer a tremendous sense of clarity. It's like suddenly having a bucket for the sand. If I know that I have a five-by-five-inch bucket in which to put my sand, I will control the grains of sand I engage with in order to be successful within that controlled structure.

So, for example, if we ask our son to put down his tablet, and he doesn't know why or for how long, and he had no prior expectation of having to stop using it, he is much less willing to cooperate. However, if we had already set a fifteen-minute time limit when he picked up the tablet, and he hears the timer go off, he will put it down of his own accord, because his expectations were clear, and now he is in control of his own destiny.

Timers

Timers are helpful for any toddler. Specifically when it comes to transitions. Almost all toddlers struggle with transitions, especially when that transition is away from something they enjoy doing.

There are several things that timers do to help with an ASD brain, in particular:

They establish forewarning that a transition is coming.

- The ASD brain is notoriously slow to adapt to change, so the advance warning that change is coming is immensely powerful in increasing the likelihood of accepting and navigating successfully through the change.

They remove arbitrary authority.

- A young child who asks why he must do something is not necessarily being disrespectful, he is being curious and wants to learn. A young child with ASD may be apt to ask even more questions than usual, to glean every detail of the logical purpose for the desired behavior.

My son asks questions ad nauseam when we tell him to do something new, not because he doesn't trust or respect us, simply because he sees all the nooks and crannies of possibilities and he wants to get to the bottom of why a particular behavior is desired, so that he can be better prepared in the future.

- On top of this, a young child with ASD may not recognize the subtle hierarchical relational nature at play underneath an interaction, and so does not realize that asking questions of authority figures can be perceived as threatening to that hierarchy.

- These two circumstances combine to make removing any potential arbitrariness from the situation beneficial to success. "The timer is going off, so it is time to get ready for school," as opposed to "It's time to get ready for school, because I said so."

They create a transparent, level playing field.

- There are few things so clear and persistent as an autistic person's sense of justice.

- When I tell my son that I need five more minutes— to finish my meal, to help his baby sister take a nap, etc.—he sets a timer for me.

- This keeps me true to my word, the same way that it keeps him true to the schedule that we need to set with him to make sure we get through our day successfully. It creates a level of transparency and fairness that speaks directly to his true nature. My "five minutes" can't stretch out to ten minutes any more than his can, and I'm not patronizing him by saying that I "just need one more minute" when really it's going to be five times that. I am being clear and holding myself to the same standard that I expect from him, which makes it easier, in turn, for him to give us the same clear, fair respect.

They offer a sense of control.

- As you'll read in the description of routines below, as much as it might feel the opposite to someone who is neurotypical, setting a timer and knowing how much time in which I have to do what I am currently doing, gives me a tremendous sense of relief, knowledge, and control over my actions.
- Instead of careening through chaotic unknown variables in uncharted space, my son has the boundaries of a spaceship—the timer—to allow him to explore safely.

Routines

One of the easiest ways to control expectations—which is why they are so comforting and often essential for people with autism—is having set routines.

Routines can be simple or complex, short or long—the only requirement of a "routine" is that it is done the same way or very similarly each time, so that you know what to expect. If done long enough and with enough consistency, they become habits, like brushing your teeth every morning and every night, or taking the same route to work each morning.

For a child with ASD, a routine is like a safety blanket. They might not need it every day, but woebegone if they don't have it on a day when they need it. For my son, a handful of very specific routines that he can count on each day to give him that boost of safety and security can carry him through the rest of a largely unpredictable day.

Here's an example of how we came to one such routine, which helped us through the transition from home to school in the morning when he was two and three years old:

"Sirus, what's wrong??" I was trying and failing to keep the concern and twinge of exasperation out of my voice, as my two-year-old tossed his whole body onto the sidewalk in front of his school.

He couldn't articulate much at that age, but I knelt down on the sidewalk and kept my arms around him so that he didn't hurt himself on the cement or get too far away from me. "Sirus, it's okay, let's talk. Let's talk. Tell me. What's wrong?"

We had cultivated this phrase of "let's talk" to help us through moments when his emotions got the better of him. It was a cue to let him know that he would be heard, that his point of view was valid, and that we weren't just going to barrel through whatever was bothering him. It had happened organically, with him asking for "Mommy, talk" during moments when we were trying to get him to understand something new or do something that he didn't appear to want to do.

"Let's talk," I said again, and he calmed in my arms. Tears ran down his cheeks as he pointed vigorously toward the front door of the school, where another family had just gone inside.

"Yes," I said, "we're going inside now. It's time for school." But I waited for him to respond, so that we could finish our conversation and he would feel like he had been understood.

He pointed again, jumping a little in his frustration. "Bell!" he finally articulated.

And I realized, "Ah, you want to ring the bell before we go in?"

"Bell! Bell!" he affirmed, and left my arms, running toward the front door.

He wasn't tall enough yet to reach the doorbell on his own, so I lifted him up, and he happily pushed the button. Then he took up a post with his face pressed against the floor-to-ceiling window right next to the door, so that he could watch one of the school aides walk down the hallway to open the door.

Once the door was opened, he dashed in, barely stopping to give me a kiss goodbye.

The next morning, he was already saying, "Bell! Bell!" as we approached the school from half a block away.

I took an extra minute putting away the stroller in front of the school, so that we could let another family go in ahead of us (nice people hold the door for each other, and I know Sirus wanted the door all the way closed so that he could ring the doorbell on his own).

We got to the front door and Sirus was already reaching for the button. But this time, when I lifted him up to press it, one of the other parents, who was still stationed inside right next to the door, popped it open less than a second after Sirus rang the bell.

"Aaaaaaahhhhhhhhnnnnnn!" Sirus wailed. I didn't understand what the issue was, and this time I had to walk Sirus inside the building myself and calm him down in the hallway before he would consent to go farther into the school. It took several long, emotional minutes, and he was still not really happy at the end of it, but he was at least complacent. Later, I realized that perhaps it wasn't just him ringing the bell that was important, maybe it was also the secondary step of seeing someone come all the way down the hall to open the door.

So the next day he and I waited a good minute after the previous family had gone inside, before we went to ring the bell. He was compliant and happy, and headed straight in after one of his teachers came down the hall to open the door.

In my mind, we had found a short, simple, specific routine that Sirus took comfort in at the very beginning of his school day, like a bookend, to help him get through the rest of a day that had any number of unpredictable variables.

Each day that I dropped him off, we did the same routine. Some days it meant we had to be quick and get to the door before another family, some days it meant we had to hang back for a minute.

One day, one of the teachers was holding the door open for us, and I had to tell her, "It's okay, he likes to ring the bell. You can let it close."

She was a little perplexed, but acquiesced, and with no effort at all Sirus rang the bell, the teacher opened the door again, and he headed inside. At that moment, I realized an even greater nuance—the teacher didn't have to come all the way down the hall to open the door, it just needed to be a teacher or a school aide, rather than another parent, who did the opening after Sirus rang the bell.

From then on, over the next year, we performed this small and simple—yet very specific—routine outside of Sirus's school every morning, and every time had quick, easy, happy drop-offs, as opposed to the protracted and emotional affair that it could have been (and was many times before we discovered this tool) without this awareness of routines.

To be clear, routines are extremely helpful for many neurotypical toddlers as well—which is why day cares will often follow the same set schedule every day. In a world where a toddler has so little control over anything to do with their own life, knowing the routine and knowing what to expect, is a very powerful tool for success.

Contingencies

Along with cultivating routines that can help both you and your children get through everyday life, it's a good idea to also cultivate contingency strategies, because it's not always possible to stick to your routines. Life gets in the way, things happen, and sometimes the routine gets thrown out of whack or has to be sacrificed for a more important whole.

For example, the other bookend to Sirus's school day—when he was transitioning from school back to home—was a regular stop at the corner deli on our way home, where he was allowed to pick out one snack to eat during our travel. Unfortunately, this routine was usually the first to go sideways, as it required us to be going home a particular way (past the deli and not around the block to stop at the grocery store, for example) and by a particular method (walking, as opposed to taking a bus). So if one day, we knew that we were going to have to stop at the pharmacy several blocks out of the way before going home, or if it was a nice day and we wanted to take him by the park for an hour before heading back, we made sure to set up his expectations before we even left the school building, and have backup plans in mind.

"So Sirus," I begin, making sure that I am talking to him at his level, crouched down in the hallway of the school, rather than standing over him. "I know we usually stop by the deli on the way home. But today I need to pick up some medicine from the pharmacy, so we are going there instead."

Inevitably, the beginnings of a meltdown surface. "Noooo," he starts to whine, his body going limp at the top in anticipation of throwing himself down.

A small change in routine like this might seem like such a superficial and tiny thing for a child to get so upset about, right? Is it just "playing into his hand" or "spoiling" him to be so sensitive? Shouldn't he learn to get over it? Remember, for the child with ASD, he has just spent all day in a sensory-overload environment, with a bunch of other kids making all kinds of noise and invading his personal space, breaking or enforcing different rules than what he has at home, obeying various authoritative sources that may be slightly contradictory and therefore confusing, eating food in a communal setting where pungent sights and smells are abundant, with very little recovery time. He has pushed himself through this all day with little protest, knowing that at the end of it, he gets to walk home with Mommy or Daddy and pick out his favorite snack at his favorite deli, like a small reward of familiarity to bring him peace after a day of chaos.

So no, he is not being overly sensitive, or manipulative. He is simply coping.

"Wait, listen, Sirus, I'm not done yet." I keep my tone light and inviting, a smile on my face to show that all is well. "Because we're going to the pharmacy instead, you will be able to pick out a snack there, just like you usually do at the deli."

"They have snacks?" he asks, his body calming as he recognizes the accommodation. I see him absentmindedly flip up the side of his shirt, where there is a tag on the inside seam. He starts to rub the tag between his fingers, shifting his weight from one foot to the other and back again. This type of behavior is common among people with autism—referred to as "stimming," and is similar to a nervous tic that a neurotypical person might have. He is outside of his comfort zone, hearing that his routine is being disrupted, but he is actively using tools he has cultivated for self-regulation and calming.

"Yes, they do," I affirm.

He continues rubbing the tag on his shirt as he answers. "Okay. But they have to have a snack that I like."

"They will. But if they don't, I have your favorite fruit snacks in my bag, just in case. Okay?"

"Just in case?" He lets go of the tag, feeling more secure.

"Yes, just in case the pharmacy doesn't have a snack that you like, I have a snack that you do like right here." I pull out the fruit snacks and show him, so that he has empirical evidence that a backup plan exists, and his "security blanket" is in place, just looking a little different from how it might usually look.

"Okay. Thanks, Mom! Let's go," he says, and bounds to the door, prepared for a new adventure.

Flexibility

If you have the blessing of sharing parenthood with a neurotypical partner, your children can benefit from your diverse perspectives and parenting
styles. If you and your partner are both beautifully ASD, your children will
benefit as well, in different ways. But if both parents are naturally routine-
heavy, you might want to consider structuring a certain amount of flexibility,
spontaneity, or other departure from your daily routine, so that your children
can begin to cultivate tolerance for—or even love of—flexibility.

While routines and setting expectations can be helpful in moving
through life more smoothly, it's also very important to learn to be flexible.

One of the ways that my husband very consciously does this for our son
is by taking different routes to get to the same places. Even if it's just walking
on the other side of the street when normally we don't cross until the next
block—little changes in the paths we traverse to show, passively, that there
are many different ways to get to the same end.

I also make a point of explicitly teaching flexibility to our son, in addition to these passive tolerance-builders, because I know he needs the low-
context, direct information.

"Sometimes it's important to be flexible," I will say to him, when we
need to make a change to our routine or when something doesn't go according to plan. "That way, we don't get stuck where we are, and we can find
a way to move on."

He has taken this learning to heart, and sometimes when we are trying
hard to help him through a moment of needing more flexibility, he surprises
us, taking the lead and saying, "Okay, just move on. Move on."

• • •

Here is an example of a moment when we explicitly showed Sirus how to be
more flexible:

"The water's too hot," came my son's voice from the bathroom. He had recently started taking showers rather than baths, which was easier for my husband to handle. Bath time used to be my territory, but when I was seven months pregnant with our second child, kneeling on the floor and bending over a tub to wash and corral an active toddler was no longer feasible.

"Okay," answered my husband. There was a pause while he adjusted the water temperature. "How's that?"

Another pause while Sirus, presumably, tested the water. "Good!" he proclaimed.

But then, a moment later. "Oh no, too cold."

"What do you mean?" Larry was keeping his tone level, despite rising impatience.

"It was too hot for my foot. Now it is just right for my foot, but too cold for my leg."

I heard my son say this and immediately pictured my husband's face contorting in pain. I put down the dish I was washing in the sink, dried my hands, and waddled as fast as I could over to the open bathroom door.

Larry had since consented to adjust the water temperature again, and Sirus was halfway into the shower. "Ooh," Sirus said, recoiling. "Now it's too hot for my arm."

I knew exactly what my son was going through. It happens to me every single time I take a shower, which is almost daily. I have learned from years of experience that there is simply no way to account for all the different temperatures that different parts of my body feel at different times, and that after a few minutes of being under the water, my body will adjust anyway.

Larry was near his wits' end, trying to accommodate our son as best he could, but saw no way out of this never-ending rabbit hole.

"Sirus," I said, keeping my voice factual. "I know the water feels a little different on different places of your body, but the water can only be one temperature. At some point you have to decide that it's good enough, not perfect for every part, and move on. So, is the water good enough?"

"Oh, okay, yes, it's good enough," he said, stepping all the way into the shower and starting to take out his bath toys.

Larry looked up at me with a face that clearly conveyed, *Thank all that is good in the world*, then said, "Pour me a whiskey please."

Clear Consequences

One of the most important aspects of setting expectations as a parent is to establish and maintain clear, consistent, and fair consequences. If I know what to expect as a result of my actions, I am more empowered to make the choices that I feel are right and that will create the end result that I want. If I don't know what to expect, it's like I've just jumped out of a plane and have no idea whether or not I have a parachute.

The best consequences are the ones that naturally occur as a result of a behavior. For example, if I don't put on my coat, I can't go outside. However, there are times when the natural consequence isn't enough to affect behavior in the way you might need.

With the coat example, at least for my son, not being able to go outside isn't necessarily a bad thing. The consequence of not going to the park might work for many toddlers to get them to put on their coat, but for a kid with ASD, who may be easily overwhelmed by all the stimulation he gets from being outside (the brightness of the sunlight, the change in temperature, the noise of the cars, the social interaction with other kids and people, etc.), staying inside might even be preferable to getting his coat on and going out to play.

When a natural consequence is not enough, it's a sign that something deeper might be going on that is a barrier for your child.

One day, for example, our son agreed to the consequence of not being able to have dessert because he would not eat the turkey sandwich that we'd made him for lunch. The fact that he would not eat the turkey, even to get his cookie, was a strong indicator that the turkey—for whatever reason—was simply inedible. It might have been the texture, the particular flavor of this brand of turkey—whatever the reason, it was a real enough issue for our son that the natural consequence of no dessert did not change his behavior and motivate him to eat the food that contained the nutrients his growing body needed. In that case, we needed to find another nutritious option for him to eat for lunch, since the natural consequence of no dessert ended up being preferable, to him, than the alternative of eating food that presented particular barriers.

Here is an example of a time when we were able to set a clear and consistent natural consequence that continues to work in affecting positive behavior change with our son:

"It's time for sleep now, Sirus. Lay down so I can tuck you in."

It was bedtime again, a source of both constant strain and precious moments in the life of any toddler.

My son was bouncing all over the bed, clearly playing for time.

"Come on, lay down please. Playtime is over. You need to sleep now." I could sense my hackles rising slightly, but I was patient. If I have one double-edged trait that is both a wonderful and also potentially harmful thing, it is my seemingly unending sense of patience.

"One more story?" Sirus asked, lying down but kicking his legs up in the air.

"No, hun. We read our story already, and we already had our five minutes of play. It's important that you get a good night's sleep." I started to layer his blankets and sheets just the way he liked them, but he was moving around so much that they were just falling off.

"Come on, Sirus," I said again.

"I need some water," he protested.

"You have your water bottle right here." I pointed to it, reminding him.

This was a solution we had developed to end the constant refrain of "I'm thirsty" and "I need a glass of water" tactics he had previously used to prolong bedtime. "You can drink from it on your own whenever you need."

"Oh, right," he said, and picked it up to take a swig. He lay down again, but then piped up with, "I'm hungry."

"You had a good dinner tonight, Sirus. And you had dessert. I don't think you're really hungry. I think you just don't want to go to sleep. But remember, you need to sleep well so that you can have energy for tomorrow."

"But I didn't have enough time to play," he persisted.

I don't remember how long this stretch of excuse after excuse for not lying down continued on, but it finally wore on my patience, which should probably have given way to firmer action several minutes ago.

"Mommy," said Larry from the doorway. "Something has to give. I know you are being patient with him, but this is really too much. He needs to know this is not okay."

Had my husband not intervened, I might have gone on like this with Sirus for half an hour or more, coming to the end completely drained and allowing Sirus to have exercised far too much control over a routine that is meant to soothe him into sleep mode by its slow and steady pace toward bed, not go on and on in response to his every whim.

But like any evolution in my usual way of doing things, I was at a loss to see how to do it differently.

"Try leaving," Larry suggested, recognizing my sense of grasping at straws.

"Leaving?" I wasn't sure what he meant.

"Yes." Larry had learned to spell new things out for me piece by piece, so that I could visualize each step and make it my own. "Not in anger, just in being done. Say good night, walk out of the room, close the door like usual, and let him fend for himself. He needs to lose something, or he won't change the behavior."

"But he won't stay in bed if I do that," I protested, spotting the problem in the change like I always do.

"I know." Larry nodded, as if that problem was the whole point of the new method. "When he gets up, ask him if he's ready to go to bed now, and then tuck him in like you usually do. If he starts making excuses, leave again. Make it clear that his time is up. Simple as that. Otherwise, you'll be in here forever and you'll lose yourself and come to a point where you have nothing left to give."

"Okay," I said, knowing in my bones that he was right and how easy it was for me to lose myself. I turned to Sirus, who had been busying himself with making a mess of his blankets. "Good night," I said to him, and both Larry and I walked calmly out of his room, closing his door behind us.

We hadn't gone two steps into the hallway before Sirus had climbed out of bed and opened his door, following us.

"Mama, come back," he said.

"Are you ready to go to bed now?" I asked.

"Yes, tuck me in please."

And he lay straight down in bed, permitted me to layer him in his sheet and blankets, gave me our customary goodnight hug and kiss, and started to rock himself to sleep while I stood in the room for another two minutes, as was our custom. When I finally blew one last kiss and left the room, closing his door behind me, he stayed in bed and went to sleep.

A year later, that simple, matter-of-fact consequence of me leaving the room with a more abrupt, but no less loving, "good night" whenever Sirus tries to turn bedtime into the song that never ends, still works. It is a clear, consistent, natural consequence that he knows to expect if he tries too many stalling tactics on his way to bed—but one that he also knows how to immediately reverse with a desired behavior.

FOLLOWING YOUR INSTINCTS

I want to take a moment here to specifically call out the power of instincts in parenting.

As someone with ASD, I don't often have real-time instincts to rely on when it comes to social cues, interpreting hidden meanings underneath what people say, or extrapolating the larger context. With time and applied analysis, though, I can often come to a very profound understanding later on, which I can begin to draw from during real-time interactions to create a facsimile of "instincts" in the moment, but this takes conscious effort and a tremendous amount of brainpower in real time. Instincts are meant to be effortless—a gut feeling—not manufactured learnings that I have to create from the analysis and interpretation of many interactions after-the-fact.

Often, my "instincts" about what might be going on beyond the surface of an interaction are entirely wrong, because of my struggles with theory of mind and high-context thinking. I might instinctually feel that someone is angry with me, for example, when in fact they are angry with the overarching situation, and it's only on the surface that their anger appears to be directed toward me.

But if you are an ASD parent of an ASD child, you have unique instincts about what your child is going through, what is going on inside their head that no one else can see, and you should trust them.

Like anything, sometimes your parenting instincts will be wrong.

But often you will find that your lived experience makes a world of difference in transcending potentially negative situations.

Here is an example of how I used my instincts to find out that a sensory barrier was getting in the way of my son's good behavior, rather than him simply being obstinate or contrary:

"Put on your coat, bud," Larry said, laying Sirus's winter jacket out on the floor for him.

"No!!!" Sirus, age three, protested.

"Come on, bud, show me your trick!" This tactic usually worked—empowering Sirus to do something cool that we all got to watch and praise him for. He was learning how to put on a coat by laying it flat on the floor, standing at the head of the coat, putting both of his arms down through the arms of the coat, and flipping the whole thing up and over his head, so that it settled down around his shoulders.

"Noooo!!!" Sirus said again, clearly upset.

"If you don't put your coat on, then we can't go to the park." Larry tried a different tack, a logical consequence for Sirus's lack of cooperation.

"No! I want to go to the park!"

"Well then—coat," Larry persisted, pointing.

Sirus stomped and flopped and was now on the floor, crying.

I had finished putting on my own coat and now engaged to offer support. In my heart I knew something was wrong. I remembered when I was young and getting ready to go outside, and how any number of things could set me off—a rock in my shoe, an itchy hat, a scarf that smelled like it needed to be washed. "Hey, Sirus," I said. "It's okay, hun. Come on, let's talk. Come sit with me."

This is one way to get your toddler out of "flopping on the floor" mode and into "sitting and listening" mode. I literally sat on the floor next to him and invited him into my lap. He picked himself up off the floor and came willingly into my arms.

"I see you're upset." This acknowledgment helps too. Just letting your child know that they are seen, they are heard, their opinion matters, even if eventually your opinion is what will carry the day because you see and know more than they do, they are still human and deserving of acknowledgment.

He nodded.

"You want to go to the park, right?"

He nodded again.

"So why won't you put on your coat? It's cold outside. You need to stay warm while we are out."

"Because!" he said. I waited, knowing he was still gathering his words. "Because, it's—" He left my lap, picked up the coat, and fingered the edge of the sleeve. "It's too hard. See?" He held it up for me to examine.

I wasn't sure what he meant, but I took the coat and felt the sleeve edge. It was quite stiff—it was one of those styles that had some kind of reinforcement at the sleeve opening to keep it round and rigid. "You mean, the sleeves are too stiff?"

"Yes, stiff," Sirus agreed. Then, feeling validated, he extrapolated. "And here." He gestured to his own neck and chin, and, coat still in hand, I moved my hands up to the collar of the coat, where again it was reinforced and rigid. "Too hard on my skin," Sirus finished, becoming sullen again as he realized that if he couldn't suffer through wearing his coat, he couldn't go to the park.

I showed the problem to Larry, who was mildly astonished that our toddler could be so obstinate about a simple sensory thing, though he was ready to support something that was obviously important to Sirus. So Larry and I pulled together a sweater and a raincoat from Sirus's other gear, and agreed that we could still go to the park if he wore both of them, instead of his winter coat. Right away Sirus was on board with the new plan.

The next day, we all went together to a children's clothing store and had Sirus try on various coats, so that he was empowered to choose one that didn't cause him so much sensory difficulty.

Since then, we engage Sirus directly in any coat-purchasing process, so that we don't accidentally get something for him that will turn going outside into an unnecessary battle. We have never had another issue of that magnitude with Sirus refusing to put on his coat.

RECOGNIZING, REGULATING, AND EXPRESSING EMOTIONS

One final set of tools I want to cover when looking specifically at parenting as an adult with ASD is emotions.

Yes, your emotions are a tool.

Believe me, I know—emotions can be a rough territory for someone with autism. Some people with ASD are overly emotive, others hardly show any emotions at all. As I mentioned earlier, some have alexithymia, which is a clinical inability to recognize emotions. Others experience emotions so deep and vast that they easily overwhelm. My experience has always been a confusing combination of all of these things—usually I exist in a kind of emotional "no-man's-land," a comfortable neutral setting that is neither too high nor too low. But given certain stimuli, I can very quickly go over an emotional edge one way or the other. And while I do have the ability to recognize and identify certain emotions, it can be very hard for me to name or explain them verbally to someone else, and if I don't know why a certain emotion is being experienced (either by me or by someone else), it can be very hard for me to recognize. It's like looking at a blank book, knowing that other people can see writing on the pages, but I can't.

Your children will learn methods for regulating their own big emotions from watching how you regulate yours. If you yell when you're angry, they will yell when they're angry. If you clap when you're happy, they'll clap when they're happy. Up until they reach a certain age, "what you sow is what you get" when it comes to emotional reactions and regulation.

Modeling Emotional Stability

You can help your child navigate through their big emotions—which often cause meltdowns or tantrums or other behavior problems—by modeling stability in the way that you regulate your own emotions.

This is especially true when you are reacting to their emotions.

A great method I have found for keeping myself grounded when faced with the unpredictable throes of toddler emotions is something I read in *Raising Your Spirited Child* by Mary Sheedy Kurcinka, Ed.D. Kurcinka talks about the "red zone"—a highly charged emotional state where your brain floods with fight-or-flight chemicals, and rational thought is difficult to find. This is preceded by the "yellow zone," which is when you start to feel the red zone coming on, recognizing warning signs of elevated heart rate, rising voice, tensing body, etc. And then of course there's the "green zone," which is when your emotions are in a happy place, or at least calm, and you can think clearly.

Young children can dive right into the "red zone" very quickly—like flipping a switch—which can be disconcerting. If one minute everything seems fine and the next your toddler is screaming and kicking on the floor, it can feel like the world just turned upside down. You can very easily start heading for the red zone yourself.

But the key is to keep yourself, as much as possible, in the green zone. Take deep breaths, give yourself a sixty-second break from the situation if you can, grab a glass of water, crouch down to the floor—whatever it is that you find helps you stay out of the red zone and keep calm.

Your child will use you as an anchor, and if you are both in the red zone, that will only anchor them deeper into the red zone. If you model staying in the green zone, it will be easier for you to pull your child back to green with you.

USING EMOTIONS AS A TOOL

That said, I have learned that there are also times when it is important, as a parent, to let your child see your emotions.

They need to learn that you are not perfect, that you get emotional, too, and they need to see what you do about it. You can develop healthy responses to your own emotions which you can show to your children in real time by "practicing what you preach."

If I just existed nonstop in complete emotional middle ground, or total "green zone" zen, my son would not learn that it is okay, sometimes, to get upset.

The key here is not to get *too* upset. It's okay—and essential—to show emotion. But measure it. Use it as a teaching and learning tool, not as a punishment or an excuse to lose control.

Be honest with your children about how you are feeling. It's okay to say "I'm upset" or "I'm sad."

Take care to frame your emotional state in a way that does not lay all the blame on your child, however. "You made me sad" is a heavy burden to put on a young child, and one that—especially if they have autism—they could easily internalize to a highly negative degree. Instead, saying, "What you did made me sad," is more accurate, and more solvable, in your child's mind.

By the same token, it's also important to show and share your positive emotions.

"That makes me very happy" or "I'm so proud of you" can go a very long way in reinforcing behaviors that you want your child to continue to cultivate.

I have found that a key emotion to model well is disappointment.

Disappointment can be an enormous source of strife for your young child, and especially if they are autistic. If something doesn't go to plan, if expectations are not met, if the vision they had in their mind is not fulfilled—it can feel like the entire world descends into chaos in that moment. As someone with ASD, if my expectations about something are not met, it feels as if the floor has suddenly disappeared underneath my feet. Everything about my existence is called into question—is the sun still at the center of the solar system? Is gravity still valid? Are atoms still the building blocks of matter? This is the level of existential crisis that my brain goes through when plans change, when something unexpected happens, when I am disappointed by something, or when I disappoint someone else.

Imagine feeling that as a child, and not knowing how it came about or what to do about it or even what it really means.

I want to reiterate that this is true whether I am the person who is disappointed, or if I am the person who has disappointed someone else. The feeling is the *same*.

So when my son does something that disappoints me, or when I experience something else that is disappointing, I try very hard to model a measured, honest response. It's okay to be disappointed. The world will not end. Life will go on. But if it's brushed away too easily, it does not become an opportunity for learning and growth.

I think that is the key for me in handling disappointment—the opportunity for learning. I have explained it that way to our son, as well. Yes, it is sad, and yes, it hurts, but it's worth it, as long as we learn from it, and endeavor to do better next time.

That way, you can show your child how to sit with the disappointment for a short while, how to realize that the world still goes on, and then how to move forward and try to prevent it from happening again the same way in the future.

Use your own emotions as learning tools for your children, and you will find yourself learning new things right along with them.

LARRY'S TWO CENTS

Kids grow up quickly! I know that may not be big news, yet the pace still surprises me sometimes. Their whole job is to grow, to learn, to evolve, each and every day. And it can be challenging, both for them and their caregivers. Parents are constantly asking themselves when they should reinforce a boundary or routine. When has the child progressed enough that what we did before is no longer appropriate and needs to change? Add in a second child growing at their own pace, and it's survival mode.

All parents can relate to this. But throw in the variable of my ASD spouse and her craving for consistency, and you have an exponentially more stressful set of circumstances.

For Sarah, each and every day seems to present a new challenge, and watching her is akin to watching a sporting event where sometimes she is on a great run and other times, it seems she can't buy a bucket. For those non-basketball fans, just imagine trying to put a couch pillow back on the sofa, only to see it mysteriously fall off, over and over again. On those good days, the kids wake up on time and the schedule goes fairly to script. At the end of them, Sarah is still exhausted and ready to go to sleep early. However, on the bad days, when they seem hell-bent on testing boundaries, Sarah is primed for a meltdown—but she knows the kids need her, so she masks her emotions and gets through the day, collapsing onto the couch after everyone's in bed, a shell of herself.

Fortunately (I think), I am a technology enthusiast, and always looking for ways to make things easier in our home life as much as I try to do professionally. Some of my gadgets or apps turn out to be helpful, like our early adoption of home grocery delivery. (Ask me about the time I dragged Sarah through a full-sized supermarket when we were dating. It's a miracle she didn't pass out.)

The more I've identified and we've incorporated such technology-based solutions into our day-to-day lives, the less Sarah has to put energy toward thinking about certain problems, like facilitating transitions (yay, timers!) or remembering to add something to the grocery list (yay, voice-activated list creation!). These home tools give her more energy to focus on the myriad of other things she needs to do as a parent, like regulating the emotions of a toddler as he gets ready for school in the morning or making sure each child has what they need ready and available in the house.

Which leads us to the number-one best purchase of my life, the Amazon Echo device(s). It turns out that kids like interacting with cool technology, and, better yet, do a reasonably good job of following through when they receive an instruction from such a device (as opposed to, say, Mom and Dad). There has not been a day where we have not set a fifteen-minute timer before turning off the TV, or an alarm to get in the bath at 7:15. Even more amazing is the willingness of our child to now set his own alarms, with a sense of pride and accomplishment.

With some reflection, Sarah realized that in her own life growing up, it was easy for her to get lost on a single task for endless hours and then loathe the energy it would take to switch gears. This awareness and understanding has helped to manage our son through transitions. In many ways, parenting has taught Sarah more about herself—which hacks work, and how to model them so our children can learn by example.

To further this awareness, I continually remind Sarah of a very profound realization she had when asked how it was being a mom to a now-walking toddler. Her answer was that it is wonderful to experience life again, through her child.

Of course, past successes do not guarantee future wins. Each day is a new, unique challenge—and a mixed blessing. Knowing there is no real chance to ever skate through a day is difficult, and very real, for Sarah. On the other hand, being mindful that challenges will inevitably arise, gives her a leg up on managing her emotions and energy. Every parent strives to feel that sense of capability, knowing you are doing the best you can for your child.

CHAPTER SEVEN

Troubleshooting and Self-Care Strategies

"I have learned to accept the fact that I will make mistakes at nearly every turn, but that those mistakes can be softened if I am honest about who I am."

—LIANE HOLLIDAY WILLEY

Sometimes, everything falls apart. Sometimes, it can feel like whatever you do, whatever you try, everything just comes out wrong.

That's okay. That's part of life.

And if you are someone with ASD or similar tendencies, that can increase both the frequency and intensity of these feelings. This chapter is about what I try to do when it happens to me, so that I can mitigate, recover from, and prevent those feelings in the future.

Taking care of yourself is the most important thing you can do to be successful, whatever your definition of success.

OVERLOAD: SENSORY AND/OR EMOTIONAL

What Does It Look Like?

Sensory or emotional overload can look and feel very different for different people.

Usually, at least for someone with ASD, sensory or emotional overload results in some form of "meltdown." For some, this will be externally focused, like an explosion—shouting, throwing, using hurtful language, walking away. For others, it will be internally focused, like depression—imploded posture, inability to move, unresponsiveness.

What we must remember, whether ASD or NT, is that a meltdown is real. It is not a put-on or a manipulation. It is not someone being weak or immature or lacking self-control. If it's you melting down, don't discount your own experience. You are human, and what you are feeling is real. Allow yourself to feel what you are feeling so you can get through it to the other side, even if the logical part of your brain is telling you it's silly. What will be important, as explored later in this section, is developing the skills to get through the melt-down without unintentionally hurting someone else—especially your loved ones, usually the most likely people to witness you going into overload.

Why Does It Happen?

Sensory or emotional overload can happen to a lot of people with ASD, and for many different reasons.

We've talked a lot about how the ASD brain can be hypersensitive to details, which can be both an advantage and a disadvantage. I have heard of this trait being described as "living life with the volume turned all the way up." And to me, that's precisely how it feels sometimes.

While someone who is neurotypical might be experiencing what feels like a completely normal atmosphere, I'm cringing from all the noise, lights, and smells that are bombarding all of my senses. My brain is taking in all the details, without my consent or control. The volume is way too loud for me, while that same volume on someone else's life might be perfectly comfort-able because they are not absorbing as much.

You can imagine how one could get overloaded.

But I can also experience a sensory overload in a relatively quiet, calm place. It might be that I just finished a hectic day or week, or I have spent all day in uncomfortable shoes or tight clothing. Something might be on my mind and taking up so much brain space that I have little room for anything else, or one tiny thing might be the "final grain of sand" that tips my scales into overload.

While sensory overload is most often triggered by sensory input, like bright lights or uncomfortable clothing or the psychological "sensation" of being very busy, emotional overload is a bit different.

When I experience emotional overload, it usually comes on because of a particularly heated or confusing interaction with someone else. For me, emotional overload is not like what I experienced when my father died. That kind of overwhelming and unparalleled grief is its own kind of hurdle, which all human beings experience. ASD-related emotional overload, on the other hand, usually happens to me for one of two reasons:

- **Analysis-Paralysis.** I can get so wrapped up in trying to understand and decipher the emotions involved in an interaction—either mine or someone else's—that my brain short-circuits. Is the other person angry or sad? Or both? Why? Are they angry with the situation, or with me, or with themselves, or all three? What about the situation could have made them angry, or what could I have done differently, if in fact they are angry with me? How am I feeling about this—is that tightness in my chest remorse, or am I actually feeling unjustly blamed, or am I just plain confused? All the while that I am trying to logically parse out whatever emotional thing is happening, I am also panicking inside that any emotion is happening at all, and that I don't know how to stop it or how to fix it.

- **Over-Empathizing.** You may have heard the myth that people with autism have little or no ability to experience empathy. This is factually incorrect. In fact, many people with ASD experience *too much* empathy. The misperception stems in part, I think, from the fact that empathy may look different coming from someone with ASD, and may require a different level of input (you might need to explain to me that you are feeling sad, and why, before I will be able to empathize, because I might not be able to intuit your emotions from your nonverbal language).

In the case of emotional overload, I can experience deep, paralyzing, unending depression from seeing a person who is homeless setting up a place to sleep for the night against the side of a building. In my mind, I am that person, and I am imagining all of the life situations I must have gone through before I got to that point, and how I must feel now, with nowhere to turn. I can't watch the news anymore because if a story comes on about a mother who was killed in a car accident or a man who was robbed on the sidewalk, my entire day can become a spiral of depression as I live inside that moment like it was me or my own mother in the car, or my husband walking down the street—or even me forced into a position of having to rob someone else to get what I needed. None of these are my own emotions having to do with my own life situation, and yet they are forced onto me by my environment and by over-empathizing with the people and world around me.

What's the Solution?

There are many different tools you can use, as someone who experiences overload or as a person who is close to someone else who experiences overload, to help while it's happening, to recover afterward, and to prevent it from getting to that point in the future. Below are a few of the tools that have worked best for me.

What You Can Do in the Moment
Grounding

One of the best tools I have found for combatting sensory or emotional overload while it is actively crashing down over me is *grounding*. Grounding is something that I have been doing since childhood, a coping mechanism developed over many years. It wasn't until recently that I read about it elsewhere and realized that, with some refinement, it is a tool that can work for many people going through similar situations.

The essential idea is to ground oneself in the present moment. Not even just in the sense of time, but physically, too. To focus your attention on the solid facts of physical reality right in front of you: *The floor is hard. The wall is white. The air is temperate.*

This helps rein in your overstimulated senses, forcing them to focus on one single, broad detail at a time. So instead of passively absorbing that there are seven distinct shades of brown in the hardwood floor, in a way that makes your brain hurt, you actively focus your attention on a singular fact: *The floor is hard.* Think of nothing else in that moment. Then move on to the next single fact: *My body is tense.* Or: *The door is closed.*

Avoid any judgment, such as "The carpet is orange. I don't like that color; it's too bright." Just observe that the carpet is orange and move on to the next solid fact.

Another way to ground, if your environment is not conducive to zeroing in on specific facts that you observe, is to play a fact-based game in your head. One by one, name and picture each species of dog that you know. Or—one of my favorites that I learned as a kid—think of the names of places, except that every place has to start with the last letter of the last place (so for example, if the first place I think of is New York, the next place name I would think of might be Kenya, then perhaps Ann Arbor, etc.). The purpose of this mental exercise is to take you out of whatever immediate stressor is triggering the overload, to remind you that you exist outside of the overload. This is only a single moment in time. The world will go on.

Grounding is a technique used in cognitive behavioral therapy to help someone "detach," in the moment, from strong emotions. Turning the focus of your attention outward, rather than inward, helps to access the rational part of your brain, to override your natural fight-or-flight response. Grounding has worked for me for both sensory and emotional overload situations, allowing me to get back to thinking rationally enough to remove myself from the situation, or to change my perspective of the interaction in order to protect my psychological health.

SOS Trigger Words

Another tool which helps in the moment, but which you will need to prepare in advance in order to be effective, is a "trigger word" you can use to signal to someone else—or to yourself—that you are in overload.

In chapter 5 on Long-Term Neurodiverse Relationships, I touched on this idea of a previously-agreed-upon word that can act as a kind of "alarm bell" that you or your partner can use to signal that something in the interaction needs to change. In the case of emotional or sensory overload, it can be easier to choke out a single trigger word in a moment of crisis than trying to have to find the words to explain that you are overloading and that you need a break.

My mother actually taught me this one when I was a kid and would fall into bouts of being completely nonverbal. It usually happened when I was experiencing emotional overload, though we didn't know to call it that at the time. She helped me learn how to recognize when emotional overload was on its way—my throat would start to get tight and hot. As soon as I started feeling that—no matter what else was happening or who was in the room or what we were talking about—I was to interrupt and say our SOS word: R2D2. I have no idea why we centered on a Star Wars character for our word—neither of us was a huge fan of the series—but I think it was important to have a word that neither of us would normally say on a regular basis, so that we both knew it was a clear signal. After we established the trigger word, I used it more than once, and every time, my mom knew it was time to take a step back and give me some space to recover, rather than try to get any further interaction out of me in that moment.

What You Can Do to Recover
Alone and/or Quiet Time

After getting to the point of emotional or sensory overload—or, if you can learn to recognize the signs, before—it can be very restorative to give yourself time to recover.

One of the best ways for me to recover from overload is to reduce external stimulation (like putting myself in a dark, quiet room where I can be on my own for a few minutes). For others, it might be listening to your favorite song, or getting close time with a loved one.

Here is an example of a time when I teetered on the edge of sensory overload, and used quiet alone time to bring myself back to center and away from the precipice:

One morning, I walked out of our bedroom, baby in hand, and immediately got a piercing headache from the living room light that we had left on the previous night. We usually leave a light on somewhere in the apartment these days, in case we have to be up in the middle of the night with the baby. Our standing lamp in the living room has two settings: Bright Light or Low Light. Moving from our dark bedroom into the Bright Light, right after an abrupt awakening by a crying baby, was too much for my head.

I put the baby down, and forced myself to move closer to the source of the light, even though it made my head pound, in order to reach out and switch the lamp from the Bright setting to the Low setting.

The pain subsided somewhat, but my body was still on high alert.

Suddenly, our toddler came stomping out of his room down the hall. "HELP ME-HEE-EE!" he screeched, his voice breaking in distress as he experienced his own sensory struggles transitioning from asleep to awake, from dark to light.

I ran to assist, already feeling dizzy.

I helped him get untangled from the blankets he was trying to bring out to the living room with him, undoubtedly seeking comfort and a semblance of temperature control as he went from warm and cozy in bed to cold and exposed in the open air of the apartment.

Bending down and straightening up again several times, to help him get his legs unraveled from his favorite blanket, left me feeling even dizzier.

My son then proceeded to climb lovingly into my lap as we settled next to the baby in the living room, pressing his face into mine, arms entwining in my hair. Normally I treasure cuddle time with my son, who doesn't often sit still long enough to enjoy it much, but this morning, his forceful advances—as he bounced all over my torso and nearly knocked me over several times—left me feeling like I was being squeezed through the eye of a needle and shoved into an active car wash at the same time.

I took one look at my husband as he came out of the bedroom half an hour later, and proclaimed, probably louder than I needed to, that I needed ten minutes to lie down in *quiet* before I could do anything else.

By this point in our relationship, I had developed enough self-awareness—and he had developed enough understanding of my needs—for us to successfully navigate what could have turned very quickly into a bad day. I could have shot vitriol at him for leaving the living room light on the Bright setting the night before. I could have lain down on the floor trying not to cry, not knowing what was wrong with me. Instead, I asked for ten minutes to recover. He was able to recognize "impending sensory overload" written all over my face and mussed hair, and did not hesitate to redirect our son's attention so that I could go lie down. After just ten minutes of decompressing alone in the dark, I was able to avoid completely melting down. I got back up, energized, no longer dizzy, and ready to help my son get dressed and off to school.

Ever since that morning, I make doubly sure that our living room lamp is either off or on the Low Light setting before we go to bed, so that I have one less intense sensory input to deal with right at the start of my day.

What You Can Do to Prevent

Sensory Protection Items

One of the best ways to help yourself never actually get to the point of sensory overload is to wear sensory protection items like sunglasses or headphones when you know you are going to be in situations that will challenge your senses.

Our son, for example, is highly sensitive to sound.

It's not just that he is physically affected by loud noises, it's also that any prolonged exposure to noise in general can start to send him reeling. Normally, he can get through most days without much strife—the noise of general city life has become something of a backdrop for him, in between the time that he spends at home or at school.

One weekend we went down into the subway system with him, and the noises of the trains as they zoomed and screeched and clanged into the stations were just too much. He bore it on our way into the city, covering his ears when he needed to, and otherwise distracting himself with other things like the fact that we were riding on the train, the people we saw, the ads on the walls, etc. But then at the end of the day, when we were about to head back down into the subway system to go home, he melted down. "It's too loud!!" was his complaint. He had had all he could take for one day.

Ever since then, whenever we know we are going to have to use the subway to get somewhere with our son, we bring a pair of big green noise-cancelling headphones that he wears over his ears, and he has no problems.

If, for whatever reason, you'd rather not walk around wearing big head-phones, there are more discreet options for ear protection, such as clear or skin-tone ear plugs. For me, just using a pair of regular audio ear buds and listening to music or an audiobook dampens enough of the surrounding sound to help me stay centered.

Another thing I do to help me survive city life is make sure that I always have some kind of scarf on when I use public transportation. No matter the weather—if it's springtime I'll use a lightweight scarf, as opposed to a heavier knitted one. If it's summer, I might have a bandana or other small piece of cloth in my pocket or bag. This is because you never quite know what smells you might encounter when using public transit in a big city—everything from strong food smells to body odor to urine. On a subway train, it can be very difficult to remove oneself from a smelly situation, at least until the train gets to the next station and opens its doors. So having a scarf around my neck allows me to discreetly cover my nose in situations where a smell that might not be bothering most other people is going to make me gag.

One other example I want to share has to do with using a preventative sensory protection item in a work setting:

We had no window in our shared, three-person office.

This was both an advantage, with little need for additional climate control, and a disadvantage, with zero natural lighting and a kind of stuffy feeling—like being in a big, comfortable closet.

Without any natural light, we had to rely on the overhead lights in order to see our work and each other. But they were quite bright.

I bought a floor lamp, so that when it was just me in the office, I could keep the overhead lights off, leaving half the office in darkness. On days when everybody was in, however, that solution no longer worked.

I started to get headaches halfway through the day, hardly able to keep my eyes open on the days when we had the overheads on. By the end of those days, I would be squinting at my computer, holding my head with one hand, unable to concentrate.

So I bought a visor to wear at work. I wanted something very discrete, small, black, and simple. I started putting it on whenever we had a full office and needed all the lights.

It blocked the overhead glare from reaching me—keeping my eyes in shade, which was all I needed.

"Sarah looks like she's ready for a card game," remarked one of my colleagues from another department as he stopped by our office, chuckling. Indeed, the visor was very much the same size, shape, and fit as the type that a card dealer would wear in a game of poker.

"These lights are giving me a headache," I responded lightly, mirroring his chuckle to let him know I wasn't offended, and gesturing to the ceiling. I had no problem being entirely honest about why I was wearing the visor, without going into any more detail than necessary.

My colleague accepted this explanation without comment—no doubt he had experienced his own light-induced headache once or twice.

I shared the above example for two reasons:

- One is to make the point that, in the case of your work environment, especially if you spend multiple hours a day there, it can be very helpful to take the time to assess what sensory needs you might have, and to implement any changes necessary to ensure that you are comfortable in your work space. If you don't have the power to alter your own work space, advocate to your boss or to whomever would make those decisions.

- And the second is to illustrate that other people may decide to comment on your sensory protection items, especially if they are outside the "norm," like big headphones or a visor. It's an almost subconscious reaction that we have as human beings—more so neurotypical brains than ASD brains, but both to certain degrees. It's part of our neural makeup to try to conform to societal norms; it evolved as a survival tactic. So if somebody sees something that they don't normally see, they may call attention to it. Hopefully, like in the above example, they do it in a lighthearted and nonthreatening way. If so, I have found that there is no reason to take it as a threat and turn it into a negative interaction. I let the other person make their comment and go on with their day. I'm as honest as I want to be in my response. However, if someone is not lighthearted about it, or if someone makes more than one comment, or makes you uncomfortable in any way, then it may need to be addressed more directly. Don't let anyone make you feel any lesser for being proactive and taking care of yourself.

NEGATIVE SPIRALING

What Does It Look Like?

On the outside, a person who has entered a negative internal spiral may not look any different from another person.

Perhaps they might seem distracted or preoccupied, or a little down. My husband, who has known me for ten years, says he can see it in my eyes when I am headed into, or deep in the midst of, a spiral.

Internally, though, a negative spiral can feel all-consuming, torturous, and unstoppable.

Why Does It Happen?

For me, it happens right after a negative interaction with someone. It could be with anyone—my husband, a friend, a colleague, a random stranger. If the interaction did not go as planned, or could have gone better in any way, I immediately fall into analysis mode, trying to work out what happened and how I can do it better next time.

Sometimes this is okay and results in good insight. Other times, however, and especially if the interaction contained any raised emotions, this can trigger a downward spiral into what-ifs and self-doubt. *What did she mean when she said that? Could she really have meant this instead? Was she being sarcastic? Did I misinterpret her meaning? Did she think I was being rude when I responded? Was I too direct? Should I have framed it differently?*

Invariably, I won't be able to work out all the intricacies of the interaction on my own, and I will end up hyper-focusing on the most negative aspects—something that the other person said to me that was particularly hurtful, or something that I said that ended up being way too awkward or tactless or taken in completely the wrong way. My brain will put them on replay, like a broken record, repeating them over and over and over again.

What's the Solution?

For me, once a negative spiral gets to the point of auto-replay, there is no "off" button.

I have to either actively distract my brain with something else, or start repeating my own contradictory phrases back to myself.

What You Can Do in the Moment
Distraction

One of the best ways I have found to stop a negative spiral in its tracks is to fully immerse myself in something entirely different. It has to be something all-consuming—like a grueling physical activity, or diving headfirst into my special interest.

The idea for a distraction tactic is not necessarily to reverse the spiral

> ## AN IMPORTANT NOTE:
> ## WRITING ABOUT SPIRALS
>
> I would *not* recommend doing this while you are in the middle of a spiral. I have tried this, and while it may work for some, for me it just made the whole thing worse because my brain's insistence on repeating the negative phrases or thoughts over and over again actually came out on the paper and all I ended up with was a written version of the spiral right there in front of me, which was even more horrifying. Instead, I wait until after the spiral has stopped, perhaps several hours or even days afterward, and then I go back and write down some of my thoughts about the catalyzing interaction.

but simply to break it—stop it in its tracks, fracture the flow of energy into the spiral so that it fades on its own.

Even then the spiral will usually still continue in the background for a short while until I get far enough into the distraction that no more brain space is available for anything else.

Positive Affirmations

If no distraction all-consuming enough is readily available, another tactic I have used successfully to combat a negative spiral is to have a set of positive affirmations—prepared in advance and perhaps written down somewhere I can access them easily—that I can say to myself over and over again.

If you have to say them out loud first in order to get them to be loud enough inside your own head, then do it—even if it means you have to step away for a minute and go to the bathroom or another private space.

Positive affirmations have often been caricatured in mainstream media as a person looking at themselves in a mirror and saying over and over, "I am worthy . . . I love myself . . ." etc.

But what's missing from this depiction is that positive affirmations can be (and often are) used by very strong individuals with a positive sense of self, just as a mental tool to escape the torture their brain is putting them through without their consent.

If my brain is yelling at me over and over, "Why don't you understand? Why don't you understand? Why don't you understand?" I'm going to need to drown out the unnecessary repetition with a more desirable repetition of my own. "I am kind, I am patient, I am learning," I might start repeating to myself in my head. Not because I don't already believe these things about myself, but precisely because I *do*, and therefore they hold enough power to drown out the negative message.

My advice is to zero in on some of the attributes about yourself that you prize above all others—your intelligence, your bravery, your creativity—and turn them into affirmations that you can pull out at a moment's notice.

Write them down—in a note that you keep in your wallet, or type it into your phone—so that as you learn to use these affirmations as a tool, you can refer to them when needed.

For a specific example of positive affirmations in action, see the "Making Space for Mistakes" section in chapter 5.

What You Can Do to Recover

Write It Out

A negative spiral can be so damaging that even after you stop it, it might still be there, waiting in the background for your brain to turn idle again.

More than once I have slipped back into a negative spiral because I didn't take the time afterward to unpack it and remove its power.

One method I have found of unpacking a negative spiral so that it doesn't happen again, is to write down what occurred.

I start by just describing the facts of what happened. What was the context, what did I say, what did the other person say, etc. Then I start with some reasoned, measured analysis—not a bunch of what-ifs and second-guessing, just conclusions that I have come to about why it went sideways. I try very hard not to speculate when writing it out—this is simply a record of where my analysis has landed, not a place to start another spiral of potentials. If I start to spiral again into conjecture while writing, I stop, let it all rest in the back of my mind for a while longer, and perhaps come back to writing later, after my brain has worked out more of what happened, or after I've had a chance to talk it out with someone.

Then I will move to writing about solutions. What will I do the next time this kind of thing happens in an interaction? What have I learned?

This process of writing it out helps to lessen its power over my idle brain cycles, and it gives my brain the space it wanted in the first place to analyze what happened.

What You Can Do to Prevent
Compartmentalize

Now that I have learned how to recognize a negative spiral before it takes root—as soon as I hear in my head a single repeat of what someone else said to me, I know it is ripe for a spiral—I have learned how to head it off at the pass, trap it in a mental "box" that gets set off to the side, and keep myself from entering the never-ending loop.

Ironically, life's other demands have helped me tremendously with this. I can't really afford to be trapped in a negative spiral when my four-year-old is begging me to play, or when I have an important event or meeting coming up at work. I *had* to learn how to compartmentalize, as we all do to some degree, just to get through life and work without breaking down.

It can be done consciously, however, which is always the most reliable way.

If you've ever heard someone say during a meeting, "put a pin in it" or "put that idea in the parking lot for now," you've witnessed compartmentalizing. Mentally, this is what I do when I spot a negative spiral starting to churn up. "Put a pin in it," I literally tell myself, and literally stick a big mental pin into the phrase that is about to start on repeat in my head. Once it's stuck, I build a metal box around it in my head and leave it off to the side until I have time to come back to it later. Usually, when I come back to it after some time has passed, it has lost a lot of its power, and when I open the box, it's just that one phrase waiting there for me to get rid of it, rather than the beginning of an unstoppable tornado.

INTERNALIZATION

What Does It Look Like?

In a way, internalizing is akin to negative spiraling, but I want to explore it separately, as it is a much broader problem.

When someone internalizes something, it means they incorporate it into their personal being. A very straightforward example of this is when someone tells a child that she is "shy," and she incorporates that descriptor into how she sees herself as a person. A less clear-cut example is when my husband tells me that he is cold, and I internalize that it's my fault for not turning the heat up in our apartment or making sure a blanket was within arm's reach of the couch.

Internalizing is also akin to what's known as "taking things personally," except that instead of taking offense and seeking to place blame externally, internalizers place the blame on themselves. To illustrate the difference: Say a colleague and I are presenting a joint report, and we are each working on separate elements of the presentation before we come together to combine our sections. When we bring our separate pieces together, my colleague strongly suggests some significant changes in the way I am presenting my sections. If I were to take this personally, I might take offense, thinking that my colleague's changes to my work are a personal attack against me, implying that I am incompetent or incapable, which upsets me. I might think to myself that my colleague is being overbearing or too controlling. Conversely, if I were to internalize my colleague's suggestions as opposed to taking them personally, I might think to myself, "Oh, they're right. I'm wrong. They are so much better at this than I am. I can never get anything right. I should just do whatever they think and never try to put together my own presentation again." I would still be reacting to a (wrongly) perceived implied incompetence, but instead of taking offense to this, I would take it to heart.

A healthier interaction would be to find a middle ground—to neither internalize my colleague's suggested changes as proof that I am incompetent, nor to take my colleague's suggestions personally as some kind of attack, but instead to feel strong and confident enough in my own abilities and position to be able to hear my colleague's suggestions and decide to either incorporate them or not, based on our mutual discussion.

Over-internalizing can also result, for me and for many others with ASD, in what appears to be a nonverbal "episode." I can get so wrapped up in my own thoughts that it becomes almost impossible to verbalize them out loud. In certain extreme situations—which happened to me routinely in childhood, but very rarely as an adult—I might be shouting something inside my own head but be unable to say it aloud.

Why Does It Happen?

A lot of people internalize, for many different reasons.

For me, the traits specifically associated with my ASD make internalizing much more automatic, and much harder to overcome.

To begin with, at the most basic level, my internal world is much bigger than my external world. I think more than I talk. I think and think and over-think. This environment is the perfect breeding ground for internalization, or placing blame internally rather than externally.

Secondly, when I do talk, it's usually for a specific purpose, like to affect a change, or to relay necessary information. I don't naturally communicate just to convey implicit or explicit emotions, as described in chapter 1. For example, I'm not just naturally going to come out with "It's a nice day," because that informa-tion is not useful (to me). Why state the obvious? But of course, many people communicate this way in order to establish an underlying emotional connection, not because the information itself is important. Because I communicate mostly for the purposes of information exchange rather than emotional exchange, my first gut reaction is always to assume that other people are doing the same—so if my husband tells me he is cold, it must be because he wants me to do something about it or because I should have done something about it before, not because he is just making light conversation or trying to share his experience with me.

This also means that I don't often share my feelings unless I have a plan for what to do about them. I might be feeling very sad about something, but unless I am specifically asking someone to help me with the emotion, I may never verbalize it. This can be problematic when the emotion is strong enough to be affecting the way that I interact with the world, or when I need help with something but don't know how to ask for it. I end up just keeping everything inside instead of bringing it up to another person who might be able to help. If I don't already have a strategy to fix it, I rarely bring it up on my own.

A third key ASD-related trait that exacerbates my internalization ten-dency is struggling with a concept we discussed earlier in the book, called "theory of mind." If you recall, this is the ability for one person to under-stand that another person might be feeling and thinking something en-tirely different when presented with the same stimuli. I understand this, intellectually. But in practice, it can be very hard for me to grasp that no-body else has any sort of access to my internal world, aside from what I communicate outward (either verbally or nonverbally). To me, my internal world is 90 percent of THE world. So how could it exist nowhere else but inside me? If I am thinking something, it takes an extra few steps for me to realize that the person next to me might not be thinking the same thing, and therefore, it would be a good idea for me to SAY the thing that I am thinking, if it is important.

This tendency to assume that other people are already thinking what I'm thinking means that I may keep more things internalized, because I won't see the need to externalize them in that moment.

What's the Solution?

Internalizing is not always a bad thing. It can be advantageous, in certain situations, to keep your thoughts to yourself. But when you start to believe hurtful or untrue things about yourself, or blame yourself for things that you shouldn't, it can become problematic.

What You Can Do in the Moment
Bird's-Eye View

One strategy I have used to lift myself out of internalization mode is to consciously take a step back and look at the bigger picture. Or take a "bird's-eye view." In my mind, I literally grow wings and fly upward so that I am high above the scene and able to see many different elements making up the whole. The key is to be able to look beyond yourself.

Take yourself OUT of yourself for a moment and bring a wider context into your conscious consideration.

So in the example above, of working collaboratively with a colleague: Is my colleague really trying to imply that I don't know how to do my job? No. What matters is the presentation, and making sure that it is the highest quality we can offer. I have to take myself out of the immediate conversation, and look at the bigger picture: We are presenting together, we are working together, we are not here to critique or put each other down, we are here to collaborate and make something bigger than either of us could do alone.

Once I take that moment to lift outside of myself, I can come back and work constructively toward that most important objective.

In the example of my husband telling me he is cold: Is he really trying to imply that I should have checked the weather this morning and thought ahead to turn up the heat in the apartment when I got home from work? No! That would be crazy, right? Looking at it from a bird's-eye perspective, I would be able to see the larger context: Both of our kids are finally asleep, we are relaxing together on the couch after a long day, and my husband wants to curl up with me under a blanket. Being neurotypical, he naturally gravitates toward a communication style that engenders implicit emotional connection via shared context, so instead of just getting a blanket or asking me outright to get one, he offers me a playful line in the hope that I will catch it and give him some play back. "Oh, you're cold? Not anymore . . ."

Recognize Red Flags

Another thing I have found helpful in stopping over-internalization is learning to recognize certain red flags.

If I hear myself start to think black-or-white things like "I *never* get anything right" or "It's *always* my fault" or "I can never be enough," I know something is wrong.

You should never be thinking things like this to yourself. If you are, something is off. But you don't need to fix it right in that moment. All you need to do is recognize that something is wrong—see that red flag. Then you know that all of these false internalized thoughts are invalid. They may still hurt, they may still be hard to stop, but they're bogus. I get a lot of things right; it's not always my fault; and, of course, I am enough.

What You Can Do to Prevent
Take the Responsibility without the Blame

A big part of internalizing is feeling like something (or everything, for that matter), is my fault. If I witness a car accident, why didn't I see it coming sooner and scream or alert the other driver or do something to stop it from happening? I blame myself for things that have absolutely nothing to do with me.

This is not healthy or accurate, and is a sign of over-internalization.

However, there are plenty of instances where something *will* be "my fault." Even if it is something indirectly related to me, like a project I had little to do with but which is being spearheaded by someone who reports to me, or a larger context I should have been aware of when it comes to my son's success in school. Just because I didn't directly do something or know something doesn't mean that I should not take responsibility for the result.

But taking responsibility is different from taking blame. If I didn't know, for example, that my son was acting up in school, is that my fault? Not if his teachers didn't tell me anything. However, my son's success in school is important enough to me that it is my responsibility to put myself in a position where I know as much as I can, regardless of whatever his teachers may or may not decide to tell me. Do I make a point of picking him up a little early once a week so that I get face time with one of his teachers? Do I explicitly ask his teacher for feedback about how he is doing? I can take responsibility for my lack of knowledge without blaming myself or thinking that I am a bad mother. When I take responsibility for things without the unnecessary internalization of blame, it is easier for me to affect positive change, because I am in control of making the situation better. Instead of blaming myself for not knowing or blaming his teachers for not telling me, I look for the opportunity to improve future results.

Self-First Time

A key element to fighting unwanted internalization is building a strong enough foundation of confidence in and respect for yourself that thoughts of incompetence or blame or shame don't stick.

If you know and respect who you are, it will be easier for you to spot the red flags of hurtful or untrue thoughts before they take root and spread.

You can practice and build a sense of self-respect by setting aside time to put yourself first.

This will look very different for different kinds of people, but the important thing is to give yourself explicit permission, during your designated "self-first time," to put your own needs above anyone else's.

For me, as a mother of two young children, this means scheduling set time periods—maybe once a month or once a week if I can—when my husband or a babysitter can take care of the kids and I can focus on myself and meeting my own needs. For someone in another circumstance, it might be every day, or just a couple of minutes here and there.

But whenever it is, it needs to be a priority.

That's the whole point—to practice making yourself a priority and valuing your own well-being, so that when over-internalized feelings of blame or incompetence come knocking at the door, you have a strong enough sense of self-worth to send them packing.

LARRY'S TWO CENTS

There comes a time in any relationship, whether with a spouse, a coworker or a friend, when you realize they are beyond rational emotion and need some time. We have all been there: when the answer to any question is "leave me alone" at best, and a regrettable snap at worst. This is challenging enough in any relationship, but with a partner who could become overwhelmed and have a meltdown, navigating what comes next becomes exponentially more difficult.

It's during these moments that relationships are truly tested, and one false step can make a bad situation much worse. At the crux of a fight, it no longer matters who or what is right, as neither of you are thinking rationally anymore.

Yes, we've all been there.

What is unique about Sarah—and which caught me off guard, especially the first time I saw it—is that she becomes quiet in that situation. Not just quiet, but absolutely silent, incapable of nearly any noise or movement. Where I would be shouting to the heavens and turning ordinary objects into projectiles, Sarah simply stops. The first time it happened, I was unsure of how to respond. So, I thought about what *I* would want in such a moment, and announced I was going for a walk and would be back later. It turns out this was a very bad idea.

When I returned two hours later, I found Sarah in almost exactly the same location I had left her in, but somehow she looked even more emotionally fractured. Suddenly, she let out a horrific sob and collapsed to the ground. For the next thirty minutes, she slowly expelled how she had felt during my absence. Only after getting through that was she able to focus on the initial problem. Of course, it was as much misunderstanding as anything else, and we were finally able to move forward. Later, I learned of similar stories from her childhood, where she developed this quiet response. She did acknowledge that it worked better as a teenager, when the world can stop with often no repercussions.

I have since learned that Sarah needs me to simply exist in the same space, even at a crisis point, to be a sort of anchor that she can see and touch, to help ground her emotions. Now I understand what is happening: an emotional overload on top of a data-processing analysis overwhelms and consumes her mind to the point that she doesn't trust any choice, and the only safe, proper thing to do is to cease speech, movement, and all emotions.

In an effort to prevent such moments in the future, we decided to adopt a squirrel. Not a real one, mind you, but a little plush squirrel that became a signaling tool for when there was a potential data-processing error mixed with emotions. It started when we watched a movie where a bounding dog in the midst of play suddenly stopped and became hyper-focused at the mere sound of a squirrel, ignoring everything he'd been engaging with just moments ago.

For Sarah, a single data point which may or may not have bearing on the matter at hand can, and does, stop her world. But now we had a trigger word—squirrel—which would signify a full stop in whatever was happening at the moment, allowing Sarah to take a step back mentally, and have a few minutes of quiet time to marshal her thoughts. At times, she can even file the issue away in her head for a later time (though of course there are also times when you have no choice but to plow through). The amazing thing is, the squirrel affords Sarah the ability to neutralize the emotional aspects of her mind and focus more completely on the matter itself. As a result, she no longer needs that elongated quiet time, which is especially important now that she is a mother. (As you may know, kids are not compatible with quiet time unless they are asleep—and even then, there is no guarantee!)

Recently, we have evolved even further, and now seldom even evoke the power of the squirrel. It has been replaced with a mixture of word choices that refactor a conversation or moment, along with a standing offer to have Sarah reach out and touch my hand or arm. As in many areas, our children have been instructive. Seeing how their needs are often assuaged by a steady, firm, loving hug has given all of us an anchor against meltdown.

As I was writing this, Sarah reminded me of one of the most important anchors in our ten years together, which started as a coping mechanism during a very stressful time. Sarah had spent four days in the hospital being induced with our first son. We had experienced what our doctor considered a high-risk turn of events, so for three days we had essentially been inundated with divergent opinions about what we (or she, really) should do every twelve hours, when a new shift of nurses came on. By the fourth morning she was fractured, and I was not far behind, so I took one of those walks I like to take (with permission, mind you) to clear my head. I ended up in the hospital gift shop, staring blankly at the various things one sees in such a place. The volunteer working the register asked politely if I needed help finding something. Laughing a bit to myself, knowing how often distraught folk must come into the gift shop looking out of sorts, I said I was seeking a way to keep present and maintain strength for my wife. At that very moment, I noticed a small stone with the word TRUST written on it. I traced the letters with my thumb, and immediately paid for it and put it in my pocket, where it remained through the (eventual) birth of our healthy boy.

Sarah remembers when I came back from my wanders, looking more like myself, with a renewed strength and ability to guide us both through the seemingly endless process. When she inquired what magic coffee I had found, I simply smiled and pulled out my anchor, the little stone. Amidst a spiral of confusion, uncertainty, and physical strain, I had found a positive affirmation to keep us both focused on the bigger picture—bringing a new life into the world. We had chosen our doctor—we trusted him with the life of our child. We had chosen this hospital—we trusted them with the life of our child. We had chosen each other—we trusted our ability to get through this together.

These anchors have empowered Sarah to continue forward motion, and further distance herself from the silent meltdowns. They gave us a healthy child, a way to not get lost or consumed by the difficulty.

Now, I am not saying meltdowns and severe emotions should never happen, nor that avoiding them is our singular goal. Indeed, acknowledging that emotions are real and healthy and need to be experienced, is paramount. However, not letting them overtake you is critical for anyone, not just Sarah, to be a strong person, a mindful parent, and a caring partner or friend.

If nothing else, I hope this recounting illustrates that everything—and everyone—is a work in progress. Finding ways to trust yourself, and others, is the best defense against the downward spiral.

Conclusion

"The most precious thing we have in the entire world
is our individuality."

—PAMELA PARLAPIANO

O f everything that we've learned through these years, and especially over the past year as we've tackled this book, it is that there is nothing so important as knowing and remaining true to yourself. To that end, the more we let go of our prejudices in using the word autistic, the more successful we found ourselves in identifying and embracing Sarah for who she was, and our partnership for what it had become.

Ultimately we have found that not only in destigmatizing the label of autism, but also in identifying traits that are specifically related to Sarah's unique perspective of the world, we have found a way to remove strong or negative emotion from much of our conversations. This isn't to say we don't have emotions when talking through things, but rather that we both realize that until we understand the mechanics of how Sarah understands a circumstance, it would be unfair to apply emotions. As a couple, this allows us to more easily move past those times when emotions have gotten the better of us.

Having this knowledge has enlightened both of us to many strategies, micro-processes, mindsets, work-arounds, and other coping mechanisms that have empowered Sarah to be true to herself and also be the person she wants to be—as a partner, a parent, and a professional.

More often than we may care to admit, the world is not calibrated for the needs of the autistic community. Even with the strategies enumerated here, there are still challenging times when Sarah has no choice but to endure a world that is not built for her. The good news is that these circumstances occur less frequently now, in part due to Sarah's increased understanding of herself and how she best operates in the NT world, and largely due to those closest in her life, including Larry, now understanding, appreciating, and supporting her needs.

In time, the realization that we all share many traits and that we are all neurodiverse in our own ways will hopefully become a normal acceptance.

Just because Larry is not clinically autistic doesn't mean there aren't traits which he shares with Sarah and others who are labeled as such. Further, the traits which qualify Sarah to be autistic are not universally shared with every autistic person, regardless of gender.

In the end, whether or not a person attains the "label" of autism has more to do with the volume and concentration of traits that add up to behavior and thought patterns that differ enough from "the norm" in order to warrant a special categorization. But a label does not define a person. It is never the be-all and end-all of a human being, and it is never a crutch or excuse. It is simply a way to get closer to a sense of true self—the true core of who a person is and what they can do to be successful, however they define that success.

Acknowledgments

First and foremost, we want to thank our dear friend Kate, without whom this book would not exist. *w00t*

Thank you to Sam Lee (may you rest in peace), Mary Shaw, Casey Sears, George Collazo, and Olivia Swomley—who, together with Sarah, met twice each month for years before this book became a reality, writing and honing their craft. Your support and commitment has been invaluable, and we treasure the day Sarah decided to take the Gotham Writers Workshop class that brought you all together.

Sarah would like to thank her mom, for her open-mindedness and encouragement through this whole journey of discovery, diagnosis, and now publication; and her sister, for her unwavering friendship.

To our children, thank you for understanding writing Mondays, when one of us was not home for bedtime. Sure the chicken nuggets, fries, and a toy were a bribe, but they were also a thank-you for allowing us to concentrate on this work.

Thank you, Pam, from the bottom of our hearts, for refusing to settle for the pretty box. Your fearless pursuit of truth and dignity and individuality—of opening the box and finding the human inside—is the only way to live.

Thank you to those mentors in Sarah's professional life, seeing her potential and supporting her pursuits. To Scott—the wind in the sails—your power is often undetectable, save for the outcomes it produces, lifting people up by their own strength; thank you for being supportive as Sarah shared her autism diagnosis for the first time. To Karen, for leading by example how to build and nurture a collaborative team. To Georgia and Densingh, for believing in her and teaching her how to lead and step forward, forging the path for others to follow.

Lastly, thank you to all those who helped along the way. Your contributions do not go unseen. To Rachel and Ginger, for your friendship, for the truest form of family. To the local coffee shops and restaurants who refilled our coffees while supplying us with wonderful treats as we worked to bring this book to life. To Emily, who waded through this entire project from start to end, breathing life into our words—your editing prowess is truly mind-boggling.

To everyone we mentioned and to the countless people who have influenced us throughout our entire lives, not just during the last year of support, we sincerely thank you.

Endnotes

Introduction

1. Amy Cuddy, *Presence: Bringing Your Boldest Self to Your Biggest Challenges* (New York: Little, Brown Spark, 2015).

Chapter One:
Communication Basics

1. Tess Eyrich, "What Makes Kids with Autism Less Social than Their Typically Developing Peers?" ScienceDaily, January 29, 2018, http://www.sciencedaily.com/releases/2018/01/180129223841.htm.

2. Daniel Wendler, *Level Up Your Social Life: The Gamer's Guide to Social Success* (CreateSpace Independent Publishing Platform, 2016).

Chapter Two:
Communication 201

1. Geert Hofstede, *Cultures Consequences: Comparing Values, Behaviors, Institutions, and Organizations across Nations* (California: Sage Publications, 2001).

Chapter Four:
Navigating Professional Relationships

1. Cuddy, *Presence: Bringing Your Boldest Self to Your Biggest Challenges.*

Chapter Five:
Long-Term Neurodiverse Relationships

1. Ashley Stanford, *Asperger Syndrome (Autism Spectrum Disorder) and Long-Term Relationships* (London: Jessica Kingsley Publishers, 2015).

About the Authors

Sarah Nannery is the director of development for Autism Initiatives at Drexel University. She holds a master's degree in conflict transformation, and was recently diagnosed with autism.

Larry Nannery is a technology consultant with experience in organizational change and life coaching, and has a lifelong love of helping others to communicate effectively.